T3-BOF-522

Justice and Democracy

'Justice' and 'democracy' have alternated as dominant themes in political philosophy over the last fifty years. Since its revival in the middle of the twentieth century, political philosophy has focused on first one and then the other of these two themes. Rarely, however, has it succeeded in holding them in joint focus. This volume brings together leading authors who consider the relationship of democracy and justice in a set of specially written chapters. The intrinsic justness of democracy is challenged, the relationship between justice, democracy and impartiality queried and the relationship between justice, democracy and the common good examined. Further chapters explore the problem of social exclusion and issues surrounding subnational groups in the context of democracy and justice. Authors include Keith Dowding, Richard Arneson, Norman Schofield, Albert Weale, Robert E. Goodin, Jon Elster, David Miller, Philip Pettit, Julian Le Grand and Russell Hardin.

KEITH DOWDING is Professor of Political Science at the London School of Economics. His books include *Rational Choice and Political Power* (1991), *The Civil Service* (1995) and *Power* (1996).

ROBERT E. GOODIN is Joint Professor of Social and Political Theory and of Philosophy at the Research School of Social Sciences at the Australian National University. He is the author of many books on political theory, public policy and applied ethics which include, most recently, *The Real Worlds of Welfare Capitalism*, with B. Headey, R. Muffels and H.J. Dirven (1999) and *Reflective Democracy* (2003).

CAROLE PATEMAN is Professor of Political Science at UCLA and Honorary Professor in the School of European Studies at Cardiff University. Her publications include *Participation and Democratic Theory* (1970), *The Problem of Political Obligation* (2nd edn, 1985), and *The Sexual Contract* (1988).

Justice and Democracy

Essays for Brian Barry

---

edited by

Keith Dowding, Robert E. Goodin and
Carole Pateman

PUBLISHED BY THE PRESS SYNDICATE OF THE UNIVERSITY OF CAMBRIDGE
The Pitt Building, Trumpington Street, Cambridge, United Kingdom

CAMBRIDGE UNIVERSITY PRESS
The Edinburgh Building, Cambridge, CB2 2RU, UK
40 West 20th Street, New York, NY 10011–4211, USA
477 Williamstown Road, Port Melbourne, VIC 3207, Australia
Ruiz de Alarcón 13, 28014 Madrid, Spain
Dock House, The Waterfront, Cape Town 8001, South Africa

http://www.cambridge.org

First published 2004

Printed in the United Kingdom at the University Press, Cambridge

Typeface Plantin 10/12 pt. *System* LaTeX 2_ε [TB]

A catalogue record for this book is available from the British Library

ISBN 0 521 83695 6 hardback
ISBN 0 521 54543 9 paperback

For Brian Barry,
Teacher, Critic, Colleague, Friend

Brian Barry

Brian Barry was born in 1936 in London. He received his first class degree in Politics, Philosophy and Economics from Oxford University in 1958 staying there to complete his doctorate in 1964. He has held positions at the Universities of Birmingham, Keele, Southampton, Oxford and Essex in the United Kingdom before moving to positions in Canada and the USA at British Columbia, Chicago and the California Institute of Technology. After a short stay at the European University Institute, Florence, he returned to England at the London School of Economics for eleven years. In 1998 he moved to Columbia University in New York. Amongst his honours are elections to fellowships of the American Academy of Arts and Sciences (1976), the British Academy (1988), and he has three times been awarded the W.J.M. Mackenzie prize awarded by the Political Studies Association (UK) for the best book published in the previous year (for *Theories of Justice*, *Justice as Impartiality* and *Culture and Equality*). The Political Studies Association also honoured him for lifetime achievement in Political Studies in 2000. He was awarded probably the highest accolade for a political scientist in 2001 when he won the Johan Skytte Prize in Political Science. The Prize Committee stated that the award was 'for his profound contribution to normative political theory performed with passion as well as clarity in the grand tradition from Enlightenment'.

Contents

Figures

Contributors

RICHARD J. ARNESON is Professor of Philosophy in the Department of Philosophy at the University of California, San Diego.

KEITH DOWDING is Professor of Political Science at the London School of Economics and Political Science.

JON ELSTER is Robert K. Merton Professor of Social Sciences in the Political Science Department at Columbia University, New York.

ROBERT E. GOODIN is Professor of Social and Political Theory and Philosophy at the Research School of Social Sciences, Australian National University.

RUSSELL HARDIN is Professor of Politics in the Department of Politics, New York University.

JULIAN LE GRAND is Richard Titmuss Professor of Social Policy in the Social Policy Department at the London School of Economics and Political Science.

DAVID MILLER is Professor of Political Theory at the University of Oxford and an Official Fellow of Nuffield College, Oxford.

CAROLE PATEMAN is Professor of Political Science at the University of California, Los Angeles.

PHILIP PETTIT is William Nelson Cromwell Professor of Politics at Princeton University.

NORMAN SCHOFIELD is the Director of the Center in Political Economy and Dr William Taussig Professor of Political Economy, and Professor of Political Science at Washington University, St Louis.

ALBERT WEALE is Professor of Government at the University of Essex.

1 Introduction: between justice and democracy

Keith Dowding, Robert E. Goodin and Carole Pateman

'Justice' and 'democracy' have alternated as dominant themes in political philosophy over the last fifty years or so. Since its revival in the middle of the twentieth century, political philosophy has focused on first one and then the other of these two themes. Rarely, however, has it succeeded in holding them in joint focus.

This volume attempts to remedy that defect. Inevitably, some chapters focus more heavily on one topic than the other. But all were written explicitly with a view to the conjunction, intersection or interaction of these two central values in contemporary political theory.

Parallel agendas?

Democratic theorizing dominated mainstream thinking about politics in the 1950s and 1960s. Philosophers were otherwise engaged: with utilitarianism dominant, and the linguistic turn in the ascendance, people in philosophy departments were mostly concerned with analytically parsing concepts such as happiness or freedom or equality. These efforts, useful though they would ultimately prove to be, had little immediate influence outside of the more rarefied corners of academe.

More influential, or anyway more directly relevant to real-world concerns, were the 'power debates' conducted mostly in political science and sociology departments. Those disputes concerned the nature and distribution of power in modern society and the salient features of modern democracy as a response. On the left, sociological critics of a more Marxist cast, from Charles Beard (1913) and the Lynds (1929) to Floyd Hunter (1953) and C. Wright Mills (1956), confidently reported the capture of American institutions by a power elite in the service of narrow economic interests. On the other side was Robert Dahl (1961), whose close examination of the processing of issues one-by-one reassured readers that the answer to the question *Who Governs?* was 'different elites on different issues'. His former research assistants pressed harder, suggesting that all was well in American democracy since the pluralist group system ensured that all legitimate interests were represented (Polsby 1963/1980; Wolfinger 1971).

Dahl's work had a massively salutary influence on political science and democratic theory. His work on democracy took a Madisonian turn, with due note of the new-fangled (or at least rediscovered) social choice results on aggregation paradoxes (Dahl 1956). His emphasis on the interest group system rightly emphasized extra-parliamentary and electoral aspects of democracy. Put together polyarchy and pluralism, and essentially you have modern democracy.

The 1950s and early 1960s also saw the birth of large-scale surveys of electorates. These studies found that few citizens were politically active and most seemed to have little interest in politics at all. These findings led some scholars to argue that apathy was a necessary component of a stable democracy. Rather than despairing that society was run by elites, and that citizens had little knowledge of political affairs, it was suggested that not only should we accept this state of affairs – stable, democratic government could only exist if most of the population were apathetic (Converse 1964).

This conservative acceptance of the indifference of the public prompted a number of political theorists to mount a defence of the ideal of active citizenship as central to democracy. Their criticism of a narrow protective view of 'democracy' overlapped with criticism of what was seen as an oversimplified conception of 'power' in Dahl's work. Lukes (1974) extended Bachrach and Baratz' (1963) analysis of non-decision-making into a three-dimensional view of power, an approach effectively utilized by Gaventa (1980) in his empirical study of a valley in Appalachia.

More generally, radical political theorists argued that, rather than viewing apathy as part-and-parcel of modern democratic life, we should view this as a major failing of democratic institutions. Theorists such as Macpherson (1973; 1977) and Pateman (1970) developed alternative participatory conceptions of democracy.

In recent years, participatory democratic theories have enjoyed a renaissance. The idea that there are democratic benefits to an inactive citizenry is not something one often reads nowadays in academic writing.[1] The dominant tendency today is quite the opposite (Verba 2000). Theorists of social capital (Putnam 2000; Skocpol and Fiorina 1999), in particular, despair of the falling levels of political participation, seeing it as part of a trend of declining sociality in community life. Where, in the 1960s,

[1] Though its benefits to those in power is hardly something they can ignore, which is surely one reason why parties in power only fiddle at the edges of encouraging participation in politics (and positively froth at the mouth when that participation gets too active).

community was seen as a radical alternative to modern democratic failings, these days bemoaning the lack of community is something that is as likely to be done by those on the conservative (rather than libertarian) right as by those on the left.

In the late 1970s, however, these debates over power and democracy seemed to have run their course.[2] Pluralist thinking remained dominant in empirical political science, albeit often in other guises, such as corporatism (Schmitter 1981), consociationalism (Lijphart 1969) and policy networks and policy communities (Heclo 1978; Rhodes 1997) were major subjects of empirical scrutiny. 'Power' seemed too hard a concept to measure empirically, so political scientists turned to other quarry. And the change in the political climate meant that active citizenship and participatory democracy fell out of fashion too. In the theoretical debates, all sides seemed to be content to declare victory and abandon the field.

Meanwhile, the publication of Rawls' *A Theory of Justice* in 1971 led to a surge of interest in social justice among mainstream political philosophers, and once again political philosophy began to flower. The number of philosophical works reacting to or influenced by Rawls are now almost beyond counting.[3] It is virtually impossible nowadays to write about justice – equality, rights, freedoms, or even virtue – without referring to Rawls, implicitly if not explicitly. Writers on the libertarian right (Nozick 1974) as well as the egalitarian left (Cohen 2000) regularly juxtapose themselves to Rawls, situating their writing in an essential relationship to the Rawlsian agenda. Whereas writing on democracy and power had centred primarily in political science departments, among people often engaged in empirical as well as theoretical research, writing on justice occurred more often in the more rarified realms of philosophy departments.

In more recent years, there has been a return once again to discussing democracy and 'democratic transitions' in response to the melting of the Iron Curtain and new democracies springing up across Eastern Europe, the Far East, South Africa and Latin America (O'Donnell *et al.* 1986; Held 1993; Hadenius 1994). Political scientists became engaged as constitutional consultants, in quasi-experimental situations, advising

[2] Except in Scandinavia, where there has been an ongoing tradition of intermittent commissions on 'Power and Democracy' (Engelstadt *et al.* 2003). More recently there has been a return to considering the measurement of power using the insights of more formal theory, see Morriss (1987/2002); Dowding (1991; 1996); Felsenthal and Machover (1998).

[3] Kukathas' (2002) four-volume collection represents the merest tip of the iceberg, as the bibliography of works cited therein attests.

as well as studying the forms in which democracies and electoral systems are there taking shape (Elster 1996; Linz and Stepan 1996; Whitehead 2002).[4]

Philosophically too, there has been a flowering of democratic theory, with the 'deliberative turn' (Cohen 1989; Bohman and Rehg 1997; Elster 1998; Dryzek 2000; Fishkin and Laslett 2003). The connection between deliberative democracy and the older participatory strand remains largely unexplored. To date, there has also been surprisingly little cross-fertilization between deliberative theorists of a more philosophical sort and empirical political theorists who might help them come to grips with how deliberation actually works (Bohman 1998). A wide gap remains between, on one side, experiments with 'deliberative polling' originated by James Fishkin (1995) or with citizens' juries and, on the other side, philosophical accounts of the requirements for deliberation – though there are signs that that gap might now be beginning to close (Steenbergen *et al.* 2002).

Indeed, what is surprising across this half century of political theorizing is not only how few people straddle the philosophy/political science divide within political theory, but how few people have written incisively on both dominant themes, 'justice' and 'democracy'. A conspicuous exception to that is Brian Barry.

Brian Barry, almost uniquely, has figured centrally in debates on both democratic theory and social justice. His Oxford D Phil. dissertation, published as *Political Argument* (1965), blended both. His critique of Rawls' *Theory of Justice*, published as *The Liberal Theory of Justice* (1973), remains the most trenchant in print. He has extended those critiques, and sketched his own positive proposals, in his ongoing multi-volume project *Treatise on Social Justice*, formally comprised of his *Theories of Justice* (1989b) and *Justice as Impartiality* (1995) and informally also incorporating *Culture and Equality* (2001) and *Why Social Justice Matters* (forthcoming). At the same time, Barry has contributed importantly to democratic theory, with *Sociologists, Economists and Democracy* (1970) and many important essays collected in his *Democracy, Power and Justice* (1989a), which also includes his forays into the power debate so central to the tradition of democratic thinking amongst political scientists.[5]

[4] This is in sharp contrast to the 1960s, when writers from both Eastern Europe and Southern Africa were defending other forms of non-competitive rule, one-party democracy as the only legitimate forms of 'people's democracy' (Naess *et al.* 1956).

[5] See also Barry (2002b). Brian Barry has also resided in both political science and philosophy departments, now holding the Arnold A. Saltzman Professorship of Philosophy and Political Science, institutionalizing his straddle across the disciplines.

Barry's thinking on both justice and democracy is subtle and complex. Essentially for Barry a just constitution is one that no one could reasonably reject, with the hard work going into what constitutes 'reasonable rejection'. Barry also defines democracy in constitutional terms, as a procedure that makes a formal connection between citizen's views and the outcomes (in referenda) or choice of representatives. He wants to leave as few issues to constitutional lawyers as possible, though recognizes that some (indeed significant) elements of justice must be built in for a system to be democratic. Brian Barry is also one of the few to consider the relationship between justice and democracy. Here his views are clear. We have few reasons for thinking that a democratic system will be a just one. Democratic decisions can be unjust, though no less democratic for that.

This collection – dedicated to Brian Barry by his friends, former students and colleagues – draws some links between thinking on justice and on democracy. Helping him to firm up connections between values that have preoccupied him for a lifetime is the highest tribute we can pay to he who has shown us how to practise political theory at its finest.

Ships in the night?

Those who write about justice often see little need to say much about the institutions required to deliver the form of justice they favour. Perhaps for this reason, those who write about justice rarely draw any very explicit links to democracy.

Most theorists of justice implicitly seem to suppose that some kind of democracy is the preferred political form, but for reasons that are usually not fully worked out. At most, there is a vague nod in the direction of democratic institutions of a fairly minimalist form, typically centring, after the fashion of Schumpeter (1950), on the electoral process.

As we saw, Brian Barry's (1991b; 1995) own conclusion – which we here elaborate – is that there is nothing inherent in democracy that necessarily makes it just. Democracy is a procedure for formally capturing the views of the citizens and translating them into outcomes. That procedure has only tangential connections to the outcomes being just. Furthermore, the justification of what he calls 'the majority principle' should lead us to accept its results even when we think the outcomes unjust (1995: 146–51). But following his favourite philosopher Hobbes, he suggests, 'Nobody but a moral imbecile would really be prepared to deliver himself over body and soul to the majority principle' – thus showing the majority principle is a 'broken reed' and its naturalness contingent on restrictive conditions (Barry 1991b: 38). Some democratic decisions can be reasonably rejected, though in rejecting them, people should keep in mind the costs of that rejection. Civil war or dictatorship might be two of the alternatives.

Democratic theorists, conversely, have been remarkably silent about justice. There are notable exceptions such as Ian Shapiro's *Democratic Justice* (1999). There, Shapiro depicts justice as consisting in part in the 'minimization of hierarchical relations in central social institutions'; and that is also of course a goal of many (if not all) theories of democracy. Notice, however, that in Shapiro's presentation justice gets pride of place, and democracy is relegated to the status of a purely 'subordinate good'.

Still, on Shapiro's account, democracy is nonetheless regarded as a good in its own right. That would be the position of many political philosophers, if not necessarily all of them (cf. Arneson, chapter 3). For many, democracy is seen as intrinsically valuable because it is a fair or impartial procedure for aggregating preferences and making collective decisions in which each citizen has a basic right to participate. For more radical theorists, democracy – extending beyond the electoral process – is intrinsically valuable because it is grounded in and upholds individual, as well as collective, self-government, and because of the effects of participation on individual citizens, including the development of a public spirit or sense of justice.

The central questions about the relationship between democracy and justice – or, more precisely, about the relationship between different interpretations of 'democracy' and 'justice' – remain largely unaddressed. Let us illustrate some of those under-examined interrelationships by reference to four areas in which justice and democracy might seem to pull in opposite directions: in relation to participation, personal satisfaction, public goods and gender.

Democracy, justice and participation

At one extreme of the possible range of positions about the relationship between democracy and justice, we might solve the problem by claiming that democracy has no intrinsic good at all. One argument (represented by Arneson, chapter 3) is that the value of democracy is purely instrumental; the choice between democracy and autocracy depends only on the results of each system measured by an independent standard of assessment. The results also determine who ought to participate. There can be no basic right of participation since autocracy may, in terms of social justice, be preferable. Everything thus hinges on the criteria of justice together with empirical evaluation of how well different institutional forms promote those criteria. (Whether, in the twenty-first century, there can be non-idiosyncratic criteria of justice that favour autocracy is an open question.)

From a purely welfarist perspective there will be no question of either justice or democracy involved if (per Le Grand, chapter 10) some individuals refrain voluntarily from political participation or participation in wider social affairs, just so long as enough are taking part to keep the society operating satisfactorily. But if welfarism is tempered or democracy is seen as having intrinsic value, then withdrawal from participation becomes a problem not only perhaps for democracy but also for justice.

When the lack of participation is involuntary (through poverty or racism, say), then both justice and democracy are obviously diminished, because some citizens are being treated as having lesser standing than their fellows. But the line between 'involuntary' and 'voluntary' abstention is not easy to draw or assess. Merely showing that poor people or ethnic minorities do not participate fully is not enough, on its own, to demonstrate injustice or a lack of democracy. There might be a number of interrelated reasons why citizens might voluntarily decide to take no part in political affairs which are democratically innocuous, even if they do correlate with people's objective characteristics.

Individuals might take no part in public affairs because they see no point in doing so. One hardly needs the tools of political economics to see that one's single vote does not make much difference (Riker and Ordeshook 1968; Aldrich 1993), particularly if one's political views seem out of line with those of the rest of the community. Similarly, if one believes that all politicians are pretty much the same and the policies of all the parties serve the same dominant interests, then bearing even the small costs of voting and of finding out the small-print differences between parties may not seem worthwhile. Apathy may come about because there seems little point in trying to engage. This apathy may be rational, but may still mask people's strong interest in politics more broadly conceived. Lack of interest cannot be simply read off from lack of participation because of the collective action problems of mobilization (Dowding 1991). Apathy does not demonstrate satisfaction with the goods provided by the political community. Even when survey respondents say they 'don't care' about the policies of politicians, this may only reveal that politicians are not engaging with respondents' interests and those goods and services they do care about, rather than that they have no cares about society at all. The fact that mainstream political activity does not capture the concerns of communities may be revealed when those communities undertake social and political activity of their own (Verba 2000): everything from community movements to Mafia-style protection agencies organized for citizens' benefit outside of the narrowly political domain.

Democracy, justice and personal satisfaction

Another possibility is that individuals might withdraw from political life because they are completely satisfied with the life they hold. How are we to judge that decision? One response might be to think that if citizens are satisfied then there cannot be much wrong with the social and political life of their community. If the political elites provide the goods that people want – markets run smoothly to provide private goods, and the state intervenes to provide public goods where markets fail – then we should not concern ourselves with low levels of participation. As long as the institutions exist to ensure the public can 'throw the rascals out', then that may be enough to get the rascals to act so that the public have no desire to throw them out. If the rascals provide themselves with a little rent for doing the job, then that is only to be expected. But we might not take such a sanguine view of satisfaction, even if satisfaction is indeed what leads large numbers not to participate.

Judging satisfaction or 'happiness' in surveys is problematic. There seems to be some kind of psychological balance to stated happiness. A person who suffers a major disability in an accident soon recovers levels of stated satisfaction or happiness close to those prior to their disability even if their quality of life has altered enormously. Similarly, at the aggregate level the degree to which a population claims they are happy does not vary much with institutional or economic conditions, though across the world (particularly the developed world) average levels of stated happiness seem to be declining. This may well have more to do with expectations than about anything objective about their lifestyle. Certainly, the economic wealth of a nation is not strongly correlated with levels of happiness, and whilst the rich on average seem happier than the poor, the difference is small (see Ng 1996; 2003 for reviews). There does seem to be a relationship between participation and stated satisfaction. Evidence from Switzerland suggests that people in more participatory cantons claim greater satisfaction than others (Frey and Stutzer 2002).

It is not clear how people judge their level of satisfaction. Do they have some kind of absolute scale, or do they make judgments based on local or global comparisons? A satisfied population may simply be an unimaginative one. People in a participatory community may claim greater satisfaction, even if they would choose not to participate without strong incentives to do so. In other words, stated satisfaction with one's political community is not, in itself, a strong reason to be sanguine even for a welfarist. If a duty, rather than a mere right, to participate were correlated with greater happiness, then a welfarist should support the duty. Those who want to go beyond welfarism within their theories of justice may also want to go beyond it in a theory of democracy. Can we prise apart democracy and justice as political theorists have been wont to do?

Suppose for example that an individual makes a choice not to pursue higher education. There may be a small social loss of that individual's (potential) talents, but the loss to the individual him or herself in the long run is the more serious problem. Do such examples come under the purview of justice? Does justice extend to individual decisions of this kind? If so, it would seem to imply that individuals must be encouraged, or even coerced, into making well-informed long-term decisions for themselves in the name of justice.

On the other hand, if participation is a basic right, then perhaps this is a question of democracy rather than justice. Yet since democracy is grounded in self-government, in individual liberty, the freedom to make mistakes would seem to be part of a democratic society. At least this is an argument that could be made in the context of a robust democracy – one that makes provision for citizens, including in their old age. In that case, there would be plenty of room for people to make unwise decisions when young that they might regret when they are older, without this diminishing their standing as citizens.

Democracy and justice in public goods

States regulate the supply of private goods, and facilitate and directly provide some public goods. Most of the literature on social justice discusses distributional issues very broadly. They are concerned with how distribution is best organized given concerns for liberty, equality and fairness. Democratic theorists have considered the distinction between private and public goods more carefully. One of the tasks that a democratic government faces is to make decisions about where to intervene in market processes to provide public goods, as well as deciding the scope and quality of provision. David Miller (chapter 8) argues that the idea that issues of justice do not arise with public goods begs not only the question of which public goods should the state provide but all the questions raised by the fact that the benefits from the provision of public goods are not equally distributed nor are the goods equally valued by all. Democratic theorists, especially those imbued with the lessons from social choice and decision theory, have carefully considered the aggregation problems associated with such decisions.

It is now widely recognized that what constitutes a 'public good' depends not only on the technical features of a product, but also upon supply and demand conditions. Markets may fail when goods are non-excludable, but may operate when technical change makes excludability feasible. Where demand is at first low, governments may step in to provide a good for all, but when demand conditions change governments can step out of the picture and allow the market to operate. Other types of goods, social insurance and pensions schemes for example, for which markets should in principle operate efficiently, may be thought to be too important to be completely left to the vagaries of human judgements about risk.

Miller argues that there are no fundamental problems about the supply of public goods in a democracy, since they are delivered through an impartial democratic procedure. However, one might take the view that the provision of a set of universal public goods is central to democracy because they are vital to the standing of citizens and the worth of their citizenship. If their health is compromised, for instance, through lack of access to adequate health-care, or if they attend poorly funded public schools, then their ability to participate fully in social and political life is undermined.

In discussions of justice this line of argument is usually treated as welfarist, as the provision of resources for individuals to use to lead their lives as they wish and to promote their well-being. The connection is not made to citizenship, that is, to democracy. This reflects the tacit assumption that democracy is only relevant to arguments about justice in the sense that a set of institutions necessary to the electoral process are required. However, some of the central concerns of a well-functioning democracy require an informed and active citizenry. But are there 'set limits' to what constitutes adequate health-care or education? If Germans want to spend more on health but less on education per capita than the French, is this a matter for a theory of justice – or indeed of democracy (Barry 1995: 97)? Nevertheless, adequate levels of each (whatever they are) may be thought as prerequisites for both justice and democracy. For example, a basic income for all citizens is one way of trying to capture a socially just society compatible with a fully-fledged market (van Parijs 1992; van Parijs 1995; Dowding *et al.* 2003).

Basic income is usually discussed only in terms of social justice. But it might be seen as a way of fostering democratization. Here the idea of citizenship in a democracy may not simply entail certain voting rights, but also other rights that have the same fundamental status as universal suffrage or property rights within the society as a whole. A basic income can allow all people, including those who provide vital non-pecuniary services, to be seen as fully-fledged citizens. Basic income might be important to democratic arguments as well as ones concerned with social justice (Pateman 2003).

Another way of looking at the provision of public goods is in terms of furthering the common good or the public interest (Barry 1964). The tricky issue here is how to determine what the public good is, even if defined as the state tracking the common interests that individuals share as citizens (Pettit chapter 9). One suggestion is that the interests will be determined through voluntary deliberative participation. Citizens, or their representatives, will debate alternative proposals and criteria will emerge that provide publicly acceptable reasons that can then be used in future decision-making.

One problem here is motivational: how to ensure that citizens and representatives debate in the right spirit and make genuine efforts to look for reasons acceptable to others and not only those that further their own private interests. Thus Goodin (chapter 6) discusses not only institutional mechanisms to help ensure that the right motivations are prompted but also 'reminders' to help this process along.

Pettit (chapter 9) looks to electoral institutions to provide the fora for such deliberation, which suggests that this is a matter of democracy, more specifically deliberative democracy, rather than justice. On the other hand he also notes that there is a convergence between this way of determining the common good and arguments about justice that rely on claims about principles of cooperation with which all can agree. Weale (chapter 5) remarks similarly on the convergence between deliberative notions of democracy and discussions of justice.

Democracy, justice and gender

The interrelationships between justice and democracy emerge particularly strikingly with respect to groups historically denied both: not least women, half the human race. The injustice of traditional gender arrangements has gone hand-in-hand with the construction of 'democracy' as a masculine preserve. It always bears emphasis that the most central criterion of 'democracy', universal suffrage, took so long to achieve even in old, established democracies. In many European countries women won the suffrage only after the Second World War. One canton in Switzerland with direct (male) democracy excluded women until 1989. And universal suffrage is still not universal, that is, global.

Women were excluded from citizenship on the grounds that they were naturally unsuited to self-government. Temperamentally they were unsuited because their affection toward particular others precluded them from principled pursuit of broader public interests (Pateman 1989). Men's government of women was exercised in the home as well as in national and local government; and the earliest feminist criticisms of men's power (Astell 1706; Wollstonecraft 1792; 1798; Mill 1869) were concerned in particular with marriage. When the legal personality of a married woman was subsumed within that of her husband, she could not be a citizen. Even now that women have won civil and political equality, marriage is not yet a just institution (Pateman 1988; Okin 1989).

Feminist political theorists have brought the question of power back into the discussion of justice and democracy and broadened the scope of political inquiry into areas ignored in conventional argument, whether by political scientists or philosophers. They have raised again, in a different context, questions asked by the advocates of participatory democracy about the connections between power in the workplace – and marriage and the home – and questions of justice and democracy. Thanks to feminists, the democratization of institutional structures, not just free and fair elections, has been put back on the agenda in a much broader context than in the 1960s and 1970s.

Feminists have also deepened arguments for deliberative democracy. Rather than the impartial and impersonal aggregation of votes cast in splendid isolation, feminists sometimes call for direct deliberative engagement of citizens with one another, not only to come to appreciate one another's understanding better (what each wants and why) but also to change our own preferences in response to engagement with others. In deliberation of this 'anticipatory and self-referential' sort, whole new constituencies are formed (Mansbridge 2003; see similarly Sunstein 1991).

Arguments about deliberation are related to another feminist contribution to the discussion of justice. Turning the accusation of women's partiality into a virtue, theorists of the 'ethic of care' scorn formal, impersonal justice as too cold and abstract. Only through close, empathetic engagement with the concerns of others can we gain the sort of perspective that we really require to do true justice to them, their needs and interests, aspirations and anxieties (Tronto 1993). This line of argument has tended to by-pass the significance for justice and democracy of the major public experiment, the developed welfare state, in instituting care for citizens in favour of attention to women's caring work in the household. Here the clash between particular relations and universal principles of justice arises in another way (to which we shall return later). Women often appeal to the courts or legislatures for equal rights against the injustices of men's dominance in the households and kin networks in which they carry out their caring work.

Democratizing formal representative institutions has been even harder than winning the vote. A widely held view is that the job of representatives is to vote for the interests of their constituents, so anyone capable of faithfully transmitting that message to the legislative vote-tallying machinery would suffice for the purpose. But male representatives might take little account of the interests of women. Criticism of this conception of representation goes back a very long way (Thompson 1825). Add recent arguments about deliberative engagement, and we get the requirement that representatives reflect identities and images, not just ideas and interests – what Phillips (1995) calls the 'politics of presence'. On this account, only women can represent women, blacks represent blacks, and so on. Certainly, empirical evidence shows that as the number of female representatives grows, so does the amount of legislation that directly concerns women's interests (Duflo and Chattopadhyay 2003; Besley and Case 2003).

Similar arguments are made about state bureaucracies and the representation of distinct groups within society. 'Femocrats' (female bureaucrats) thus represent the politics of presence in the executive, justified by deliberative logic on a par with that governing an inclusive legislature (Sawer 1990; Sawer and Simms 1993; Eisenstein 1996).

Such measures can be justified as producing a more empathetic understanding of the identities as well as the interests and ideas of everyone in the community. But they also have a more straightforward justification, at least in the case of women. Women are half the citizen body (often somewhat more). Unless they are equal participants in decision-making in all authoritative bodies then both justice and democracy are still lacking (Hawkesworth 1990).

Mapping the interrelationships

Generically, there are basically three different ways of viewing the relationship between justice and democracy.

On the first view of that relationship, the two concepts inhabit, and rule over, 'separate spheres' that are hermeneutically isolated from one another. Any issue of conflict between them is thus obviated. Questions here tend to be phrased in terms of the proper 'scope' of justice and of democracy, respectively. The problem, on this view, is simply to determine whether an issue falls within the sphere of 'democracy' or of 'justice'. Once that is settled, the precepts governing that sphere dictate the outcome, without any reference to precepts applicable only in the other sphere.

On a second view, the two concepts are different sides of the same coin. Either one implies the other, or else the same underlying value implies them both. Thus, either there can never be any genuine conflict between 'justice' and 'democracy', rightly understood; or any conflict between the two can be straightforwardly adjudicated by appeal back to the underlying value that gives rise to them both.

On yet a third view, 'democracy' and 'justice' are genuinely distinct and genuinely competing values that might both be in play simultaneously. In any given case they might pull in different directions; and when they do, there is no straightforward way to adjudicate the conflict by reference to any underlying value that underwrites them both.

What is at stake in choosing among these three views? Does it make any material difference which one we adopt? In one way, it may not. The recommendation for political institutions and public policy will presumably be much the same in any event: 'democracy tempered by justice' or 'justice tempered by democracy' (depending on which concept is allowed to 'wear the trousers', in Austin's (1962: 70) patriarchal phrase). The rationale will be different, as will the particular blend, depending on which view we adopt. But the basic structure of the solution will not – at least not in the standard sorts of cases to which the concepts are ordinarily applied. The need for really hard choices between them arises only if 'democracy' and 'justice' become greatly at odds with one another; and the distance between them will deepen the nearer societies are to being truly 'divided' rather than merely 'multicultural' (Barry 1975). We return to this issue at the end of this chapter.

Family resemblances and potential resolutions

Philosophers in quest of the true 'essence' of things seem to suffer an almost irresistible temptation toward trying to trace all values back to some one core value, and to show that all appearances of competing values are merely surface manifestations of that same underlying value (cf. Barry 1965/1990: 58, xl–xliv; Hampshire 2000).

On the face of it, this might look like a promising approach to reconciling the twin values of 'justice' and 'democracy'. After all, most of the main approaches to political philosophy – utilitarian, contractualist, proceduralist, participationist – all prescribe both justice and democracy. Of course, it is utterly implausible that all our moral intuitions can really be captured by one underlying value. If that were so we might wonder why there is so much political and moral disagreement, and so many moral dilemmas: we return to those issues later.

Our focus for the moment is on whether this strategy will necessarily work, even if there were a single value underlying both 'justice' and 'democracy'. Brian Barry has insisted that there is no good reason for thinking that the correctly specified democratic procedures will always provide truly just outcomes. There is no guarantee that the democracy that each approach prescribes will necessarily deliver the form of justice that it desires. Justice and democracy are not the same thing, even if the same (sorts of) values underlie both.

The tension that is famously endemic in 'social democracy' offers one particularly clear example of this pervasive problem. When the vote of the people goes against them, social democrats must decide whether they are first and foremost socialists, or first and foremost democrats. That is to say, do they see themselves as justified in pursuing their preferred theory of justice, even in the absence of a democratic mandate? Or do they see themselves as obliged to respect the democratic verdict, even when that precludes the pursuit of justice as they see it? Can it license renegotiation through authoritarian means in order to create a new settlement that is more likely to produce continued socialism through future democratic procedures? Or are the dangers of dictatorship greater, from a social democratic perspective, than those of a democracy that seems unwilling to legitimize socialist or egalitarian outcomes?

Every political philosophy that wants simultaneously to endorse justice and democracy seems to confront a similar conundrum. There is no guarantee that the form of democracy any given philosophy prescribes will necessarily end up embracing the form of justice that it endorses. When it does not, we need to trade off justice for democracy. Alternatively, we need to renegotiate the terms of that democracy, either democratically (which may not provide a path out of the conflict) or non-democratically (with its obvious costs and dangers).

There is nothing necessarily incoherent or shallowly intuitionistic about making such trade-offs (cf. Rawls 1971: 34–40; see Barry 1973: ch. 7 for critique; also Barry and Rae 1975). There are principled reasons, within the terms of each philosophy, for tipping the balance one way or the other. Our point is simply that there is always a balance to be struck, a choice to be made.

Utilitarian justice, utilitarian democracy

Take first the case of utilitarianism. Utilitarianism offers an account of justice: the just constitution is one that maximizes utility across the society as a whole. That bare-bones formulation acquires more flesh when utilitarians such as Bentham (1823) add two further empirical conjectures. Assuming (1) everyone's underlying preferences are pretty similar to everyone else's, and (2) most goods have diminishing marginal utility, a broadly egalitarian distribution of goods will be that which maximizes social utility (Carritt 1967).

Utilitarianism can also be shown to imply democracy, after the fashion of James Mill (1820; Macpherson 1977). On this account, the value of having a vote is to protect oneself against the arbitrary exercise of public authority. And assuming everyone has an equal interest in such protection, rule by majority vote is once again the utility maximizing strategy. All else being held equal, the balance of utility lies with the greater number. This old thought finds modern formalization in the work of Rae (1969) and Taylor (1969).

Both derivations involve problematic assumptions. But leave those aside. What emerges is that there is no reason to suppose that the form of democracy that utilitarianism prescribes will necessarily yield justice of the form that utilitarianism describes. At the very least, aggregating utilitarian preferences into such a welfare functional would require completely honest citizens: no strategic voting, here.

In more familiar majoritarian ordinal voting schemes that utilitarians like Mill prescribe, office-seekers are likely to concentrate their attention on the median voter at the cost of those further from the centre (Downs 1957). On some accounts, this leads to a systematic exploitation of those at the extremes by those at the centre: for example of the rich and poor by the middle classes (Stigler 1970; 1988). On other accounts, it leads to a systematic exploitation of minority groups by majority ones (Rogowski 1974). Neither form of exploitation could plausibly qualify as just, from a utilitarian point of view.

Schofield (chapter 4), using formal argument and empirical evidence, argues that median voter convergence does not occur. Showing the restrictiveness of the 'mean voter theorem', Schofield argues that the more problematic the decision (especially if it involves a new or suppressed issue dimension), the greater the divergence of candidates and positions. He uses a Madisonian argument to suggest that, when issues are uncertain, citizens need to make a judgement on the 'fit choice' of the best candidate. That frees utilitarian democracy from the median voter theory and its potentially exploitative consequences, perhaps. But still, a majority will count: the decision will be made, and some will win and others will lose out.

The inevitable focus of majoritarian politics means that it will not necessarily display impartial concern for the interests of all, in a way that the aggregations of utilitarian justice are supposed to do. True, majoritarian democracy is more egalitarian than other political systems (Jackman 1972; Verba *et al.* 1978). Nevertheless, majoritarian democracy is not *perfectly* egalitarian. Where utilitarianism might depart from egalitarian solutions, majoritarian democracy may do even less well, unless the majority act with some perfect empathy toward others.

Perhaps this is merely to say that classical utilitarians have traditionally plumped for the wrong form of democracy, from the point of view of their own theory. Maybe they should have gone for more consensual modes of democratic decision-making instead (Lijphart 1999). But there is no guarantee that consensus politics will maximize utility. The vetoes it offers certain individuals or groups constitute invitations to extortion that are far from utility maximizing (Barry 1965: 245–9; Rae 1975, Schofield chapter 4).

In short, utilitarianism may well imply one form of justice and one form of democracy. But there is no reason to suppose that the form of democracy that utilitarianism recommends will necessarily deliver justice as utilitarians conceive it. Some utilitarians might resolve that conflict by prioritizing utilitarian justice over utilitarian democracy, saying that departures from utilitarian democracy may (but may only) be justified in terms of utilitarian justice. But that smacks of introducing substantive constitutional principles into a democratic settlement that Brian Barry, for one, has suggested should not be seen as part of principles of democracy. Utilitarians following that line of thought might be tempted to prioritize utilitarian democracy over utilitarian justice, instead.

Contractarianism

Broadly the same pattern emerges when we look at contractual, consent-based theories. Consent underwrites democracy. Free and fair elections are typically seen as a mechanism for securing 'the consent of the people'. That is what, in the eyes of many, most fundamentally legitimates democratic rule.

The trouble is that collective consent of the sort secured by a democratic election does not necessarily give rise to just outcomes. Any democratic rule short of unanimity almost certainly yields outcomes with which someone has a legitimate complaint – unless the scope of democratic decision-making is constrained within the terms of the rights people are supposed to have (which is to say, the scope of democracy is constrained in the name of justice). And this is why many of the theorists of an original contract argued that 'the law of nature' and 'natural rights' operated in civil society and provided a standard of justice by which to judge governments. Down to our own day, contractual theories specifying particular principles of justice, such as Rawls', cannot guarantee that any specific democratic aggregation mechanisms will ensure that those principles are implemented without taking them out of the reach of democratic procedures altogether.

Contractarians might reply that the consent required for purposes of contractarian justice is consent not to particular outcomes, but rather to institutions and procedures. Once we have secured universal consent to the democratic institutions and procedures in view, we will *ipso facto* have consent (of the sort that is supposed to count, here) to anything done through them. Albert Weale (chapter 5) points out, contracts signed behind the veil of ignorance suffer from there being various ways in which we can axiomatize concepts of rationality and rational agreement. How do these map onto the practical concerns of a functioning democracy? Securing universal consent to democratic institutions assumes we can have unanimity for majoritarian principles. But libertarians would argue that such agreement could only be possible by severely constraining the scope of the preference aggregation procedure. If so, most of our lives would be left untouched by democratic decisions.

If we imagine both the principles of justice and those of the democratic procedure to be part of the contract, then as Dowding (chapter 2) suggests, that contract should specify the scope and form of democratic decision-making within its principles of justice. If democracy in practice departs too far from the principles of justice, then people may legitimately ask for renegotiation. He wonders if the potential conflict between ideal justice and practical democracy is any greater than that between ideal justice and any practical system of justice. Or as Weale puts it: reasonable individuals without a veil of ignorance will have to appeal to substantive ideals to make their proposals acceptable. The content of justice cannot be avoided through a 'contractual solution'.

Libertarian theories should be distinguished from other contractual theories. After all, before Rawls, one utilitarian famously derived an egalitarian result from utility maximizing from behind a veil of ignorance combined with empathetic preferences (Harsanyi 1955). But, as noted above, in the absence of a social welfare functional derived from that original contract, we can hardly expect that egalitarianism to be sustained in subsequent democratic votes once the veil is lifted.

Libertarian-contractarians face a different problem. They do not specify any substantive principles of justice. Their motto is instead a proceduralist one, 'from each as they choose, to each as they are chosen' (Nozick 1974: 160). There is no particular pattern that libertarians can identify, *ex ante*, of people's actual choices, as the uniquely just distribution. *Ex post*, they confidently commend whatever has emerged from individuals' free choices, in the market and elsewhere, as the just distribution. But this resolves the problem of how to reconcile libertarian-contractarian forms of justice and democracy by fiat. The market is not the same as democracy; libertarian-contractarians simply privilege their form of justice (free choice in the market) over their form of democracy (free collective choice of rules by which to live). In addition, the libertarian-contractarian privileging of one kind of rights – property rights – involves a further, different sort of constraint on justice.

Contractarians can, of course, find various ways of resolving the tension between justice and democracy. Note well, however, that they are all ways of resolving the tension, not of denying its existence. We inevitably face a trade-off between justice and democracy, conceived in contractarian terms. For contractarians as for utilitarians, then, justice and democracy are not the same thing, even if they are seen as proceeding from the same principles.

Proceduralism

We see similar tensions between democracy and justice arising with procedural accounts. At first blush it might seem that there are certain formal properties of 'fairness' and 'impartiality' that run through both justice and democracy, thus uniting them (Goodin, chapter 6; Elster, chapter 7). But those 'same' standards are applied to different objects in those different realms. As Little (1952) long ago suggested, the impartial aggregation of preferences turns out to be different, in important respects, depending on whether we are doing that for purposes of compiling a social *welfare* function or a social *decision* function.

Procedural democracy is usually defined simply in terms of the processes by which individual judgements are translated into authoritative decisions. Procedural democracy is standardly contrasted with substantive accounts of democracy, ones that incorporate substantive principles of justice within the scope of democracy. Even fair-proceduralists, however, almost invariably agree that substantive constitutional constraints need to be imposed on the operation of democratic rule (Sunstein 2001). From the point of view of justice, the whole point of constitutional requirements of due process is to protect principles of justice from the vagaries of democratic decisions. Proceduralism in respect of social justice is thus virtually the counterpart of proceduralism with regard to democracy.

Again, we could try to bring these two proceduralist arguments together. A just democracy would have a constitution which defines the scope of democratic decision-making and constrains actual decisions by ensuring the just constitutional provisions are not overturned through the legislative process. How constraining a constitution turns out to be, however, may depend on the substantive principles of justice accepted by those sworn to uphold the constitution. As Waldron (1999a) points out, constitutional courts make their decisions through majority voting, too. Only a belief in the higher virtues of the elite (at least those with law degrees) as opposed to the mass makes constitutionally-entrenched principles of fair-proceduralism more just than procedural democracy.

The real problem for the tension between justice and democracy with regard to proceduralism is that proceduralism in all its forms cannot deliver substantive justice. All it can deliver is procedures. Is this enough?

Participationism

Participation, both in the minimal form of periodic voting and the more expansive activities emphasized by participatory democrats, is a familiar democratic value. Participation can also be seen as one way of construing the ideals of justice, as emphasized by recent work on social exclusion. Everyone having the capacity to take full part in the life of their society is one form of justice; or anyway the opposite, some being excluded, is one clear form of social injustice (Goodin 2003b: ch. 10; Le Grand chapter 10).

Tension nonetheless remains between participatory conceptions of justice and of democracy. There can be no guarantee that a fully participatory democracy will not vote to exclude some people from enjoying the full benefits of their society, in various other respects. Participatory and deliberative democrats hope, and may have some good grounds for believing, that this is less likely under the arrangements that they propose than at present. Still, the uncertainty and potential need for trade-offs between participatory democracy and participatory justice remains.

Of course, here as before, there are ways of squaring the circle. The democratic principles one wants in participatory democracy can be constitutionally built into a conception of participatory justice; or participatory democracy can contain the requisite principles of justice.

Participatory conceptions face a particular difficulty in pursuing such strategies, however. A key thought in such conceptions is that the participants are supposed not to be held to any pre-set list of constitutional norms (interpreted by courts). Instead, they are supposed to participate in order to reconfigure their social arrangements and circumstances as they see fit, after deliberation. How can we build in more than absolute minimum requirements for full participation or deliberation in a participatory democracy? Is this enough for participatory justice?

Participatory democrats might well reply, 'Certainly not!' That is precisely why they do not place all their hopes for justice on elections and procedural constraints. They give as much, if not more, attention to democratizing institutional structures and to measures increasing substantive social equality. Tensions remain, but such an approach offers the possibility of constructing a bulwark against social exclusion, and against the persistence of perceptions of sections of the citizenry that open the way to votes that diminish their standing.

Justice and democracy in multicultural and deeply divided societies

Strict consensus is hardly required for a well-functioning democracy. If it were, two-party democracies would be doomed, or they would have nothing to argue about. What democracy requires is merely something like 'single-peakedness' in people's preferences (Black 1958). We can take different positions on the issues before us. But we must see the shape of our disagreement in broadly the same way. We need not agree, but we must at least broadly agree on what constitutes each end of the spectrum.

Most discussions of democracy and justice assume that this criterion is ordinarily well satisfied. Political life may be like a 'divide-the-dollar' game, with our interests strictly opposed (each of us wants as much as possible, and the more we get the less is left for the others). But at least we completely agree on the nature of the struggle.

Of course, even where the ends of the spectrum are seen in the same fashion, the character of the problems and solutions may not be. This was illustrated by the controversies over power and citizen apathy in the 1960s and 1970s. It was illustrated more recently in the way that many problems discussed by feminist scholars are still not seen as problems in many accounts of justice and democracy. Multiculturalism occupies a similar position.

The problems of multicultural conflict in multicultural societies bring out most forcefully the tensions between justice and democracy that we have been discussing. As we quoted Barry above, if a democracy gets too out-of-kilter with the interests of some groups in society, we cannot expect those groups simply to lie back and think of procedural democracy. Groups may wish to reconsider the procedures of a democratic settlement if those procedures do produce outcomes that are completely unacceptable to them (Dowding chapter 2). In Barry's terms, groups might reasonably reject outcomes if they are too exploitative and may reasonably wish to renegotiate the precise procedures of their democracy (although this, of course, cannot license renegotiation through mere disagreement with the outcomes).

Democratic principles of freedom of association and religion and collective self-government seem to support multiculturalism and to contribute to justice (Kymlicka 1995). Yet autonomy for cultural groups to control their own affairs can run counter to justice and democratic rights for individuals within those groups, especially in the case of women whose position is seen as central to the preservation of religious and cultural traditions (Okin 1998; Shachar 2001). Brian Barry (2001) has most forcefully argued that no special treatment, rights or benefits need to be meted out to different groups in society. The equality principle, properly applied, can ensure each person may live their idea of the good life in conformance to the harm principle.

Debate about multiculturalism has focused on immigrant communities in Western countries, and here the equality principle is well embedded. But in other countries 'multiculturalism' is about national minorities. Some of those countries are such deeply divided societies that agreement about the ends of spectrum, about the nature of the conflict, or even over what is important in life is precisely what is lacking. Even where divisions are not so deep, minority groups are often wary of democratic domination, and may feel the need for specific constitutional protections. Yet, as Brian Barry has pointed out, such constitutional provisions often highlight conflict and deepen the battles as the constitution, rather than mere legislation within it, becomes the battleground.

Problems for working liberal democratic states can occur as ethnic conflicts are encouraged as the economic prosperity of modern capitalism extends its global reach. With the exception of radical Islam, however, these problems are usually concerned with conflicts between close neighbours rather than globalization itself, as Russell Hardin (chapter 11) points out. Liberal democratic solutions include giving greater autonomy to some, or protections against exploitation or domination. But it only takes an ethnically-based diversity in income or wealth to encourage hostility over other 'cultural' effects. People feel their identity is threatened when economic progress leads the younger generation to embrace new cultural artifacts in music or dress or behaviour, even if they would do exactly the same in their own culturally homogeneous state. Men feel even more threatened when women try to embrace new ways or appeal to human rights. Indeed, it is almost certainly for this reason that globalization is exacerbating such conflicts.

Liberal-democratic solutions for injustices to minority groups may include greater autonomy, or, more radically, secession. These are only really practicable, however, where groups are geographically concentrated. Constitutional provisions may be required to satisfy the demands and assuage the fears of minority groups in diverse societies but as we have pointed out, these can exacerbate problems.

If liberal-democratic political thought has a problem particularly with conflicts in deeply divided societies, it is that liberalism has never really developed a theory of the state. Liberalism does not specify how large states should be, or whether it is good for societies to be socially or ethnically homogenous or heterogeneous. Instead, liberalism specifies universal practices for treating all in the same way. But what does liberalism have to say about groups who wish to opt out completely from a liberal state; what does it say about secession?

Allen Buchanan (1991) argues that secession is an embarrassment for liberalism because its universalism leads it to be suspicious of separatist movements. Once all the correct liberal principles are adopted, presumably there can be no reason for desiring secession. There can be no liberal theory of just secession from a just liberal state (Dowding 1998) – only theories justifying secession when states treat groups unjustly. On the other hand, Harry Beran (1984) has long argued that government by consent requires that secession be allowed if desired by a territorially concentrated group. A simple majority in a referendum should be enough to justify secession of one geographic region; and if the opponents were geographically concentrated they could then secede from the new state, and so on.

These two contrasting views on liberalism and secession might stand as an exemplar of the issues we have been exploring between justice and democracy. Buchanan suggests that there can be no just reasons for seceding from a just state. Beran suggests that if people democratically decide to secede that is all that is required, *no matter what their reasons are*. Buchanan's views on secession tickle our intuitions over justice, Beran's tickle our views on democracy. We do feel that there should be self-rule, both for individuals over their own lives, but also by extension for groups that self-identify. But we also have a theory of justice that may lead us to believe that secession for the wrong reasons – to set up an unjust society, or for exploitative reasons – cannot be justified. To some extent this may also explain contrary intuitions about multicultural conflicts within states.

Conclusion

Justice and democracy are two separate concepts, though they are inextricably intertwined. Whilst some may believe a just society could be undemocratic, most would think that democratic procedures are those most likely to sustain socially just societies in the long run. On the other hand, few would doubt that democracies can and do produce injustices.

The arguments for justice, howsoever one conceives it, and those for democracy in its various ideal guises also take many forms. The intuitions that lead us to our ideally just society, on the one hand, and to our preferred form of democracy, on the other, may conflict. We ordinarily accept that our views on what should happen may not be the views of the majority of our society. When we lose the vote in a democracy we ordinarily accept the decision and work within it, accepting the laws that proceed from that decision. We nonetheless think that it is still legitimate for us to lobby and work to overturn legislation we do not like, or bring down governments we disagree with, or work to change institutional structures, gender relations or to further social equality. Those are as much a part of the democratic process as accepting the result of the democratic vote. However, when decisions made in a democracy are felt to be too unjust then, in the name of justice, that democratic decision may be challenged undemocratically. As Brian Barry warns, the costs of any such challenge must be weighed carefully; and often the costs outweigh the injustice. We have not tried to suggest any hard and fast lines where justice should prevail over democracy. We have been concerned instead merely to highlight the tensions that exist within and between theories of justice and democracy.

2 Are democratic and just institutions the same?

Keith Dowding

Democratic procedures and just social outcomes are clearly not the same thing. A majority of the electorate can easily vote for a politician or a party that promotes social injustice (Barry 1991b). Given the competitive nature of democracy and the fact that most, if not all, political issues concern the distribution of scarce resources, unjust (re)distributions (under some theory of justice) are likely to be the norm rather than the exception. Unless, that is, the competitive aggregative procedures (voting and pressure politics) can be rigged to ensure that just distribution follows; or people can be persuaded somehow not simply to vote in their own self-interest but to look more broadly at social welfare in their society (Goodin 2003b). In fact, we know that sociotropic voting occurs and people do not uniformly vote for their own self-interest. And whilst the voting systems are not normally 'rigged' to achieve just distribution, most liberal democracies do have some constitutional provisions to control rent-seeking. Nevertheless, democratic procedures and just social outcomes are far from being the same thing.

Despite this obvious fact, I am not convinced that extant theories of justice and arguments for democracy are as analytically distinct as most theorists maintain. I will argue that the fundamental justifications for having democratic procedures lie essentially in the same realm as arguments for social justice. Of course, there are many competing theories of justice. And they do not all envisage the same 'good life'. Even those liberal theories that do seem to entail much the same structure of society have quite different justificatory frameworks. So if my argument is to include all such theories it must be drawn with a broad brushstroke. There are also, of course, competing justifications of democracy. Some defend democracy largely in terms of the representation of interests, recognizing that some rights and liberties are also necessary. More recent democratic thought has concentrated upon deliberative democracy that

I would like to thank Bob Goodin for his penetrating comments and useful suggestions on the first draft of this chapter.

has much greater expectations of political institutions, and more particularly of citizens. Again, my argument will try to encompass these different justifications of democracy.

Arguments for democracy

Early arguments for democracy derive from principles concerning the protection of interests. That is, to stop exploitation of citizens by their government (Bentham 1823; Mill 1820; Macpherson 1977; see Weale 1999: ch. 3 for a short discussion of such arguments). More recently, democracy has been justified in more positive terms, with suggestions that it allows individuals to express their preferences and input these into the decision-making process (Dahl 1989; Dahl 1998). Voters do not always get what they want, but they can feel that governments must take account of their wishes. Indeed, democracy is often defined simply in terms of the aggregation of preferences and more particularly in terms of the majority principle (Barry 1991b; McLean 1991) with its known nice properties (May 1952). However, few extant electoral systems ever deliver the majority winners of first preferences of the electorate (or the Condorcet winner by pairwise comparisons), let alone the citizenry as a whole. At best, governments are chosen by a plurality of first preferences of the electorate or some other summative procedure of preferences down voters' orderings (see International IDEA www.idea.int for information on electoral systems across the world). The specific mechanisms of preference aggregation give different aggregations, of course (Riker 1982; Saari 2001; Reeve and Ware 1992), but the general procedural principle is that individual preferences are represented in the final decisions over representatives and policies.

Beyond the electoral system itself, democracy requires other rights and freedoms, if only because individuals need the space that these provide in order to discover or develop their preferences. Rights of assembly, to form parties, pressure groups, a relatively free media, and so on, are required in order to give a point and purpose to having the right to vote. Even those who wish to define democracy simply in terms of the majority principle recognize that its normative gravity derives not only from its technical features but also from those technical features being valuable to the electorate. Other rights and freedoms are thus necessary features of democracy. Democracy is still justified procedurally, however. Certain rights and freedoms are required as a background to the aggregation rules, but it is these rules that lead to the choice of the electorate, whatever that happens to be. And that choice may be unjust.

In recent theories of deliberative democracy the simple aggregation of preferences is not seen as the most important aspect of a democracy, though usually it is understood as a necessary condition for a working democracy (Cohen 1989; Dryzek 2000). Deliberative democrats see the processes of democracy as involving the interchange of ideas and arguments in such a way that citizens can come to understand others' interests and reach accommodation in a less antagonistic and competitive manner. The justification is still procedural, though not aggregative, since the aim is to reach more consensual outcomes where the results of the procedure are thought to be more objective. In that sense deliberative democracy might be thought to be less clearly procedural than theories that concentrate upon fair representation of interests. Deliberative democrats also champion the referendum to give citizens a more direct input in governmental decision-making than provided by voting for independent representatives (Barber 1984; Parkinson 2001; Pateman 1970). For deliberative and epistemic democrats Condorcet's jury theorem, rather than the Condorcet procedure, is the paradigm consideration. The jury theorem (arguably) requires that there are right answers to the questions posed to the electorate, and that each person is more likely to choose the correct answer than any wrong one. Hence majority verdicts are likely to track the truth (Estlund 1989; Estlund 1994; List and Goodin 2001).[1] The types of outcomes that democratic procedures produce relative to rival forms of government thus enter strongly into the justification for democracy. Democracy is no longer being justified on simple procedural grounds once it is claimed that one of its desirable features is that it is also more likely to get the right answer than a dictatorship.

We should not make too much of this contrast between traditional aggregative defences and deliberative defences of democracy. Traditional arguments proceeding from the protection of interests also have at least one eye on the outcomes of democratic procedures for their justification. After all, protecting the interests of the citizens can be seen as a 'better outcome' than their interests being trodden on. We might also think that such protection is just, and a procedure that protects interests 'tracks' *that* truth. On the other hand, we cannot be assured that voting through referendums or using a deliberative process produces more just outcomes than representative democracy unless we specify that the 'right answers' tracked by issue-voting and deliberation are just ones. The 'right answer' one set of deliberators may be considering is how best to extract resources from some other group in society. Or the 'right answer' may be

[1] In fact this requires that the mean probability of being correct across the jury is above one-half and the distribution of error is symmetric (Grofman and Feld 1988).

how to ensure the lowest tax level without destitution for some in society – which may be far from the requirements of some theories of social justice.

The justifications for democracy are generally procedural, though not without one eye on the types of outcomes we should expect from democratic routines. And we cannot expect that even if democratic procedures are correctly and legitimately followed the outcomes they produce will be unjust. At least we cannot fault the democracy as a *democracy* if they are. Or can we? I will suggest below that indeed we can fault a democracy on *democratic* grounds if the working of that democracy is systematically unjust.

Arguments for justice

One way of trying to contrast arguments for justice against those arguing for democracy is to contrast the largely procedural form of the latter against the largely patterned nature of the former. Theories of justice tend to set out conditions of distribution of rights, welfare, resources, primary goods, capabilities or whatever (hereafter the 'distributandum'). They might be thought to defend end-states rather than procedures. Of course not all theories of justice are 'end-state' ones. Nozick (1974) contrasted his own account with liberal and egalitarian theories by its procedural rather than end-state qualities. But this is a false dichotomy between historical and end-state or patterned theories of justice. Nozick saw the libertarian theory of justice as the working through of a series of just transactions given an initial just distribution of (property) rights. In that sense it is historical. His claim is that we cannot expect to see any pattern in the allocation of the distributandum so that at any given moment thereafter, different sets of just transactions might result. These may subsequently produce virtually any distribution imaginable.

Contrast this with patterned principles of justice that imply assigned allocations. Egalitarians require that the allocation of the distributandum conform (to some extent) to their preferred pattern at each historical moment. Market transactions cannot be allowed to disrupt the patterning and hence must be carefully regulated. Nozick derides such arguments, suggesting that patterned principles do not allow any form of transacting and massively curtail liberty. But the distinction here is not between historical principles and patterned ones, but in the type of history that is allowed. For Nozick the just history is one that comes about from the just original distribution through free transfers alone. Any form of coerced transfers such as taxation is unjust. But 'patterned' theories of justice only require a structure or set of institutions defining legitimate market transactions and then constantly intervene in these transactions to ensure that the results of the market process do not lead to great social injustices. This simply requires regulation of markets (for safety, to stop exploitation and domination, and indeed to ensure fair and proper competition), and a tax and benefits system – that is, a welfare state – to ensure the 'patterning' remains in place despite legitimate transacting. It might be believed that such a welfare society may lead to lower economic growth than a less regulated market society, but social justice may require that price to be paid for its other social gains. History is allowed to unfold under such structures, and there can be winners and losers, both through merit and through luck of one sort or another.

The distinction between historical and patterned principles of justice melts away once we realize that the fundamental justification for justice is to develop the basic structure of society and political institutions (Rawls 1971: 274–5; Rawls 1978). Nozick's distinction between patterned and historical principles of justice crucially depends upon his stark views about any attempt at redistribution not following simple market procedures. History is not allowed to encompass redistributive taxes. All principles of justice allow 'history' to unfold within them – but do so according to different standards of what is permissible. Nozick is not defending a 'historical theory of justice', merely defending one that privileges free transfer above all else.

All the fundamental justifications for liberal social justice can be seen as historical in Nozick's sense. They pattern outcomes by setting up institutions through which people act. Socially just institutions must take into account the incentives they create for people in order to shape a society in accord with their justificatory principles. They all follow this same logic. 'Justice as mutual advantage' imagines a contract signed in the state of nature that is thought to be to the mutual advantage of all contractors once they find themselves in the society at large (Gauthier 1986; Rawls 1971; see Barry 1989b for discussion). In justice as impartiality institutions are designed to be neutral between competing claims. Interests are promoted by a defence of liberty through the harm principle (Barry 1995). In both cases there are ideal end-states (though how inegalitarian a society may become due to the difference principle (endorsed by Barry 1989b: Appendix C) is not so clear) but the aim is to produce institutions designed to lead to the end-state of maximizing the condition of the worst-off.

Egalitarian debates are largely about what is to be equalized and maximized – utility, welfare, resources, opportunities, capabilities, power, real freedom – and all too often say little about the institutions which are to deliver the goods. One obvious exception is van Parijs (1995) who has been leading the arguments for a basic income. Basic income is one of the simplest institutional processes to allow the market to operate with its attendant good features whilst ensuring a (maximum) level of realizable equality.

Even utilitarian theories can be represented under this same logic. Harsanyi (1953) makes use of the veil of ignorance device that Rawls later made famous. He imagines what distributional principles individuals would make if they had an equal chance of being anyone in a society, given that they would want to maximize their utility. We can view this calculation behind the veil as being about the nature of the individual decision procedure that each should adopt once they are in society. This could be an argument for each choosing to maximize social utility each time they make a decision. But it can also be seen as a device to secure political institutions to maximize social utility (which is Harsanyi's intention).

In this sense utilitarianism as an institutional theory (Hardin 1988; Goodin 1990; 1995) is teleological (rather than merely consequentialist). By teleological I mean that the rightness of an act should be seen in terms of the purposes for which the act was designed.[2] Utilitarian institutions are designed to maximize utility (which under Harsanyi's own axioms is highly egalitarian). My point, however, is that the logical form of this argument is the same as that for other accounts of justice. Whilst end-states are used to justify the design of the social institutions, those institutions are supposed to stand as just, *whatever they deliver in detail.* The arguments for principles of justice are supposed to deliver the institutions that are thought to follow from those principles. To the extent those institutions deliver the end-states used to justify them, the better the justification. But we should not claim that the institutions are *unjust* simply to the extent that they fail to deliver those end-states.

To be sure, we judge actual institutions in society by holding them up to the ideals of the justification for the principles of justice. But we must not be led to dismiss all possible institutions because they fail to deliver in detail the principles our justification has upheld. In other words, to the extent that theories of justice are about just *institutions* it seems less than assured that those institutions will always deliver outcomes that are just in every detail. Some people will lose out – through bad decisions, through bad luck, through failure of others to do their duty within their institutional roles (including those whose job it is to secure compensation for those who have failed through the failure of others, etc.). What we

[2] The distinction is closer to the dictionary definition than that of Feinberg (1973) which seems to me to have misdirected many in classifying moral and political theories.

can say is that institutions are more or less just to the degree in which they deliver the just outcome for which they were designed.

We can think about these procedural implications from so-called 'end-state theories' by considering the role of incentives in Rawls' theory of justice which has taxed some recently (Cohen 1995; Cohen 2000 and is the subject of Barry 1989b: Appendix C). Barry succinctly summarizes the problem:

> On the one hand, when he is seeking to establish equality as the baseline from which departures have to be justified, Rawls relies on the premise that whatever makes people more or less capable of producing is morally arbitrary. On the other hand, in the course of making his move from equality to the difference principle he makes use of the premise that people in a just society will respond to material incentives. But the implication of any system of material incentives is that those who produce more will finish up with more. The charge is that, if it is accepted that productive advantages are unjust, there should be no need for material incentives. For the members of a just society should be motivated by thoughts of the injustice of inequality to work loyally in pursuit of the goal of maximum income equally distributed. (Barry 1989b: 396)

The claim of Narveson (1976; 1978), Carens (1981), Cohen (1995; 2000) and Murphy (1999; 2000) is that the truly just society on Rawls' argument leaves no room for inequality. If institutional incentives are required in order to motivate moves towards equality then this can only be second best, and we cannot have a just account of the difference principle. It must rely upon pragmatic grounds, not ones of social justice. This argument is interesting for my account here since it tries to force a disjunction between the justification for institutions of redistribution and what a just distribution should look like. On Cohen's (2000) account, only a society where everyone behaves (always) in accordance with the principles of justice is actually a just one. My claim that we cannot expect just institutions to always deliver just outcomes is denied, since for Cohen the only just institutions are those norms of behaviour which lead everyone (always) to act in accordance with the principles of justice.

I must admit to the kind of impatience with this argument that Cohen (1988: 253–4) displays against historical property entitlement theories when applied to actual distributions of property. If theories of justice are to be directed solely at persuading people to change their behaviour then they are resolutely moral and not political. But I take political philosophy to be directed at producing organizing principles for a just society that provide incentives for people to behave justly. If we are entitled to the expectation that the only institutions which are required are those constituted by the behaviour of people – through the norms, morality and conventions of behaviour 'recursively organized' and 'recursively implicated'

(Giddens 1984: 25) or more simply their equilibrium strategies – then institutional design is easy. But here's the rub. Institutional design is not easy since the behaviour has to be demonstrated to be the equilibrium strategies either of people or of their genes (Binmore 1994; 1998; Gintis 2000). One cannot simply assume that if we have a theory of justice people (even if they buy the theory) will follow its principles.[3]

As Barry (1989b: 398–9) argues, Rawls' own position is that the liberties contained in the first principle and the constraints placed on the difference principle in the second half of the second principle allowing for the freedom to choose one's occupation under equal liberty and fair competition entail individuals being able to choose the type of job they want, and, given the constraints of holding on to that job, how hard they work at it. Conscripting people to the jobs they are best fitted for and ensuring they work at maximum productivity does not allow for individual liberty.

We do not have to assume that all people are knaves and design institutions accordingly. Indeed, the design of institutions should take into account the incentives that lead some to be knavish, and those that lead some to virtue (Brennan and Hamlin 2000; Le Grand 2000; 2003). But we cannot expect to be able to design a set of institutions that are perfectly incentive-compatible, so that the end-states we would ideally like to attain will automatically follow when the institutions are in place. Just institutions do not guarantee just outcomes in detail any more than democratic procedures guarantee them. It does not follow, of course, that arguments for just institutions are the same as arguments for democracy simply because neither guarantee just outcomes. However, I would now like to suggest that arguments for changing the institutions of society – whether they are the institutions designed for justice or the institutions designed for democracy – have the same logical form. In both cases, legitimate arguments for changing the institutions of society will come from the *injustice* wreaked on some by the operation of those institutions.

Contrasting democracy and justice

Democracy is procedural, but then so is justice. Systems of justice may be set up for specific distributional or social reasons, but those systems are constituted of procedures for ensuring that the distributional and social consequences result. Similarly, democracy is a procedure, but if that procedure leads to injustices then we cannot expect reasonable people to accept those procedures indefinitely. One cannot forsake a democratic

[3] As someone who buys 'revealed preference' theory, I have to add that of course people do not truly buy theories unless they behave in accordance with them. Talk is cheap.

decision just because one does not like it, but that is not the issue. But no matter what the procedures of justice or democracy are, they should be open to challenge because the *results* of those procedures do not conform to what was expected when those procedures were formed.

What I have in mind is the simple contractual analogy. We enter into a contract to form a set of rules to govern our democracy. Some of the rules are set up to ensure we have entered a society that is just. We assume that those signing the contract did so willingly, and there was no domination of one group by another. Nevertheless, at some future time, some of the contractors wish to renegotiate. What they wish to renegotiate are the procedures or rules. Under what conditions might we say they are entitled to demand such renegotiation? When is such renegotiation just? When is it democratic? Are the conditions of such renegotiation the same?

In what sorts of ways can it be right to demand that the rules be rewritten? First, it may be that you did not realize how the rules would work out.[4] You didn't realize that a particular institution would favour some people against others. Here, for your claim to have legitimacy, it cannot be merely that you did not realize that you would miss out. It is no good arguing once the veil has been lifted, that whilst you understood the poor would suffer ill health, you didn't realize that you were going to be poor. The claim has to be that you had not realized that these rules would leave the poor with such wretched health. One of the claims of injustice against the use of QALYS (quality adjusted life years) as objective judgements about who should receive health-care, is that the procedure (at least in some forms) disadvantages the poor because their lifestyle in terms both of those aspects over which they have little control (such as the poorer quality food they are forced to purchase) and over those which they may be thought to have greater control (such cultural facts as the relatively higher proportion of smokers in lower social classes) leads to lower life expectancy amongst the lower than that of the middle and upper classes. One may agree that QALYS seem to be a good objective way of rationing health-care when they are discussed in theory at the contract stage, but once it is realized how they work in practice it is not unreasonable for the poor to want the contract renegotiated.

We may argue similarly for democratic procedures. We may agree to an electoral system composed of a set of constituencies, voting rules, an

[4] Of course in most contractual myths, such as Rawls (1971) the contractors are supposed to have full information about how everything will work out. But I am taking the view that if we are to compare justifications for the actual institutions for justice and those for democracy we need to take a more realistic account of our knowledge. Binmore (1994; 1998) uses the contractual device that can be constantly renegotiated through his 'games of morals' and 'games of life'.

assembly (or two) and so on. We may consider how each of these elements shape up when signing the contract, yet once the electoral system has been working for a while some contractors may legitimately ask for changes in the rules. Perhaps it was not clear just how non-proportional the system might be. Perhaps it was not clear how manipulable the particular voting rules would prove. It is not unjust to ask for changes in a contract once the contract is in place if the results turn out to be particularly biased in some regard.

Another aspect that may lead contractors to demand renegotiation is that the world has changed in some way. We regularly examine electoral constituencies because the geographical mobility of the electorate changes the relative size of voting districts and their social composition. Boundaries are redrawn to reflect changing circumstances. There is nothing unusual or unjust in such changes to the electoral landscape (even though, of course, redistricting is subject to much political lobbying for electoral advantage). Notwithstanding lobbying for gain, gerrymandering and so on, the process of redistricting can hardly be claimed to be undemocratic or unjust as a process. Similar considerations may be applied to reconsidering other aspects of the voting game due to the changing social composition of the electorate through social or geographical mobility. A plurality voting system may produce majoritarian results if the ideological split is bipolar and two large parties represent the interests of two large groups of voters (with the swing median voters deciding the outcome each election). But if the social spectrum divides further into new camps, the plurality system may no longer reflect those changed circumstances. It is not unjust for groups to demand modifications to the voting system in order to reflect those social changes and allow greater proportionality of first preference votes to a larger number of parties. Of course, the median voters (in the parliament if not the electorate) will still swing the votes to create the government. Nevertheless, coalition governments may feel the need to reflect a broader spectrum of society and even if they do not that is no reason to besmirch the reasonable claims for greater proportionality to reflect the changing social bases of the society.

Demands for changing the rules may also legitimately be made when the way people respond to those rules alters over time. In sports, rules are often changed when competitors play within the rules, but start to break the spirit of the game. In tennis, rules have been introduced for how quickly the server must serve after the end of a point, and how many times they may call for their physiotherapist or doctor, as it was felt that some competitors slowed matches down when it was to their advantage. In soccer, managers and coaches are now restricted as to how close they may get to the pitch and players must leave the field of play if they ask for the physiotherapist, because it was felt that coaches were coaching from the sidelines (not illegal but restricted) and players were faking injuries for team gain. New rules are introduced because the players start behaving differently. Or perhaps more precisely, when the way some always behaved becomes widespread it becomes a problem. So too in a democracy. As Easton (1965) argued, it is not enough to have formal institutions for stable democracy; the people must also behave in the right manner. The institutions and the culture must work together.[5] We may have the formal rules of a democracy, but people must also behave properly within them. A society may be able to function well whilst carrying a few racists who stand for election, incite racial hatred, and so on. It may not function so well with many, and depending upon the nature of the racist behaviour, new laws controlling that behaviour may be thought appropriate. Of course, those to whom such laws are directed often complain about losing democratic rights. And of course they do, as indeed does everyone, whether or not they wished to exercise those rights. But the considerations of stability, as well as the rights of others, are thought to trump them, and others' rights and the stability of society are equally a part of democratic considerations. We can view such restrictions as the renegotiating of contracts as a consequence of the way some behave within the terms of the old contract.

Similarly we will find that when we come to write the detailed provisions of the institutions of justice, these rules will need to be altered as people respond to the rules as written. This may be illustrated with a simple example. One of the beauties of basic income as an institution for social justice is that it is so simple and efficient to operate. It also requires fewer regulations to ensure less exploitation and domination in the labour market. But one issue over basic income is whether all should receive exactly the same amount or whether the disabled should receive extra on account of the extra costs to them of attaining the same as the able-bodied. The problem with giving extra to the disabled is that the numbers claiming to be disabled, in one way or another, is bound to shoot up.[6] For

[5] I am using the term 'institution' here (and indeed throughout this chapter) in the old-fashioned sense traditional in Easton and in old public administration texts, rather than in terms of the 'new institutionalism' where it becomes difficult to draw a distinction between institutions and cultural practices.

[6] In the United Kingdom claims for disability allowances increased fourfold from 1972–95 in the age ranges 50–54 and 55–69 and two-and-a-half times in the age range 60–64, before beginning to fall (Social Security Estimates 2000: Chart A2). Part of this increase occurred with the collusion of government, to remove people from the unemployment register, but clearly doctors were ratcheting up their assessments of disabilities. The fall in claims occurred as the government attempted to redress the ratchet effect through

this reason, most of the proponents of basic income wish to restrict the payment of extra resources at most to the 'severely disabled'. One can see, however, that in practice, given the pressures of electoral politics, the line around 'severe disability' is likely to be drawn and redrawn. That is not to say that the arguments for the redrawing will be illegitimate on either side, but judgements of the justness of specific claims will have to be weighed, given how the rules, howsoever they are written, are interpreted. These claims are likely to be made on the grounds of fairness and equality. If person X gets more because of that disability, then person Y should also get more because in practice her disability entails equal or greater costs.

Can we make a similar argument on the grounds of the fairness or equality of outcomes to changing the precise institutional rules governing democratic procedures? Brian Barry argues that the procedural justification for democracy is that our equality of input – 'one person one vote' – does not lead to any expectation of equality in respect of outcomes. This would suggest that inequality of output cannot justify changing the voting rules. Barry attacks the idea of the 'wasted vote' along these lines. He says that, since any vote cast for a non-winner may seem to be wasted and the voter 'effectively disenfranchised' it is absurd to think that some systems waste more votes than others, or that it can be claimed that, to that extent, those systems are unjust and so justify being altered (Barry 1991b; Barry nd). Whilst the argument is indeed silly in respect of one voter whose vote does not contribute to the winner in one election, the argument is not so silly when applied to the majority of voters in any given election (the actual argument of the proponents of proportional systems of voting whom Barry is attacking) nor to a large group of voters who lose at every election – the problem of persistent losers (Dahl 1956; Dahl 1989). The larger the subgroup the less silly the argument appears. The problem of persistent losers has worried many democrats (Dahl 1956; Jones 1988) and there is no simple answer to the problem. The problem is not simply that some people do not get the government they want, but rather that minorities do not get what they want on issues which are of importance to them but to which the majority is relatively indifferent. In these instances, the other side of democracy – pluralism and the pressure group system – might help deliver these goods. Where there is direct conflict, however, the losers may feel that they need further protection against the tyranny of the winners. Those losers with whom we are likely

information and further assessment. Similarly, the expenditure on people with long-term illness and disability increased over fourfold between 1978/9 and 1997/8 (Social Security Estimates 2000: Table B4).

to feel most sympathy are those who lose on 'an issue of identity' rather than an 'issue of competition' (Sartori 1987).

In order to explain this difference I want to make use of a distinction that was first introduced by Barry (1991c). In the context of the power index approach to measuring power, he suggested a distinction between power and luck. Power is getting what you want despite resistance, whilst luck is getting what you want without trying. The power of a voter (*i*) in a group *n* is the number of times the voter is pivotal in *n!* sequences of votes (Shapley and Shubik 1969; see Dowding 1991: 56–63 for a simple exposition). In a constituency of 40,000 with each person getting one vote, each voter's Shapley-Shubik voting power would be 1/40,000. But some might always get the candidate they prefer, and some might never do so. The difference between the probability of getting what you want and your power is your luck. Being on the winning side is usually more dependent upon luck rather than Shapley-Shubik power, and the larger the electorate the less likely that one's vote is decisive. For example, in the USA, if there are two presidential candidates, then Mueller (1989) calculates that for each voter the probability of being decisive is 1/16,666 as long as we assume that each voter chooses their candidate by tossing a fair coin. Even this small probability of being decisive is misleading, since the maximum probability of being decisive occurs when the probability of voting for one or other candidate is equal across all voters, but the gradient around the function is very steep. If the expected probability of the vote for one of the candidates is 0.499, then the probability of a voter being decisive falls to $1/10^{90}$ (Carling 1995). This makes clear the obvious point that the citizens who get the President they want are lucky not powerful, whether or not they bothered to vote for him. In this sense, considering the 'wasted vote' from the individual voter's point of view is indeed a waste of time. But is it from a group perspective?

Some may be systematically lucky and some systematically unlucky (Dowding 1991; 1996; 2003). Systematic luck is getting what you want irrespective of your resource holding, simply because the luck of getting what you want attaches to certain locations within the institutional and social structure. When this comes to preferences within the voting game, it is because the preferences you have are systematically attached to a given location in the social structure that is always winning because of the rules of the particular aggregation system in use (Dowding 1999). Preferences are not things which one simply decides to have. Rather there is something about one's social location that structurally suggest them (Dowding 1991). But can losers, even systematic losers, expect to be given special dispensation in the democratic game simply because they are losers? On the contractual argument above they can. If they hypothetically agreed to the rules without realizing how those rules would play out, then they have a claim to change those rules once their effect is apparent. For example, a minority ethnic group may have been allowed to live their lives according to their conception of the good life for many years, but then at some point the majority group may start to encroach upon that life by treating them differently within the same laws. For example, as economic times become harder perhaps the majority group refuses to trade with the minority, or will only trade under exploitative conditions. Here, the minority group may demand new protections in law. Or the majority may use their majority to change laws that deleteriously affect the minority.

How are we to recognize such minorities as being systematically unlucky requiring special treatment because their luck leads them to be treated unjustly? It cannot simply be that you never win. There are many people who have never got the government they wanted, and never will, simply because their preferences are so out of line with everyone else's. (I think I'm one of them.) But on its own that cannot be considered a legitimate claim to renegotiate the democratic institutions. ('I did not realize from behind the veil that I would have such odd preferences.') In reality people do not have any old preference ordering and people from similar backgrounds tend to order their preferences over certain sets of issues in particular ways. We might see a 'people' who have a legitimate claim to be treated in a special way by the democratic process as a set of individuals (1) who tend to order their preferences with regard to certain issues in much the same way, (2) to whom these issues are important or 'urgent' (Scanlon 1975), (3) for whom these issues are historically conditioned through institutionally transmitted means, and (4) who tend to recognize themselves as a 'people' by this ordering tendency (Dowding 1998: 81). People tend to see themselves as a 'people' when they feel hard done by; when they feel they are being dominated or exploited (or when their own exploitation or domination of others is under threat). But that is precisely when their claims for special treatment need most urgently to be examined. (Of course, we do not require that a people recognize themselves as such – under point (4) – in order to believe that morally something should be done for them. We may wish to fix gerrymandered constituencies, even if those whose votes are diluted by the gerrymander are unaware of the problem. Politically, however, groups make demands when they feel injustice.)

We should also not make too much of the distinction between the defence of the background conditions for procedures of democracy and those procedures themselves. Waldron (1999a) reminds us that the arbiters of constitutional provisions also vote their decisions and the same issues and ideologies split their votes as split the electorate at large. Constitutional provision should at best give pause to the democratic processes in the wider society, just as the deliberations of lawyers and politicians may also be extended through wider deliberation to all in society (Goodin 2003b).

In fact, the times when 'special treatment' for minorities is required by justice should be relatively rare. The equal liberal constitutional protections that I suggested give a point and purpose to democratic aggregation procedures should also provide the protection that most need (Barry 2001), but we should not discount 'fancy franchises' without considering the cases one by one. And here is the upshot. When deciding which preferences need to be protected from the tyranny of the winners (majority, plurality or minority) in a democracy we can only select those that we feel should be protected given our theory of justice. The reasonableness of withdrawing from the particular aggregation procedures used in one society, can only be decided against the background of what are considered reasonable reasons for such withdrawal (and the violence and conflict such withdrawal implies) within a theory of justice.[7]

Of course democracy and social justice are not precisely the same. But our arguments for just institutions and for democratic ones have the same logical form. And arguments for changing the institutions we have for promoting both democratic outcomes and just ones also proceed from the same basis, that is the unjust consequences which follow from the institutions we have. It is no more a defence of democracy to say 'but that is the result given our voting method' ('it is the majority decision') when some are reasonably claiming they are systematically losing in 'urgent' matters given the way that decision procedure works in practice, than it is a defence of a constitution to say that it was written to promote social justice when some make reasonable claims they are systematically losing their entitlement given the way the constitution works in practice.

[7] We might consider one of the most famous footnotes in American constitutional law, 'whether prejudice against discrete and insular minorities may be a special condition, which tends seriously to curtail the operation of those political processes ordinarily to be relied upon to protect minorities, and which may call for a corresponding more searching judicial inquiry' (Stone 1938). Widely cited on issues not only of minority representation in apportionment decisions, but equally in cases of positive discrimination. The fundamental moral issues remain much the same whether we are querying representation, participation or distribution.

3 Democracy is not intrinsically just

Richard J. Arneson

In Bertolt Brecht's glorious Communist propaganda play *The Caucasian Chalk Circle*, a character who is a mouthpiece for the author declares that 'things belong to people who are good for them'.[1] In other words, you are entitled to ownership of some item only if your exercise of ownership promotes the common good. This should be understood to be a maximizing doctrine. If one person's ownership of land prevents another person from using the land more productively, the first is wasting resources.[2] At this point in the play what is at issue is rights to use land, but later the same point is applied to politics. The wily judge Azdak displays Solomonic wisdom and demonstrates that it is a grave misfortune for the country that his political rule is coming to an end. Political power rightfully belongs to those people who are good for it.

I am an egalitarian liberal and a democrat, not a communist, but I accept the principle of political legitimacy that Brecht espouses. Systems of governance should be assessed by their consequences; any individual has a moral right to exercise political power just to the extent that the granting of this right is productive of best consequences overall. No one has an ascriptive right to a share of political power. Assigning

I first encountered Brian Barry's work when I was a graduate student who wanted to do political philosophy but was clueless as to what the enterprise was or how it might profitably be conducted. Barry's essay 'Warrender and His Critics' made a deep and lasting impression. Since then I have continually found in Brian Barry's writings an inspiring combination of analytic rigour and sharp intelligence, originality and verve, and humane and sensible political engagement. I admire the man and have the greatest respect for his immense wide-ranging intellectual achievements. It's an honour to honour him by contributing to this *festschrift*.

1 Brecht (1947). Why call this a 'propaganda' play? At the time of its writing, Brecht aims to cast in a favourable light Stalinist political regimes, the horrific nature of which is reasonably described in Glover (1999: ch. 5). Why then call the play 'glorious'? In my judgement, it has considerable aesthetic merit and addresses significant issues in intellectually interesting ways.

2 John Locke asserts a version of this idea in the form of a 'no waste' condition on justified appropriation of land. He writes, 'Nothing was made by God for man to spoil or destroy'. He does not interpret the 'no waste' condition as requiring maximally productive use, however. See Locke (1980: ch. 5).

political power to an hereditary aristocracy on the ground that the nobles deserve power by birth is wrong, but so too it is wrong to hold that each member of a modern society just by being born has a right to an equal say in political power and influence, to equal rights of political citizenship and democratic political institutions. The choice between autocracy and democracy should be decided according to the standard of best results.[3] Which political system best promotes the common good over the long run? Many types of evidence support the conclusion that constitutional democracies produce morally best results on the whole and over the long run, but this judgement is contingent, somewhat uncertain, and should be held tentatively rather than dogmatically. In some possible worlds, probably some past states of the actual world, and possibly in some future actual scenarios, autocracy wins by the best results test and should be installed. Democracy is extrinsically not intrinsically just.[4]

Many contemporary political philosophers addressing the issue of the justification of democracy reject the purely instrumental approach this chapter defends.[5] The alternative view is that democracy is a uniquely fair process for reaching political decisions. Democratic political procedures may be valued for their tendency to produce morally superior laws and policies than would tend to emerge from other procedures, and democracy may also be valued for other good effects that it generates. But even if the results overall of having a non-democratic political regime would be better than the results of having democracy, given that democracy itself qua fair procedure is a substantial intrinsic component of justice, it

[3] In this chapter I leave it an open question, what is the moral standard for assessing results that determines which ones are best. Some of my formulations suggest that the best results standard is consequentialist, or more specifically a consequentialism of rights. But non-consequentialist moral views could embrace a best results standard for assessing forms of governance. For example, a version of a Lockean natural rights view might hold that a state is morally more acceptable, the more it promotes the fulfilment of natural rights (without itself violating any). John Locke suggests such a view though he does not fully commit to it. See Locke (1980).

[4] Mill (1977: ch. 8) defends this position, see also Dworkin (1977: ch. 5) and Arneson (1993: 118–48).

[5] Theorists who hold that democracy is intrinsically just include Beitz (1989); Christiano (1996; 2001); Estlund (1993; 1997); Brighouse (1996); Cohen (1997: 407–38; 2003); Waldron (1999a); Rawls (1993; 1999); Nelson (1980); Dahl (1989); Buchanan (2002: 689) asserts that 'where democratic authorization of the exercise of political power is possible, only a democratic government can be legitimate'. But as he develops this claim he leaves it open that the choice of democratic governance is only morally required when democracy 'can produce laws that satisfy the requirement of equal regard for all persons' basic interests' (2002: 712). If 'can produce laws' means 'actually produces laws', then Buchanan is only committed to the claim that a moral preference for democracy is a tie-breaker to be employed when democratic and non-democratic governance procedures would equally satisfy the relevant best results standard.

might well be that opting for democracy would still be morally preferred all things considered.

Formulating the issue as a dispute between those who assert and those who deny that democracy is intrinsically just can be misleading. The former do not hold that a democratic system of government is unconditionally morally valuable in virtue of its non-relational properties. Most would say democracy is conditionally valuable. It is valuable only given mass literacy and the presence of other cultural background conditions, according to its advocates. The idea rather is that democracy is not merely instrumentally valuable but also qualifies as a worthwhile moral goal and also that democracy is one of the requirements of justice, so that other things being equal, the more democratic the society, the more just it is.

Some philosophical accounts of political democracy take a more radical position. They hold that what constitutes justice for a given society is in principle indeterminable apart from consulting the outcome of proper democratic procedures.[6]

A related view holds that although we cannot ever know what is just, we can reliably distinguish fair from unfair procedures for determining how to cope with persistent disagreement about what we owe to each other. Democracy is a fair political procedure, and moral knowledge extends only to judgments about fair procedures.[7] From this standpoint the idea that we should judge democracy – the intrinsically fair procedure – to be morally required, optional, or prohibited depending entirely on the degree to which it contributes to some supposed substantive standard of 'justice' is a non-starter.

Refuting the radical positions just described is not the aim of this chapter. My position is that democracy, when it is just, is so entirely in virtue of the tendency of democratic institutions and practices to produce outcomes that are just according to standards that are conceptually independent of the standards that define the democratic ideal. Democracy, in other words, should be regarded as a tool or instrument that is to be valued not for its own sake but entirely for what results from having it. I take it to be obvious that we have a lot of knowledge about the substance of justice – that slavery is unjust, for example, or that it is unjust if some people avoidably face horrible life prospects through no fault or choice of their own. Moreover, our grounds for holding these beliefs are

[6] Dahl (1989) endorses something in the neighbourhood of this position.

[7] See Hampshire (2000) for a subtle discussion that finds insistence on fair procedures more sensible than insistence on any conception of substantive fairness of outcomes. Hampshire does not endorse the radical affirmation of the instrinsic fairness of democratic procedures as I characterize it in the text of this paragraph.

independent of any convoluted account one might give to the effect that these positions would win a majority rule vote under procedurally ideal conditions.

My focus in this chapter is on the moderate and seemingly reasonable position that political institutions and constitutions should be assessed both according to the extent to which they promote substantively just outcomes and according to the extent that they conform to standards of intrinsic fairness for political procedures. This chapter argues against moderation.[8] I also target a view that lies between the moderate and radical positions as just described. This view holds that even if, as a matter of moral metaphysics, there are truths about substantive justice, they are epistemically unavailable when what is at issue is the justification of democracy, because the need for politics stems from the fact that deep and intractable disagreement about what justice requires persists in modern times even among reasonable people.[9]

The purely instrumental approach to democracy can sound more extreme than it needs to be. The instrumentalist holds that democracy is to be assessed by the consequences of its adoption and operation compared with alternatives. Some might hear this as implying that 'we' now have infallible knowledge of the correct moral standards, the principles of justice. This is not so. The instrumentalist as I conceive her is a realist about morality but can and should be a fallibilist about our present moral knowledge. There is moral truth, but our current epistemic access to it is uncertain, shaky. Hence one crucial standard for judging a society's institutions and practices is the extent to which they are efficiently arranged to increase the likelihood that as time goes on our epistemic access to moral truth will improve. All of this is perfectly compatible with pure instrumentalism. Analogy: we are searching for genuine treasure, and our practices should be assessed instrumentally, by the degree to which they enable us to gain treasure. Our current maps guiding us to treasure are flawed, and our current ideas about what 'treasure' is are somewhat crude, and we have reason to believe there are better maps to be located and better

[8] 'Moderation' as conceived here includes a wide array of possible views. At one extreme, the moderate might hold that the right to a democratic say is just a tie-breaker that favours a democratic over a non-democratic regime if the results of each would be equally good. At the other extreme, one might hold that the right to a democratic say is the right of rights in the sense that it trumps all others combined, and one should always prefer the more democratic over the less democratic regime, allowing the justice of the results of the operation of the system only to act as a tie-breaker among equally democratic regimes. Of course, there are indefinitely many intermediate views.

[9] Christiano (1996; 2001) and Waldron (1999a) develop versions of this position. For Christiano, the intrinsic fairness of democratic procedures follows as a uniquely uncontroversial inference from a conception of substantive justice whose other significant implications are controversial.

conceptions of 'treasure' to be elaborated. So our practices should be judged by the degree to which they enable us to attain genuine treasure, and the extent to which our practices improve our understanding of the nature of treasure and help us locate better maps is an important aspect of their instrumental efficacy.

The idea of democracy

The question whether or not it is intrinsically just that society be governed democratically cannot be addressed without some specification of the idea of democracy. As is well known, the idea is complex. In a society governed democratically, elections determine what laws will be enforced and who will occupy posts that involve political rule. In these elections, all adult members of society have a vote, and all votes are weighed equally. All adult members are eligible to run for political office in these elections, or can become eligible by some non-onerous process such as establishing residency in a particular state or federal division. Majority rule determines the outcome of elections. Political freedoms, including freedom of association and freedom of speech, are protected in the society, so the group or faction that currently holds power cannot rig election results by banning or restricting the expression of opposing views.

A democratic society may operate in indirect rather than direct fashion. That is, rather than its being the case that all citizens together vote on proposed laws, citizens might vote for the members of a representative assembly, whose members enact laws. But indirectness does lessen the degree to which a society qualifies as democratic. This becomes clear if one imagines indirectness iterated many times – voters vote for an assembly that votes for an assembly that votes for another assembly that votes for a political group that votes for laws and votes in officials to administer them. Indirectness diminishes the democratic character of a regime because it lessens the extent to which the present will of a majority of voters controls political outcomes. The contrast between direct and indirect democracy is connected to another, between immediate and mediate accountability of elected rulers to majority rule of citizen voters. In a political system that allows for immediate recall of officials by citizen initiative, the accountability is more immediate, other things being equal, than it would be if recall by this means were not permitted. If some part of the law-making power is exercised by a judicial branch of government, top members of which are appointed by some process that is more rather than less indirect, the political process is to that extent less democratic. If political officials in any branch of government, legislative, executive, or judicial, may not be removed from office once they are validly appointed, this factor also lessens the extent to which the society qualifies as democratic.

Another dimension on which a political system can register as more or less democratic concerns the scope of the authority of the majority will of the citizen voters. If there is a substantial set of restrictions, for example, a list of individual or group rights, which are constitutionally specified as the supreme law of the land, and which may not validly be altered or extinguished by majority will vote, the greater the extent of these limits on majority rule, the lesser the extent to which the political system qualifies as democratic. A provision here is that there are some individual rights that are themselves conceptually required by democracy itself, and the insulation of these rights from majority will control does not render a society less democratic.

Finally, a political system qualifies as more democratic insofar as all citizens have equal opportunity for political influence. This norm admits of various construals. Let us say that citizens have equal opportunity for political influence when all citizens with the same ambition to influence politics and the same political talents will have equal prospects of influencing political outcomes. The idea is roughly that if such factors as one's wealth or family connections affect the impact one could have on the political process if one worked to achieve an impact, then opportunities are unequal and the society to that extent less democratic. If only ambition and political talent, which includes administrative and entrepreneurial skill and the ability to persuade others and build coalitions, affect the chances that one could influence the outcomes of the political process if one tried, then opportunities in the relevant sense are equal and the society to that extent more democratic.

The statement of equal opportunity given above takes individuals as they are, with the political talents they happen to possess at a particular time, as setting the standard of equal opportunity. One might view this statement as inadequate in view of the following sort of example. Society might give access to the opportunities for training and developing political talent only to a restricted social group. If some individuals lack the opportunity to become politically talented, then one might hold equal opportunity does not prevail even though the equally ambitious and talented enjoy equal opportunities. One might then, in a Rawlsian spirit, hold that citizens have equal opportunity for political influence only when all citizens with the same native potential for political talent and the same ambition to develop and exercise it have equal prospects for affecting the outcomes of the political process. This version of equal opportunity for political influence might seem better as a theoretical formulation than the one stated in the previous paragraph, but in practical terms it has the defect that it may be hard in many situations to tell whether it is being fulfilled, given that the idea of potential for political talent is a vague notion.

Democracy is, then, a complex ideal. The judgement as to how democratic the political process of a given society is combines several dimensions of assessment, each of which varies by degree.

Against the right to a democratic say

Consider the proposition that each member of society has a basic moral right to an equal say in the political process that determines the laws that the government enforces and also which people shall be political rulers or top public officials. One has an equal say when one could, if one chose, have the same chance of influencing the outcomes of the political process as any other member of society with equal political skills and equal willingness to devote one's resources to participation in politics. Saying the right to an equal say is a basic moral right includes denying that one has the right merely derivatively, on instrumental grounds. Call this right the 'right to a democratic say'.

The right to a democratic say so understood is a right to political power – a right to set coercive rules that significantly limit how other people will live their lives. With this right secured, one has power over the lives of other people – a small bit of power, to be sure, but power nonetheless. My position is that there is no such basic moral right, because one does not have a basic moral right to exercise significant power over the lives of other people, to direct how they shall live their lives. Rights to power over the lives of others always involve an element of stewardship. If one has such a moral right, this will be so only because one's having the right is more conducive to the flourishing of all affected parties than any feasible alternative.[10]

Parents standardly have extensive power to control the lives of their children who have not yet attained adult age. My position is that there is no basic moral right to have such power. The system of parental control is justified just in case it is maximally conducive to the flourishing of those affected. In just the same way, no one has a basic moral right to be the chief warden of a prison or the director of an insane asylum.

This position has attracted the objection that any substantive moral right involves power over the lives of other people. If you have full private

[10] 'Flourishing' here is just a place-holder referring to whatever the correct best results standard turns out to be. That standard might be a consequentialism of rights position along the lines developed by Sen (1982). For some doubts about Sen's position, see Arneson (2001).

property in some object, you have the right to determine what shall be done with it and to forbid other people from interacting with it. Since all rights involve power to direct the lives of others to some degree, nothing yet has been said to single out the right to a democratic say as specially problematic and not an appropriate candidate for inclusion in the class of basic moral rights.[11]

In response: everything is like everything else, I suppose, in some way or to some degree. Still, a rough line can be drawn between rights that confer on the right-holder the power to direct how another shall live and rights that do not confer such power. Consider the moral right not to be 'bashed' – severely injured by unprovoked non-consensual violent physical attack. If this right is enforced, the right-holder has power over the lives of others to an extent, since she can give or withhold consent to attack and thus determine by fiat whether any other person may attack. But a right that constrains other people from engaging in a certain type of conduct toward the right-holder differs from a right to set rules that might specify what others shall do across a broad range of important types of conduct. I concede this is a difference in degree but when the difference in degree is large the difference is large and in my view morally significant.[12]

[11] Christiano (2001) makes a criticism close to this one in his note 13. Griffin (2003) develops this and other criticisms of the purely instrumental view of democracy. See Arneson (2003) for a reply. Sugden (1993) first developed the criticism.

[12] The claim in the text that rights vary in the extent to which they confer power over the lives of other people and that rights that involve significant power over the lives of others require a best results justification might be challenged. The challenge repeats the point that any moral right involves power over others. Consider many people's exercise of their private ownership rights over small resource holdings. In the aggregate, these exercises of a very small degree of power might very significantly restrict other people's life options. Millions of people might exercise their rights in ways that leave some individuals with just a single employment option or access to just one person who is willing to sell them food needed to live. How does this differ from the way that many people's exercises of the franchise might aggregate to issue in coercive rules that specify how others shall live their lives? In reply: I don't deny that any moral right you might care to name might in some circumstances confer power over the lives of others. I deny this must be so. Consider a world in which small groups of voluntarily associating adults live at great distance from each other. The members of each group may have many moral rights that do not, in isolation or in the aggregate, involve significant power over the lives of others. Moreover, in the case just imagined, where many people exercise rights over small bits of property that in the aggregate significantly begin to restrict the lives of others, I would say the 'intrinsic moral right' gives way and a best results standard becomes operative. Here I intend to contrast moral rights that confer lots of power over the individual's own life and moral rights that involve significant power to direct the lives of others. One might hold that moral rights that confer significant control over the direction of one's own life are justified by a principle of autonomy or personal sovereignty. Hence your right to act as you choose so long as you do not harm others in certain specified ways might be thought not to require a best results justification. Your right stems from a right of personal sovereignty, not from the fact that you are more competent to run your own life than others are to run it for you.

A second response is that perhaps we should acknowledge that many ordinary rights, such as rights to private ownership, do often involve significant power over others. These rights, then, on my view are not appropriate candidates for the status of basic moral right. Consider the owner of a factory, the sole employer in a region, who is also the owner of a company town. Here, private ownership definitely gives the right-holder significant power over others. Perhaps, strictly speaking, only rights to capabilities (real freedom to achieve important human functionings) or rights to opportunities to genuine well-being or the like should count as appropriate candidates for the status of basic moral rights. Even if, in particular circumstances, one's right to capability is secured by control over resources that give one power over others, what one is strictly morally entitled to on an approach that takes capabilities to be basic will never be the power over others but the freedom to achieve and enjoy in the ways central to human flourishing, where these core freedoms could always in principle be secured in some alternative way without the control and the power.

These two responses have some force, but to the advocate of the right to a democratic say they might seem close to question-begging. After all, what rules it out that the freedom to participate on equal terms with others in collective decision-making is a core human capability, on a par with the capabilities to attain knowledge, friendship and love, and achievement? Saying no one has a basic moral right to power over others invites the counter-assertion that the examples of parental rights and democratic rights show that people do indeed have such moral rights. To make further progress we need to investigate the positive arguments for the right to a democratic say. The case for instrumentalism would be strengthened if the search turns up empty pockets. The rest of this chapter follows this roundabout strategy.

What free and equal rational persons can accept

We are looking for the strongest and most plausible arguments for the right to a democratic say, regarded as tantamount to the claim that democracy is an intrinsic component of justice. My search strategy is to elaborate simple considerations, raise objections, then attempt to refine the argument to see if it becomes more compelling.

Start with the idea that each person is owed equal concern and respect. Each person's interests should be given equal consideration in the design of political institutions. But any system that violates the right to a democratic say, assigning or allowing some people greater rights to participate than others, manifestly violates the basic right to equal concern and respect. This argument might be put in a contractualist formulation: free and equal rational persons would not agree to principles that give some greater basic political rights than others. Any such principle would be reasonably rejectable.

The instrumentalist will maintain that principles of equal concern and respect are best satisfied by choice of political arrangements that maximize the fulfilment of basic human rights (other than the disputed right to an equal democratic say). We show concern and respect for people by showing concern and respect for the fulfilment of their rights. It would be question-begging to say in reply that one can only show equal concern and respect by showing respect for all basic moral rights including the right to a democratic say. This argument is supposed to establish, not presuppose, the existence of such a right.

Much the same applies to the contractualist formulation. The instrumentalist need not reject the contractualist idea that what is morally required is what free and equal rational persons would agree to as morally required. But if the choices of ideal moral reasoners determine what is moral, it should be noted that these ideal reasoners are choosing principles for a world in which human agents are not perfectly rational. There is nothing *prima facie* puzzling in the thought of ideal reasoners choosing moral principles that require that some actual persons, less than fully rational, be denied equal rights to political power if that is necessary to produce morally best results.

Persons are not equally free and equal in ways that matter for the question, whether democracy or autocracy is morally superior as a form of governance for people under modern conditions. People vary significantly in the degree to which they are motivated to discover what is just and conform to its requirements. They vary significantly in their capacity to figure out what the requirements of justice are, either in general or in particular circumstances. They vary significantly in their capacity to figure out what ways of life and conceptions of the good are choiceworthy. They also differ significantly in the extent to which they are motivated to exercise whatever practical reasoning abilities they have in order to bring it about that they end up affirming more rather than less reasonable conceptions of what is valuable and worthy of human pursuit. Moreover, all of these significant inequalities bear directly on the issue, who should have political power. These differences in competence render it the case that it could be that under some types of circumstances some autocratic constitution of society would predictably and reliably bring about morally superior outcomes to the outcomes that any feasible form of democracy would reach. In such circumstances (which may not be the actual circumstances of our world), autocracy would be the morally superior form of governance. Given all of this, persons who are free and equal in the threshold sense specified above may reasonably accept an undemocratic political constitution for their governance.

Recall that the question at issue is not whether autocracy is morally required all things considered, but rather whether autocracies (non-democratic political arrangements) are intrinsically unjust, other things being equal.[13]

Must competence tests be objectionably controversial?

Perhaps we can make headway toward understanding the claimed intrinsic justice of democracy by noting that substantive claims regarding the shape and content of people's basic moral rights are controversial in modern diverse democracies. Reasonable members of society do not converge to agreement. Nor is there a long-term tendency toward agreement.

In the face of such disagreement, any assertion that this particular group of persons is more competent than others at determining what rights people have and designing laws and policies to implement rights is bound to be intractably controversial. Why this particular group and not some other? Any proposal of a set of qualifications that determines who is more competent and should rule will run up against the objection that it is morally arbitrary to favour this particular proposal over many alternatives that might have been advanced. The claim that the specially competent should rule thus conceals a naked preference for some conceptions of justice and against others with just as much rational backing.

David Estlund urges a similar argument against what he calls the doctrine of Epistocracy – rule by competent knowers. Estlund (1993: 88) asserts that 'no knower will be so knowable as to be known by all

[13] Why do not the pro-autocracy considerations adduced here suffice to establish at least a strong presumption in favour of the claim that autocracy is morally superior to democracy all things considered? Three countervailing concerns are pertinent. One is 'Quis custodiet custodies?' Concentrating political power in the hands of an elite can produce horrible consequences if the elite becomes corrupt or incompetent. In choosing forms of governance, we should give special weight to preventing moral catastrophes. (A system of Madisonian checks and balances might mitigate this problem.) A second consideration is that political science has not devised a feasible reliable procedure for distinguishing competent from less competent agents and installing only the former as rulers. A third consideration, prominent in democratic theorists such as J. S. Mill, is that aside from a possible tendency to produce better legislation and policies and better implementation of these laws and policies, democracy tends to produce other indirect morally valuable results such as social solidarity and the moral and intellectual development of the democratic citizens. A fourth consideration is that if people are somewhat disposed to use whatever power they have to advance their interests, it is better (though not good), other things being equal, that laws and policies cater to the interests of majorities than to the interests of smaller groups.

reasonable persons'.[14] Disagreeing about justice, reasonable people will also disagree about proposed criteria of competence and about who is more qualified than others to rule. He combines this assertion with a contractualist premise and concludes that political rule by a knowledgeable elite could never be morally legitimate. The contractualist premise is that it is wrong to act in ways that affect people except on the basis of principles they could not reasonably reject. The conclusion is that any version of Epistocracy is reasonably rejectable, hence morally illegitimate.

This line of thought collapses when one asks what counts as a 'reasonable' person. If a reasonable person makes no cognitive errors and deliberates with perfect rationality, then reasonable people will agree in selecting the conceptions of justice and rights that are best or tied for best. There are other conceptions of justice that attract the allegiance of less than fully reasonable persons, but these can be set aside. The notion of competence that figures in the idea of a competent political agent can then be calibrated in terms of the best conceptions of justice. This notion of competence will not be controversial among reasonable people. So if a 'reasonable person' is identified with the idea of a maximally reasonable person, a notion of competence can be non-arbitrarily selected.

Suppose instead that we use the idea of a satisficing threshold to identify the 'reasonable person'. A 'reasonable person' is reasonable enough. The lower the satisficing threshold level is set, the more plausible becomes Estlund's conjecture that 'no knower [or knowledge standard] will be so knowable as to be known by all reasonable persons'. The question then arises, why set the threshold at any particular less than maximal point? Estlund's set of reasonable persons might be unable to agree on a competence standard for political rule because some of them are adding two plus two and getting five or making some comparable subtler mistake of reasoning. Given that the political rulers will be charged with the task of designing and administering laws and policies that will maximize fulfilment of human rights, it is incorrect to accept any satisficing standard (unless in context the maximizing strategy calls for satisficing). Only the best is good enough.

One might attempt to defend a satisficing standard for identifying the 'reasonable person' by appeal to a requirement of respect. If a person has sufficient rational agency capacity to be able to recognize and formulate reasons and debate about principles, then it is wrongfully disrespectful to act toward him in ways that dismiss or slight this rational agency capacity, as though he were a mere tool to be manipulated for the common good.

[14] It should be noted that Estlund himself is trying to defeat the claim that authoritarianism in the form of rule by moral experts is morally required. I am treating his argument as though he were making a positive argument for the right to a democratic say. For commentary on Estlund, see Copp (1993).

The requirement that the principles on the basis of which we interact with people, including the principles that determine the proper mode of political governance for our society, should be able to elicit their assent at least if they qualify as reasonable, expresses a fundamental norm of respect for persons.

The reply is that appropriate respect for an agent's rational agency capacity is shown by recognizing it for what it is. It shows no wrongful disrespect to me to notice that I am imperfectly rational and to take efficient steps to prevent my proclivity to mistakes from wrongfully harming others or for that matter myself. This is true in face-to-face personal interaction and it is just as true in a context where what is at issue is identifying institutional procedures and norms for collective decision-making. Respect for rational agency should not be interpreted as requiring us to pretend that anyone has more capacity than she has or to pretend that variation in capacity does not matter when it does. Respect for rational agency in persons requires treating them according to the moral principles that fully rational persons would choose, the principles best supported by moral reasons. Supposing there is a divergence between the principles that threshold reasonable people would unanimously accept and the principles that ideally reasonable people would accept, I submit that the latter not the former are the norms, acting on which manifests respect for persons (beings with rational agency capacity). The point I am trying to make in this paragraph was stated clearly by Mill (1977: 474) long ago: 'Every one has a right to feel insulted by being made a nobody, and stamped as of no account at all. No one but a fool, and only a fool of a peculiar description, feels offended by the acknowledgement that there are others whose opinion, and even whose wish, is entitled to a greater amount of consideration than his'.[15]

In passing I observe that those who deny that standards of political competence that in some circumstances might justify non-democratic forms of governance can be non-arbitrarily and rationally identified seem to have no trouble with the idea that minimal competence standards can be non-arbitrarily formulated.[16] But if we say correctly that insane and feeble-minded persons lack rational agency capacity and are in virtue of these facts rightly deemed incompetent in certain contexts for certain purposes, we are pointing to traits that vary by degree above whatever threshold level is singled out as 'good enough'.

[15] Mill's statement occurs in the course of an argument for a plural votes scheme, in which more educated citizens, and those who pass a political competence examination, are allotted extra votes beyond the single vote that every adult citizen gets.

[16] Christiano (2001: 207–8), accepts a minimal competence qualification for the right to a democratic say.

Of course, nothing guarantees that fully reasonable persons will be able to select a single uniquely best conception of justice, which can serve as the reference point for defining a non-arbitrary standard of political competence. Suppose ten conceptions are tied for best, given the best moral theorizing and reasons assessment that is presently ideally available. In that case, it would not be unreasonable to implement a political system geared to achieving any of the ten. From the possibility of reasonable disagreement one gets a loose disjunctive standard of moral acceptability, not an argument for the unique fairness of democracy. Note that the fact that several conceptions of justice are equally acceptable for all we can know is fully compatible with there being a plethora of popular and decisively unreasonable views concerning the requirements of justice, any of which might command a majority vote in a democracy.

In the face of disagreement about what justice requires, one might flatly deny that the opinion of any member of society can be dismissed as unreasonable. In that case one is abandoning the moderate position about justice and democracy that is my main target in this chapter and is instead dismissing the possibility that a standard of justice can be available to provide an independent standard for assessing the political outcomes produced by the democratic process. The moderate, as I imagine her, agrees that we can have knowledge about justice but insists that democracy is an intrinsically just and fair procedure independently of its tendency to produce good results. Perhaps moderation, when pressed, slides toward radicalism.

Some readers will suspect that my position involves an illicit sleight of hand. What we observe is the members of society disagreeing about justice. From their different standpoints they will affirm opposed standards of political competence. Even if one grants that metaphysically there are right answers to questions about the substance of justice, one cannot in this context invoke these right answers to justify some elite form of political rule, because our agreed circumstances preclude any claim that any of us has epistemic access to the truth about justice. If we disagree, then we disagree. Jeremy Waldron (1999a: 253) expresses the sense that the instrumentalist is playing an illogical trick when he writes that 'any theory that makes authority depend on the goodness of political outcomes is self-defeating, for it is precisely because people *disagree* about the goodness of outcomes that they need to set up and recognize an authority'. Or again: 'rights-instrumentalism seems to face the difficulty that it presupposes our possession of the truth about rights in designing an authoritative procedure whose point is to settle that very issue'.[17]

[17] For criticism of Waldron, see Estlund (2000).

These are sensible concerns.[18] There are sensible ways to address them. Consider a simple example with epistemic uncertainty. A violent altercation is underway in the street. Many people observe some of it. It is not certain who has done what to whom, with what justification or lack of justification. Among onlookers, some have a better vantage point to see what is happening, some make better use of the observational data they get, and some have a better, some a worse grip on the moral principles of self-defence, provocation and proportionality that determine who of those involved in the altercation have right on their side. There is no consensus among reasonable spectators as to what is taking place or what should be done. Any proposal as to what intervention is justified meets with reasonable suspicion from some person's standpoint. Still, none of this excludes the possibility that you in fact perceive correctly what has happened and judge correctly what ought to be done and are rationally confident that your opinions on these matters are correct. If you happen to have the power to implement this correct assessment, you should do so, despite the fact that your assessment will not attract the unanimous assent of those affected. As Anscombe (1981: 52) observes, 'Just as an individual will constantly think himself in the right, whatever he does, and yet there is still such a thing as being in the right, so nations will constantly think themselves to be in the right – and yet there is still such a thing as their being in the right'. Paraphrasing this to highlight its relevance to our topic, we should say that just as people think they are acting justly, whether they are or not, yet there is such a thing as acting justly, so also people will think their preferred standards of competence and criteria for eligibility for political office are correct, yet there is such a thing as there being correct standards of political competence and correct inferences from these standards to judgements as to what form of political governance in given actual circumstances is just.

The resourceful Waldron (1999a: 250–1) has another arrow in his quiver. He argues that to suppose that an individual possesses moral rights is already to suppose that the individual has the competence to exercise them. A being that lacks rational agency capacity is not the sort of being who can be regarded as a right-bearer. Hence, there is tension and perhaps incoherence in arguing that to achieve the overall fulfilment of the rights of all members of society we must deny some the right to

[18] However, Waldron overreaches in stating that the point of political procedures is to settle the truth about what rights we have. A vote can fix the content of legal rights in some political jurisdiction, but this does not settle the issues (1) whether it is morally right that these legal rights are instituted and enforced and (2) whether these legal rights coincide with the moral rights that people have in this setting.

participate as equals in the political governance process on grounds that they are incompetent. If they are incompetent, how can they be right-bearers at all?

The tension Waldron sees eases when we look more closely. Competence is not all-or-nothing. An individual might be fully competent for many tasks but less competent at some. I may have rational agency capacity that a snake or even a gorilla lacks, and so be a candidate for ascription of moral rights that they could not sensibly be thought to possess, yet lack political competence at the level needed to contribute in a positive way to the determination of what laws and policies should be passed in order best to protect human rights. Also, the ground for ascribing some rights to people need not include strong claims about their competence to exercise the rights. I may believe that each individual has the right to live her own life as she chooses within wide moral limits. I may believe that each person has this right of autonomy without for a moment doubting that some persons have marginal or problematic competence to make good life plans and execute them. (Notice that one might believe there is a presumption in favour of each person being free to live her own life without believing that there is any presumption that everybody has an equal right to participate on equal terms in the governance of everybody's life.) The particular nature of the putative right to a democratic say is such that competence requirements apply with special force to it.

Publicity

Some theorists who claim that democratic governance is intrinsically just point to the requirement of publicity. It is not enough that justice is done, it should be manifest that justice is done. Moreover, this requirement that justice be visible at least to a reasonable and careful observer is itself a further requirement of justice.

In a narrow sense, a society satisfies publicity when all members of society can check for themselves that the practices and institutions of the society as they actually function fully satisfy the norms and rules to which it is committed.[19] In a broader sense, publicity requires in addition that all members of society if they engage in reflective deliberation can see that the rules and norms to which the society is committed are themselves morally justifiable.[20]

[19] Christiano (2001) deploys a narrow publicity requirement in his argument.

[20] On wide publicity, see Rawls (1999: ch. 3). For an interesting deployment of this publicity requirement in a controversy concerning what distributive justice requires, see Andrew Williams (1998).

This asserted requirement of publicity is parlayed into an argument for the intrinsic justice of democracy. The idea is that in a world rife with reasonable disagreement about morality and the good, it can be difficult to discern whether or not a government's policies conform closely to elementary requirements of justice. Consider the fundamental norm that each person should be treated with equal consideration and respect. All persons are of fundamentally equal worth; no one's life is inherently worth more than anyone else's.

The fact that a society is autocratic thereby fuels a suspicion that some people's lives are being counted as more valuable than other people's. A society that is substantively democratic, that brings it about that all its citizens enjoy equal opportunity to influence political outcomes, goes further toward manifesting a commitment to the principle of equal consideration. The society with democratic governance, other things being equal, satisfies publicity to a greater degree than it would if it were undemocratic, and since publicity is a component of justice, this democratic society simply in virtue of being democratic is more just.

In reply: neither the wide nor the narrow ideal of publicity qualifies as an element in the set of basic moral rights definitive of justice. That it is manifest that the rules a society claims to enforce are actually fully implemented likely tends to elicit people's allegiance and in this way contribute to the long-run stability of the system. If the rules manifestly conform to principles that almost all citizens accept, this tendency is likely reinforced. If these speculative hunches are empirically corroborated, publicity promotes justice and should be valued in this purely instrumental way.

None of this provides any support at all for the quite different claim that there is a basic moral right to publicity, that publicity is intrinsically just. Consider cases in which the aim of achieving publicity and the aim of achieving justice (aside from publicity) conflict. Let us say we must choose between a policy that over the long run secretly prevents more murders or an alternative policy that prevents fewer murders but does so in a way that satisfies publicity. Once we get the issue clearly in focus, and set aside the here irrelevant likely instrumental benefits of publicity (that it possibly might prevent more murders overall in the long run), I submit that publicity should have no weight at all in conflict with other justice values.

I deny that publicity is an intrinsic component of justice. But I also deny that autocracy inherently is incompatible with publicity. If instrumental or best-results justifications of democracy in a particular setting do not succeed, and autocracy would in that setting produce morally superior results – let's say, more just results – then autocracy can satisfy publicity.

In the argument from publicity to the claim that democracy is intrinsically just, the fact that society is democratic evidently conveys a message to members of society. Democratic governance procedures are used to signal the commitment of society to the principle of equal consideration. But messages can be communicated in various ways. Why suppose that the only effective way to convey a commitment to justice is through instituting and maintaining democracy?

If autocracy is chosen on the ground that it leads to morally superior results, and this surmise is correct, then over time autocracy will produce justice, or at least more justice than would be obtainable under any other type of political regime. What could manifest a commitment to doing justice more obviously and credibly than actually doing justice over time? We are not talking here about private acts performed in people's bedrooms, we are talking about the public policies pursued by a government and the changes over time in its institutions, social norms and practices.

The claim is made that in a diverse society whose members fan out to embrace a wide array of conflicting views of morality and value, there will inevitably be a degree of uncertainty and a lack of precision in people's estimation about the extent to which their government over time brings about basic social justice. So publicity cannot be satisfied merely by aiming at morally better policies. More is needed. The symbolism of democracy – everyone counts for one, nobody for more than one – has an important role to play in securing that it is manifest that justice is done, or approximated to a good enough degree.

If the fact that the government over the long haul enacts policies that bring it about that social justice requirements are fulfilled across the society does not suffice to satisfy publicity, because people of diverse standpoints disagree about justice, I do not see why the fact that the society is democratically run must succeed in conveying the message to all that the society is committed to justice. Some may see democracy as catering to the lowest common denominator of public opinion.

The thought might be that the very existence of an autocratic system, a clique of persons who wield power and are not accountable to those over whom power is wielded, must fuel suspicion. But an autocracy need not select the members of the ruling group by a hidden process. The process by which membership in the ruling group is set may be open for public inspection, and conform to the norm of careers open to talents or a stronger meritocratic principle such as the Rawlsian norm of equality of fair opportunity.

For concreteness, imagine an egalitarian social justice party that overthrows a clearly unjust regime and institutes autocratic rule. Any adult member of society is eligible to apply for party membership, and the criteria for membership are a matter of public record. Applications are assessed on their merits, and those deemed most qualified are admitted to the ruling group. Moreover, education and other forms of societal assistance to child-rearing practices are set so that any individuals with the same ambition to participate in political rule by joining the ruling party and the same native (potential for) political talent have identical prospects of success in gaining party admission. In other words, the political process satisfies norms of formal equality of opportunity and also substantive equality of opportunity (Rawlsian equality of fair opportunity). Here, then, is a further response to the demand for publicity. The imagined autocratic society makes manifest its commitment to social justice, especially to the fundamental norm that all are entitled to equal consideration and respect, by bringing it about that its policies and practices achieve justice and also by regulating access to membership in the group that exercises political power according to meritocratic norms. So if publicity were itself an intrinsic component of justice, this would not tend to show that democracy is intrinsically just, because some versions of autocracy can satisfy publicity.

Fans of publicity and democracy have a riposte to the argument made to this point. The idea is that the meritocratic ideal that political rule should be exercised by the competent, not by all citizens, unravels and reveals itself as inherently unfair as we try to specify it. There are no neutral criteria of competence. The criteria of political competence will inevitably be calibrated in terms of some controversial moral ideal, which the ruling autocrats label 'justice'. But this gambit takes us back to the claim – already discussed and rejected in this chapter – that standards of political competence invoked to support some type of non-democratic regime must be morally arbitrary and capricious.

Conclusion

This chapter has searched without any success for sound arguments for the claim that there is a non-instrumental moral right to a democratic say. This is good news for the purely instrumental approach that I favour. The victory for instrumentalism is nonetheless incomplete pending a full account of human rights that enables us to see why the justifications for the fundamental human rights do not include a justification of a fundamental intrinsic right to a democratic say. This is a story for another day.

4 'The probability of a fit choice': American political history and voting theory

Norman Schofield

Madison, Condorcet and the ratification of the constitution in 1787–1788

[I]t may be concluded that a pure democracy, by which I mean a society, consisting of a small number of citizens, who assemble and administer the government in person, can admit of no cure for the mischiefs of faction . . . Hence it is that democracies have been spectacles of turbulence and contention; have ever been found incompatible with personal security . . . and have in general been as short in their lives as they have been violent in their deaths.

A republic, by which I mean a government in which the scheme of representation takes place, opens a different prospect . . .

[I]f the proportion of fit characters be not less in the large than in the small republic, the former will present a greater option, and consequently a greater probability of a fit choice. (Madison in Rakove 1999)

This argument in *Federalist 10*, written in November 1787 by James Madison, may still be relevant today. However, modern theories of democracy have not constructed formal models of voting able to develop Madison's distinction between pure democracy and the republic (or what we call representative democracy). My intention in this chapter is to present a model that can be used to interpret certain aspects of American political history in order to gauge the validity of Madison's argument.

The theoretical problem that Madison addressed in *Federalist 10* was the generally accepted belief that democracy was unstable. This view, due to Montesquieu (and earlier British writers) also influenced Alexander Hamilton, during the debates in the Constitutional Convention. We can illuminate this argument about democracy with reference to Figure 4.1, which draws on modern social choice theory. In a direct democracy (or in Madison's term, a pure democracy) using the majoritarian principle there can be no veto groups. Any *alternative* proposed as a democratic choice

This chapter is based on research supported by NSF grant SES 0241732, undertaken in collaboration with Gary Miller and Andrew Martin. I am grateful to Claude-Anne Lopez and Nicolas Rieucau for comments on bibliographical details on Condorcet, Franklin and Jefferson, and to Alexandra Shankster for typing the manuscript.

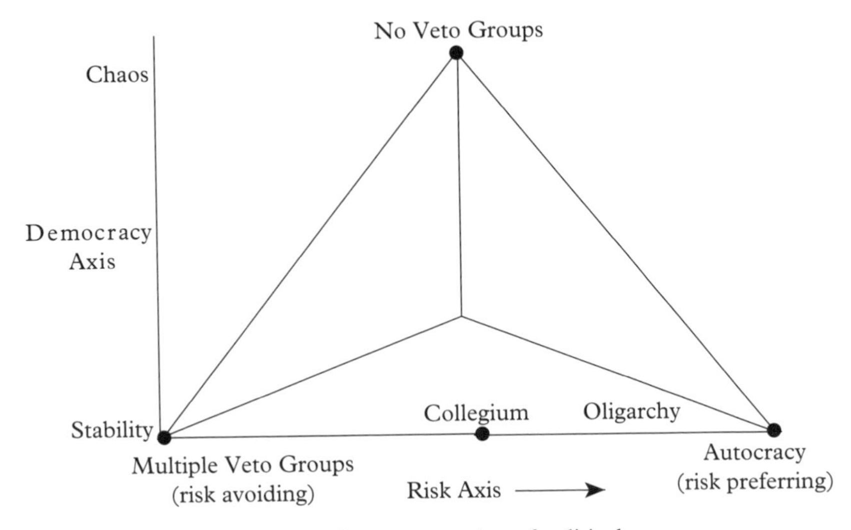

Figure 4.1 A schematic representation of political power

can be overturned by some majority. As Madison wrote in *Federalist 62*: 'It will be of little avail that the laws are made by men of their own choice, if laws be so . . . incoherent that they cannot be understood; if they be repealed or revised before they are promulgated, or undergo such incessant changes that no man who knows what the law is today can guess what it will be tomorrow' (Rakove 1999).

Madison also used the term 'mutability' for this incoherence of the law. And note here, Madison implies that the choices made by the representatives, themselves, can be mutable or chaotic. The key to understanding Madison's meaning is that a law is an alternative, *not* a person. I shall argue that the phrase a 'fit choice' in *Federalist 10* refers to a *person*, not an alternative.

To return to the Montesquieu (1990 [1748]) argument represented by Figure 4.1, since turbulence is a characteristic of any direct democratic voting body, the way to restrain chaos is by some exercise of veto power. Such veto power creates the element of risk. For example, it was well understood that monarchical power induces stability, and provides leadership. Adair (1943; 1974) has used the phrase 'energy, secrecy and dispatch' to characterize the monarch. Monarchical power can become autocratic, and as any student of British history knew, autocracy (by Cromwell, for example) could lead to war, and the intolerable indebtedness of the nation. The quandary that British political theorists of the late eighteenth century faced was how to maintain monarchy, for its advantages of leadership and stability, and yet curtail the probable risk-taking of the monarch. The device adopted was to give Parliament what can be called 'collegial' power. What I mean by this is that Parliament, if united, could overwhelm the monarch if he exceeded the power that had been granted to him. The English Civil War had made it clear that Parliament had, in fact, the physical power to overwhelm the monarch. Since the parliamentary collegium would necessarily be less risk-taking than the monarch, this social choice theory suggested that risk could be balanced. Of course, as Figure 4.1 suggests, Parliament could fragment into many different veto groups. Such a situation could lead to the opposite of risk-preferring autocracy, namely excessive risk avoidance. (A more detailed presentation of this social choice theory of legislative balance can be found in Schofield 2003a, from which Figure 4.1 is adapted).

Madison and Hamilton were both well aware of the Montesquieu balance theory involving monarchy, aristocracy and democracy (and its antecedent theory in the writings of Henry St. John, Viscount Bolingbroke). In the Federal Convention, on 4 June 1787, Hamilton had argued for an absolute veto by the Chief Magistrate. Madison, fearing autocracy, declared, 'to give such a prerogative would certainly be obnoxious to the temper of the country' (Madison 1977). Later in *Federalist 51*, he suggested that:

> [A]n absolute negative on the legislative appears at first view to be the natural defence with which the executive magistrate should be armed. But perhaps it would be neither altogether safe, nor alone sufficient. (Rakove 1999)

Madison's point here is that an absolute veto by the Chief Magistrate, while not endowing him with autocratic power, nonetheless gives power great enough for him to extract what we today would call 'social surplus'.

The 'checks and balances' instituted in the federal apparatus – the division of authority between federal and state governments, the separation of powers between the executive, legislative and judiciary branches, and the bicameralism of the legislative branch – were devices designed to satisfy the requirement that 'ambition must be made to counteract ambition' (Madison 1977). Present day pluralist theorists (Melissa Williams 1998; Dahl 2002) are partially correct in their interpretation of this institutional balance when they argue that it can induce stability. However, they neglect two points arising out of the social choice theory represented in Figure 4.1. The fact of complex institutional veto arrangements means that multiple veto groups can be brought into being with the power to protect their own particular interests against the public good. As I suggested above, such veto groups may induce risk avoidance. As an illustration of this phenomenon, Caro (2002) comments on the ability of Southern

Democratic Senators to implement the filibuster (or even the threat of its use) to void all attempts to pass Civil Rights Legislation in the 1950s. The resulting 'political risk avoidance' meant that the American polity could not address an intractable social problem. It was only by heresthetic manoeuvres that Lyndon B. Johnson, as leader of the Senate, could push through the 1957 civil rights legislation. Later, as President, he could use public opinion to force further civil rights legislation against the resistance of the Southern Senators.

I contend that Madison, in his writings in *The Federalist*, directly faced the dilemma that this presented. The requirements of the office of Chief Magistrate were (i) that he be able to overcome the potential mutability of the legislative branch and (ii) act with the proper dispatch in dealing with the urgent problems (such as war, or fundamental economic decisions) with which the polity had to deal. At the same time, if the Magistrate was endowed with excessive power, then he would frequently sacrifice the 'happiness [of the voters] to his ambition' (as Madison wrote in his *Vices of the Political System of the United States*, in April 1797).

In this earlier paper, Madison began to develop the Humean argument that the extended Republic can be modelled into a commonwealth with 'compass to refine the democracy', to prevent any measures 'against the public interest' (Hume 1985b [1777]: 528). But Hume was also aware of the dangers of the selection of the Chief Magistrate:

> The filling of the [position of elective magistrate] is a point of too great and too general interest, not to divide the whole people into factions. Whence a civil war, the greatest of ills, may be apprehended almost with certainty, upon every vacancy. (Hume 1985b [1777]: 18)

In *Federalist 10*, Madison proposed a theory of the selection of the First Magistrate, which, in large degree solved this dilemma. The key phrase is 'the probability of a fit choice', where I interpret 'fit choice' to mean person 'pre-eminent for ability and virtue' (to use Hamilton's phrase from *Federalist 68*). The characteristics of 'ability and virtue' are inherent features of a person, which may not be directly or accurately perceived by the members of the voting body. Consequently, the election of a Chief Magistrate can be viewed as a collective decision problem under risk (or even uncertainty). This means that though the interests of the voters will necessarily be involved in their choice, their beliefs about the characteristics of the contenders will also play a role. Preferences and beliefs are not the same, and how these are modelled will affect what we infer about elections.

I contend that Madison's logic in *Federalist 10* is a development of Condorcet's *Essai sur l'application de l'analyse à la probabilité des voix* (Condorcet 1785; McLean and Hewitt 1994).

Condorcet's *Essai* dealt with the theoretical problem of jury decision-making. A person (in truth) is either innocent or guilty, and each voter (or juror) has an intrinsic probability of selecting the true option. Condorcet showed essentially that if the average of these juror probabilities exceeded one-half, then the jury, using majority rule, would select the true option with a probability higher than this average probability. Moreover, if the jury was increased in size, without limit, then this probability of correct choice would approach 1 (this theorem is discussed in Black 1958; Barry 1964; 1965).

There are two intellectual avenues through which Madison could have learned of Condorcet's result. One, merely conjectured, is through Franklin, and one, much more certain, is through Jefferson.

Franklin had sailed for France in October 1776, ostensibly to negotiate Treaties of Alliance and Commerce between France and the United States. The more important (and secret) reason was to arrange a subsidy (of two million livres, or 330,000 dollars) from France for the American Revolution. This subsidy was followed by grants of six million livres (January 1778), three million (in December 1779), and six million (in December 1782). During Franklin's stay in France until July 1785, he was lionized by the French, and became a habitué of the salon of Madame Brillon and others. Franklin came to know Condorcet well, and they exchanged many letters (Lopez 1966). From about 1774, Condorcet worked on what has been called 'l'Arithmétique politique . . . l'application du calcul aux questions socials, juridiques et politiques' (Badinter and Badinter 1988: 191). Condorcet's biographer, Baker (1975), used the term 'social mathematics' for this work. By May 1785 Condorcet had finished his *Essai* and sent a version, *Probabilité des jugements rendus à la pluralité des voix*, to Frederick the Great of Prussia. The publication of the *Essai* in 1785, and Condorcet's appointment as permanent secretary of l'Academie des Sciences, confirmed his fame as one of the most eminent *philosophes* of France.

On Franklin's arrival back in the USA in September 1785, he created a Society for Political Inquiry in Philadelphia, and recommended Condorcet's election to the American Philosophical Society.

From the Annapolis Convention of September 1786 to the Constitutional Convention in Philadelphia in 1787, Madison concentrated on a study of the 'literary cargo', a history of politics and commerce that had been sent by Jefferson from Paris (Ketcham 1971: 183).

I conjecture, first, that Franklin knew of Condorcet's jury theorem because of his contact with Condorcet in Paris, and secondly, that he discussed its implications with Madison, during the period 1786 to early 1787. The chronology makes sense, and Madison's work on *Vices of the Political System of the United States* (April 1787) shows some general influence due to Condorcet. What is clearly documented, however, is that Madison received some of Condorcet's work from Jefferson by 6 September 1787 (the date of a letter from Madison to Jefferson acknowledging receipt of work by Filippo Mazzei).

This work, *Recherches historiques et politiques sur les Etats-Unis de l'Amerique septentrionale*, was an 'encyclopedia of information about America, much of it supplied by Jefferson and worked over by Condorcet, who vetted the translation into French and added two essays of his own, the *Lettres d'un bourgeois de New-Haven* and *De l'Influence de la revolution d'Amerique sur l'Europe*' (Darnton 1997). In his first essay, Condorcet contended that it could be proven rigorously that 'increasing the number of legislative bodies could never increase the probability of obtaining true decisions' (McLean and Hewitt 1994: 325). Madison, in *Federalist 51*, rejected what appeared to be Condorcet's argument for unicameralism. This seems, on the face of it, to support the inference of Urken (1991) and McLean and Urken (1992) that Condorcet's theory had no influence on Madison. However, the fact that Madison specifically rejected Condorcet's argument implies that he had, at least, read Condorcet's essay.

I contend that Madison not only understood the argument, but saw that it was applicable to the dilemma over the choice of the Chief Magistrate. Condorcet believed the jury theorem applied to a political outcome, or proposition, either true or false. As I have suggested, however, Madison conceived of legislative decision-making over alternatives as potentially mutable. In particular, the domain of legislative decision-making is not restricted to two alternatives, as demanded by Condorcet's theorem. Finally (though this point may not have been obvious to Madison), the jury theorem required that each voter's choice be independent of every other voter's choice. In a legislature, this property will clearly fail.

However, consider a situation where each voter judges whether or not the candidate for Chief Magistrate is in fact 'pre-eminent for ability and virtue'. If there is some information available about the candidates' abilities and degrees of 'virtue', then each voter will be in a position to form a judgement, which may, in fact, be correct. It is a plausible conjecture that the average value of the probability of a correct judgement exceeds one-half. We may thus rephrase *Federalist 10* as Madison's conjecture.

Consider two republics, of size N_1 and N_2, with $N_2 > N_1$. Suppose that the proportion of fit characters (ρ_2) in N_2 exceeds that proportion (ρ_1) in N_1. If individual judgements are mutually independent, and are based on ρ_1, ρ_2 respectively, then the probability of a fit choice by N_2 exceeds that by N_1.

Independence is dealt with implicitly in Madison's scheme, by supposing that the extended republic involves heterogeneous interests, thus inducing choices that are independent.

The logical structure of Madison's conjecture in *Federalist 10* dealt with the Humean problem of factional conflict over selection of the Chief Magistrate. For Madison, 'men have different and unequal faculties for acquiring property' (*Federalist 10*), and therefore differing interests, or preferences. However, if their judgements over 'a fit choice' are independent from their interests, then the selection of the Chief Magistrate will not be dominated by interests. In this case the electorate will have reason to accept the future decisions of their principal representative.

Of course, interests cannot be entirely removed from the judgements of the electorate. For example, in voting for a state representative, or for a member of the House of Representatives, it is probable that each representative would indeed be characterized by the local interests of his constituents. Consequently, Madison's conjecture would not be appropriate. As a consequence, members of State Houses, or the US House of Representatives would embody heterogeneous or diverse interests. Moreover, since the representatives themselves do not choose a person, and therefore do not judge over 'fitness', the Madison conjecture does not apply. Consequently, choice in a legislature can be expected to be mutable.

Barry (1965: 292) adduces a somewhat similar logic as regards 'fitness' in Madison's conjecture to Rousseau's conception in the *Social Contract*. He suggested that the 'right answer in politics' is akin to the correct answer in arithmetic. The reason for this is that the voters 'are more likely than not to arrive at the correct answer because the individual biases . . . will tend to balance out'.

Obviously, this property of independence of judgements from interests may or may not hold in the scheme of representation called the Republic. As I have suggested, it is unlikely to hold for methods of selecting representatives for the legislature, for example.

To determine whether it is indeed a property likely to hold in the selection of the Chief Magistrate, I shall offer, in the next section, a formal model of voting that does involve both interests and judgments. My purpose is not to determine whether Condorcet's jury theorem is applicable, or whether Madison's conjecture is valid, but rather to use this theoretical apparatus to gain some insight into the nature of the political conflict in the Republic.

A model of belief and interest aggregation

The spatial model of voting has been used since at least the work of Black (1958) and Downs (1957). The 'stochastic' variant (Hinich 1977) allows voters to be uncertain in their choice, and it is this model that I shall adopt. The primitives of the model are:

(i) some 'policy' space X which characterizes both voter interests, and candidate declarations;
(ii) the electorate, N, of size n, is described by a set $\{x_1, \ldots, x_i, \ldots x_n)$ of 'bliss points', one for each voter, i;
(iii) the set of candidates, P, of size p, is described by a set $\{z_1, \ldots, z_j, \ldots, z_p\}$ of declarations, one for each candidate, j;
(iv) the latent utility, $u_{ij}(x_i, z_j)$ of i for j has the form

$$u_{ij}(x_i, z_j) = -A_{ij}(x_i)(z_j) + \varepsilon_j \qquad \text{(Eq. 1)}$$

Here, $A_{ij}(x_i, z_j)$ is some function of the 'disutility' to i because of the difference between x_i and z_j. Thus, $A_{ij}(x_i)(z_j) = 0$ if and only if $x_i = z_j$.

A_{ij} is usually taken to be some quadratic function based on 'distance' between x_i and z_j. Later in the analysis, I shall allow for individuals to have different saliencies for different 'axes' of X.

The set X^N of bliss points is fixed, and the set X^P of possible declarations is strategically chosen by candidates. Given the data X^N, X^P, each voter, i, is characterized by the probability ρ_{ij} that i votes for j. This probability can be written $\text{Prob}[u_{ij} > u_{ik}$, for all $k \neq j]$. This stochastic feature involves the 'errors' $\{\varepsilon_j\}$, for $j \in P$, which are assumed to be drawn from a normal distribution, each with variance σ^2 (perhaps also involving co-variance terms).

Hinich (1977) assumed each candidate, j, adopted a declaration z_j to maximize V_j, the expected vote share (obviously given by $1/n\Sigma\rho_{ij}$).

He argued (in the special case of $p = 2$) that the resulting 'Nash equilibrium' would be one in which both candidates adopted the same position, $z_j{}^*$ at the mean of the voter distribution ($1/n\Sigma x_i$). This theorem has recently been extended to the case of arbitrary p. However, there is one proviso. For the theorem to be valid, it is necessary that the errors be independent, with variance σ^2 'sufficiently large'. In fact, Schofield (2004) has examined this result more carefully and shown that 'sufficiently large' can be interpreted in terms of a constraint, that every bliss point $\{x_i\}$ must lie in a 'sufficiently small' neighbourhood of the mean. To illustrate, if we assume $A_{ij}(x_i)(z_j) = \beta\|x_i - z_j\|^2$ and renormalize, so that the mean Σx_i is the origin, then the domain constraint becomes $\beta\|x_i\|^2 < \sigma$. (This constraint is required because the cumulative normal distribution has a point of inflection at $-\sigma$).

However, there is a second, more serious, difficulty with the so-called mean voter theorem.

Empirical analyses of voter behaviour show clearly that a superior model has the form

$$u_{ij}(x_i, z_j) = -A_{ij}(x_i, z_j) + \overline{\lambda}_j + \varepsilon_j$$

Here, the term $\overline{\lambda}_j$ may be regarded as the 'valence' of candidate *j* (Stokes 1963; Ansolabehere and Snyder 2000; Groseclose 2001). In the empirical analyses, $\lambda_j = \overline{\lambda}_j + \varepsilon_j$ is a stochastic valence, with expectation $\overline{\lambda}_j$, where the stochastic component is described by ε_j, with expectation 0. Thus, $\overline{\lambda}_j$ is the average 'popularity' of candidate *j*, throughout the electorate.

Suppose that all candidates adopt the identical mean voter position ($z_j{}^* = 0$). Then a comparison by *i* of candidate *j* and candidate *k* involves a comparison of $u_{ij} = \overline{\lambda}_j + \varepsilon_j$ and $u_{ik} = \overline{\lambda}_k + \varepsilon_k$. Then, when there are just two candidates, and the policy space is of dimension *w*, the constraint necessary for equilibrium at the mean is $2\beta(\overline{\lambda}_j - \overline{\lambda}_k)\Sigma_i \| x_i \|^2 < nw\sigma^2$ for every *j*, and *k*. Obviously, if candidate *k* has much lower valence than candidate *j*, and if σ is not large, then this condition is likely to fail (Schofield 2004).

Empirical analyses of elections in Britain, the USA, Israel and elsewhere (Schofield 2004; Schofield, Miller and Martin 2003) demonstrate that the empirical values obtained for σ, β and $\lambda_1, \ldots, \lambda_p$ imply this constraint fails. Consequently, it can be inferred that candidates will generally not converge towards the electoral mean in an attempt to maximize vote shares. Even with two candidates, it is difficult to calculate the relationship between σ, β, and λ_1, and λ_2 and optimal positions. What is clear, however, is that if $\lambda_1 \ll \lambda_2$ then the low valence candidate will tend to flee towards the electoral periphery.

The conclusions of this valence model suggest why convergence to an electoral centre is a very rare occurrence. Indeed, it is only plausible when the election involves such a high degree of uncertainty (or high variance σ^2) that policy differences are almost irrelevant.

This model can be interpreted in terms of Madison's conjecture. We may view $\overline{\lambda}_j$ as the average electoral judgement that candidate *j* is a 'fit choice'. The particular weighting that *i* gives to *j* is a stochastic variable, $\lambda_{ij} = \overline{\lambda}_j + \varepsilon_j$ where ε_j is drawn from the normal distribution. It is clearly possible in this model for a voter actually to vote for candidate *j* over *k* even though, in terms of explicit policies, candidate k has declared an intended policy that more closely matches i's interests.

Notice, however, that Condorcet's theorem cannot be used in this context to argue that the selected candidate is necessarily superior. Because the probabilities ρ_{aj}, ρ_{bj} (that voters a and b choose j) depend on x_a and x_b, they will not be independent. However, if σ is large with respect to the parameters $(\beta, \lambda_1, \ldots, \lambda_p)$, then voter choice will be almost pairwise independent. In this case, if one candidate, 1, say, has a clearly dominant valence then this candidate will win the election, with high probability.

To interpret this observation, suppose that $\beta \to 0$ so that policy does become irrelevant. Suppose further that there is information available to the electorate which is consistent with the judgment $\overline{\lambda}_1 > \overline{\lambda}_2 > \ldots > \overline{\lambda}_p$, say. Irrespective of the policy choices of the candidates, it will be the case that, for every voter i, the probabilities $\{\rho_{ik}\}$ for $k = 1, \ldots, p$ will be ranked $\rho_{i1} > \ldots > \rho_{ip}$. From the multinomial theorem it then follows that the majority rule preference will choose 1 with greater probability than 2, etc. This is an analogue of Condorcet's jury theorem.

In other words, if there is some linkage between data and valences, then the stochastic spatial model just presented can be interpreted as a generalization of the jury theorem.

Since the model can incorporate interests, which were of concern to Madison in writing *Federalist 10*, we may also view the model as a method of studying the balance of interests and judgements in a polity.

However, when interests are involved, then it is necessary to examine the equilibrium behaviour of candidates as they respond to electorate incentives. Unfortunately, computation of equilibria in this model is quite difficult. However, one general inference that can be made is that if candidates adopt vote-maximizing positions, then they necessarily must keep their distance from one another. If the individual judgements are correlated in some fashion, then this phenomenon is more pronounced.

If there is a single dimension involved, as I shall argue was the case in the Jefferson election of 1800, then it is plausible that there exists only one possible pair of equilibrium positions for the two candidates. If there are two dimensions, as I shall suggest is plausible for the election of 1860, then the equilibrium will depend on the number of candidates. Figure 4.3 positions the four presidential candidates for 1860 within a two-dimensional policy space, characterized by a land/capital axis and a labour/slavery axis. In a pure stochastic model for such a situation there would be multiple possible equilibria. However, Miller and Schofield (2003) and Schofield (2003b) propose a variant of the model involving activists for the candidates. Assuming activists generate support for their preferred candidates, and this support enhances the valence of their candidate, then there will indeed be a unique equilibrium (that is a set of positions, one for each candidate).

It is implicit in this model, that contention, rather than compromise, is the fundamental characteristic of politics.

One final remark: this model is appropriate for the selection of the Chief Magistrate. It is not obvious that it is relevant to the behaviour of a legislative body. In this latter case, judgements over the appropriateness of a particular policy will be highly correlated with interests. In such a case, the variance (σ^2), since it is relevant to judgements, will be zero. The model, therefore, reduces to a deterministic spatial model. There are two differing views of the appropriate conclusions to be drawn from the deterministic model. One (due to McKelvey and Schofield 1986) is that the behaviour is inherently chaotic or 'mutable'. A second is that mixed strategy equilibria exist near the centre of the distribution of the legislators' preferred points (McKelvey 1986; Banks, Duggan and le Breton 2002). However, it is difficult to see how the notion of *mixed* strategies makes sense when legislators must choose actual policies. It seems far more likely that equilibria occur, at least in the American context, precisely because of the strong veto power of the President. As I understand the sentiments of the Founding Fathers, this is precisely what they intended.

Jefferson and the election of 1800

A recent empirical analysis of voting behaviour in the USA (Schofield, Miller and Martin 2003) shows quite clearly that, from at least 1960, it is necessary to use two cleavages, or dimensions, to interpret presidential elections. One is the standard left-right economic policy dimension, and the second involves civil rights.

In principle, there may even be three axes of political decision-making, derived from the three economic factors of capital, land and labour (Rogowski 1989). The relationship between the economic factors and their political analogues depends on particular historical and social conditions. For example, for the period of Ratification of the Constitution in 1787–8, Beard (1913) argued that conflicts over capital were the prime reason for differences between federalists and anti-federalists. But Beard's emphasis on capital – on the different interests of creditors and debtors – obscured a latent dimension involving land. The landed gentry, including George Washington, had been motivated to some degree to fight for independence because of the British attempts, under the Quebec Act of 1774, to remove the Ohio Valley from settlement (Schofield 2002a).

After the War of Independence, this landed interest was less concerned over the question of debt, and more concerned with the manner by which the territory east of the Mississippi would be made accessible. Thus, the axis of conflict at the time of the Ratification may be interpreted as a political cleavage involving a hard money principle on the Whiggish right, and an expansionist principle involving land on the left. Although Madison and Hamilton were generally agreed in 1787 over the need to deal with government debt, by 1789 their disagreement over the future development of the United States had become apparent. This disagreement was based on their differing views about the appropriate relationship between commerce and the agrarian economy.

The disagreement between Hamilton, on the one hand, and Madison (together with Jefferson after his return from France in late 1789) on the other was over what I shall call a 'quandary' over the future development of the USA. This quandary is discussed in more detail in Schofield (2003c), but I shall use it as an example of the application of the stochastic model of voting just presented. For Hamilton, the public interest lay in the creation in the USA of a political economy akin to that established in Britain from 1720 on. For convenience, I shall use the phrase the 'Hamiltonian point' (as in Figure 4.2) to briefly characterize what Hamilton had in mind. In Hamilton's *Report on Manufactures* (Freeman 2001: 651) he basically argued from Adam Smith (1981 [1776]) that an increase of capital was necessary for economic growth. However, this understanding of the causes of British economic development demanded a number of related policy choices. Britain's growth depended on the implementation of a particular institutional arrangement between Parliament and its fiscal system. To provide credit, and deal with debt, the Bank of England had been constituted shortly after the Glorious Revolution of 1688 (North and Weingast 1989). Although it was intended that Parliament would credibly commit to the repayment of interest on government debt, through land taxes, it was obvious by 1710 that the Tory landed interest was motivated to repudiate the rapidly growing debt (Stasavage 2003). After the debacle over the South Sea Company in 1720, Walpole instituted an arrangement where debt was covered by tariffs and customs on British imports (Brewer 1988). This had a number of consequences. Since imports were land intensive, the price of land was kept high. This placated the landed interest and allowed for increased investment in agriculture. The required switch from a need for unskilled agricultural labour to skilled labour may account for the lack of growth in real wages for unskilled labour. This brought about extensive urbanization and the flow of labour into industry (Crafts 1994). To maintain this institutional arrangement required limitation on political enfranchisement (Brewer 1976: 6). Its successes led to a 'hundred years of stable single party Whig government' (Plumb 1967: 158). It was only in 1846 that this mercantilist system of protection was repealed (McLean 2001: 33–54). Enfranchisement was extended by the Electoral Reform Acts after 1867 (McLean 2001: 61–86).

Hamilton's scheme involved the creation of institutions parallel to those instituted by Walpole: a National Bank (proposed in February 1791) and a system of tariffs to raise government revenue. However, because American imports were manufactures, rather than food, as in Britain, the scheme would necessarily benefit capital, rather than agrarian interests (Beard 1915).

The letters between Madison and Jefferson (prior to Jefferson's return from Paris) show the development of a theory of political economy based on free trade and agriculture. In formalizing this theory, Jefferson was much influenced by Condorcet's writings in this matter (and those of Turgot, Condorcet's patron) arguing for free trade. Indeed, Condorcet's optimism in this matter found later expression in his *Esquisse d'une tableau historique des Progrès de l'esprit humaine* (Condorcet 1794).

In the House of Representatives, in February 1789, Madison asserted that 'though he was a friend to a very free system of commerce', he believed tariffs were 'justifiable to discourage luxury spending . . . and to retaliate against unfair commercial regulations by other countries' (Ketcham 1971: 280). The proposed tariffs were on rum, liquors, wine, molasses, tea, sugar, spices, coffee and cocoa, all goods intensive in land, rather than capital. In April, Madison called for the encouragement of 'the great staple of the United States . . . . agriculture' (Madison 1979).

On his return to the USA, Jefferson wrote to George Washington asserting that he 'disapproved of the system of the Secretary of the Treasury [Hamilton] . . . and this is not merely a speculative difference. This system flowed from principles averse to liberty [and] was calculated to undermine and demolish the republic' (Peterson 1984: 994).

In discussing Jefferson's opposition to Hamilton, historians have often focused on the relationship between Jefferson's views and the writings of Viscount Bolingbroke arguing against the institutional arrangements of Walpole and the Whig hegemony in Britain (Kramnick 1992). Bolingbroke, like Jefferson, rejected what he regarded as the corruption flowing from government debt and the institutions of capital. It is clear, however, that both Madison and Jefferson had a very clear conception of a particular possible path of economic growth for the USA. In their view, the availability of land in the USA meant that the country could become the granary of the world. In this, Jefferson in particular was influenced by Condorcet's writings. However, the rejection of the Hamilton scheme would limit the industrial growth of the country, particularly of the North-east. Moreover, the fact that Britain was already well on the way to predominance in industrial strength and was protected by a mercantilist system of trading arrangements, could lead to American subservience or dependency.

Enlargement of agriculture would, of course, benefit what we may call the agrarian interest. However, an additional axis of policy (distinct from the land and capital axes) is necessary for understanding the particular combination of interests involved in the lead up to the election of 1800. Free labour would be divided between the Hamiltonian, or Whig, option, and the Jeffersonian, or Republican, strategy. Limiting the availability of capital would affect the productivity of agriculture, and thus agricultural wages. Those enterprises based on slave labour, cotton, tobacco, indigo, etc., could more readily obtain investment capital from abroad. This would lead, in the long run, to the relative expansion of that component of the American economy founded on the slave-owning agrarian interest (North 1961). Clearly, there is an inherent conflict of interest between free labour, whether agrarian or based in manufacture, and such slave-owning agrarians.

Figure 4.2 represents the Jeffersonian point as one favouring land.[1] However, for such a policy point to gain a majority, it is evident that the conflict between free labour and slave-owning agrarians (represented by the labour axis) had to be suppressed in some fashion. What is surprising is that the issue of slavery was suppressed for so long. Riker (1986) attempted to argue that the issue became explosive in the late 1850s because of a successful political manoeuvre by Lincoln in the Senate race in 1858. I shall argue instead that the 1860 election, like that of 1800, involved a matter of deep contention in the society, with candidates standing for quite different opposed principles to do with the 'correct' path of development in the future.

[1] In Figure 4.2, I have drawn the left-right axis as a single dimension, with 'land' on the left and 'capital' on the right. This is for convenience of representation. However, it is reasonable to infer that Hamilton's position could be described as a hard money principle, favouring creditors, and commercial development, while Jefferson believed in the logic of an agrarian economy. Though he was opposed to government debt, he presumably favoured a soft money principle, or the availability of credit to finance agrarian expansion to the West. This axis of conflict has been clearly evident throughout American history, particularly at the end of the nineteenth century, in the conflicts between the commercial interests and the populist William Jennings Bryan (Schofield, Miller and Martin 2003). By the mid-twentieth century, the relevance of land was not so clear. Even in the 1930s, however, debt was the problem facing the impoverished farmers. Clearly, they contributed to F.D. Roosevelt's successful bid for presidency.

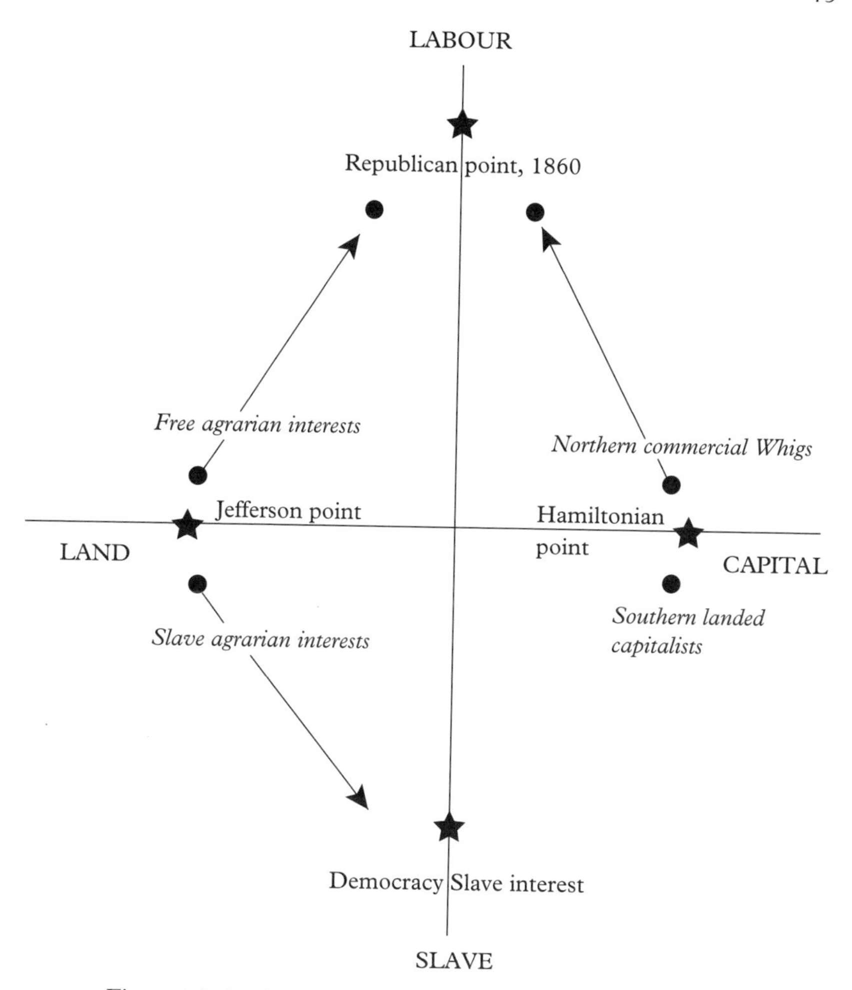

Figure 4.2 A schematic representation of land and capital in the USA in 1860

The quandary over slavery in the USA, 1800–1860

Figure 4.2 is intended to imply that, with two independent axes of choice in the American polity, there are at least four potential electoral coalitions, corresponding both to regions of the country, and to particular coalitions of interests. In the election of 1800, there were indeed four presidential candidates; Jefferson, Adams, Pinckney and Burr. Because of the particular electoral law, the choice between Jefferson and Burr went to the legislature where Jefferson won as a result of a political manoeuvre. The Republican victory was seen by both Jefferson and Madison as a vindication of the theory of political economy discussed above.

It is clearly impossible to form any clear estimates of the underlying parameters of this election. Assuming that the spatial model outlined above is qualitatively appropriate, we can make some inferences. First, because the election turned on the future development of the USA, the variances associated with the valences of the various candidates must have been relatively high overall. Obviously enough, the valence, or judgement over the validity of Jefferson's position, would be high for voters (or for members of the electoral college) from states like Virginia (dependent on slave-based agriculture) as well as from Western free states. Even voters from more urban, Eastern states, involved in industries linked by trade to Britain, could judge Jefferson highly. Overall, there would be a weak geographic relationship between judgement and interest. Given these electoral relationships, there is no reason to suppose that vote maximizing candidates would converge to an electoral mean. In fact, it seems quite clear that the various candidates did stand for quite different policy positions. Even though Burr became Jefferson's Vice President, there is evidence that Burr and Jefferson disagreed over how the balance between land and capital was to be maintained.

As I have indicated, it was important for the maintenance of the Republican coalition after 1800 to supress the labour axis representing the potential conflict between free labour and slave-owning interests. Miller and Schofield (2003) suggest that this can be done, at least in a plurality system, by tacit agreement between the two principal parties. This argument depends on the role of activists in providing support to the parties. In this version of the stochastic model, activists who find the policy declarations of their party candidate acceptable provide resources to further enhance the valence of that candidate. However, if one dimension of potential conflict is suppressed, then potential activists, who are concerned about this latent dimension, may disrupt the two-party equilibrium.

To illustrate this possibility, consider again the Jefferson point (representing the Republican party position) and the Hamiltonian point (representing the position of the federalist or Whig position). Given the suppression of the labour axis, both parties gain support from both Northern and Southern states. If, however, an anti-slave activist coalition were to form in support of the Whigs, then that would increase the Whig vote in the North, but reduce it in the South. Whether that increased the overall Whig vote would depend on the intensity of support. As long as the issue of slavery could be suppressed, the creation of such an activist coalition was unlikely.

In 1824, the successful Republican (or Democrat) coalition almost fragmented as a result of the competition between the 'Whigs' John Quincy Adams and Clay, and the Republican Democrats Jackson and William Crawford. Although Jackson won a plurality of the electoral college, John Quincy Adams became president because of the support of Clay, and the election in the legislature. Jackson won in 1828, and 1832, followed by his Vice President, van Buren, in 1836. In 1844, the intersectional compromise to suppress the labour axis was broken when Southern activists rejected the Democrat contender, van Buren, and declared James Polk the presidential candidate for the Democracy.

The 1844 election was extremely close. A switch of 5,000 votes in New York would have given that state to the Whig, Clay, and with it, the presidency.

Figure 4.2 suggests that, from approximately 1840 on, the issue of slavery could not be suppressed. Partly as a result of van Buren's handling of the 'Amistad' affair in 1839, the House of Representatives passed a permanent gag rule, forbidding any petition on the abolition of slavery. John Quincy Adams's efforts to rescind the rule were eventually successful because of the support of both Northern Whigs *and* Northern Democrats. Northern Democrats voted against the gag rule because of their anger at their Southern partners over the veto, exercised against van Buren (Miller 1995; Schofield 2001; 2002b). As the influence of the pro-slavery interest group in the Democracy grew, so did a small, but anti-slavery, group in the North. By 1856, the Republican, Fremont, took 76 electoral college votes in the North (out of 110), while the Democrat, Buchanan took all 88 in the South. That year, the candidate for the remnant of the Whig party, Fillmore, only gained 22 per cent of the popular vote and 8 electoral college votes (all in the border states).

For a Republican candidate to win, there had to be an activist anti-slavery coalition, to lend support and enhance the candidate's valence in Northern states.

Figure 4.3 gives a very schematic representation of the positions of the four presidential candidates in 1860 (Schofield 2003d) in the full dimensional policy space. Lincoln's share of the popular vote was overwhelming in Northern states such as Vermont (79 per cent). Even in Illinois, where Stephen Douglas was popular, Lincoln gained just over 50 per cent. Obviously, Douglas stood in a sense for a Jeffersonian expansionism, associated with free labour. Schofield (2003d) argues that Lincoln's success was due to two causes. First, because of the *Dred Scott* decision by the Supreme Court in 1857, Lincoln was able to press home the inherent

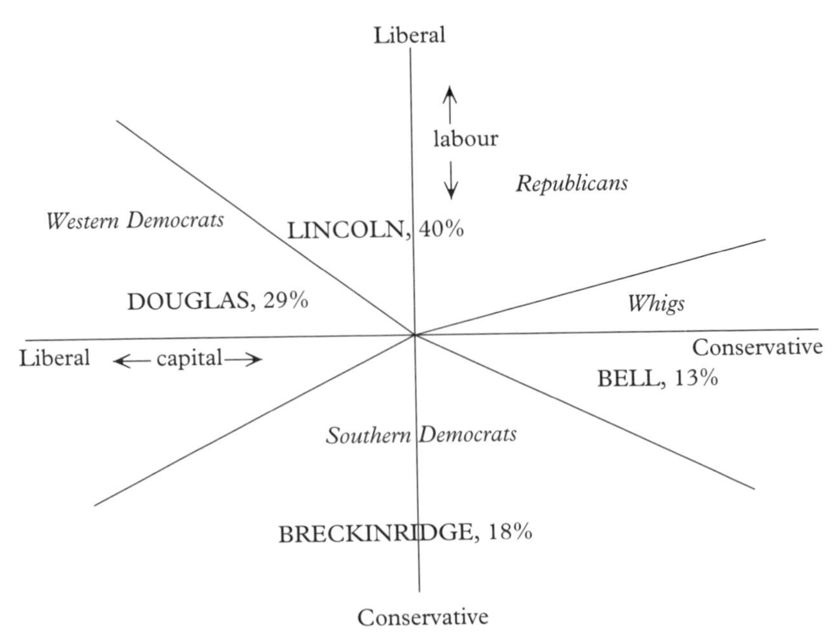

Figure 4.3 A schematic representation of the presidential election of 1860, in a two-dimensional factor space

conflict between free and slave labour. Indeed, he argued that the *Dred Scott* decision could lead to the employment of slave labour in Northern free states. This decision, due indirectly to the creation of a Southern pro-slave activist coalition, led, in turn, to the creation of a significant prohibitionist activist coalition.

Lincoln's speeches in New York and New Haven also contributed to the increase of the value of his valence (the estimation that Lincoln's argument was correct) among voters in both Northern and Western states. Thus, although voters in Illinois, for example, might consider that the position of Douglas, with respect to states' rights and expansion, was close to their own, they judged Lincoln to have logic on his side.

I have suggested that prior to Lincoln's speeches, the uncertainty (or variance) in the Northern electorate about the relevance of the issue of slavery was very high. This uncertainty can be viewed as the crucial component of the 'quandary over slavery'. However, once Lincoln's arguments over the intention of the South had been made, this uncertainty became much less pronounced. This effect of increasing valence for Lincoln can be called a belief cascade in the Northern electorate.

At the same time, the valence for the Southern Democrat, Breckinridge, also increased in the Southern electorate. After the election, new quandaries made themselves obvious, different in the North and the South. These, of course, were over the choices to secede from the Union in the South, and to prevent this secession in the North.

Valence and interest in the North and South were obviously correlated, so it is impossible to refer to Condorcet's jury theorem to form a judgement about the validity of Lincoln's interpretation of Southern intentions. Nonetheless, we can perhaps agree that Lincoln's election in 1860 was indeed a 'fit choice'.

Conclusion

The point of the extensive discussion of the periods 1787 to 1800 and 1840 to 1860 is to emphasize that polities can involve deep and apparently irreconcilable quandaries over the proper course of action. Madison hoped that the resolution of such uncertainties would come from the aggregation of judgements, uncontaminated by interests. Formal models of electoral processes have focused on the aggregation of preferences, and have tended to conclude that rational political actors will compromise in their choices, through convergence to an electoral mean, for example. Such convergence, however, is seldom observed in political life. Indeed, at times of great uncertainty, it seems that political competitors become more polarized. This polarization is particularly relevant when latent electoral coalitions are activated over concern about a policy dimension that has been suppressed. Miller and Schofield (2003) argue that the relationship between potential activist coalitions and candidate policy positions can only be understood with reference to the suppressed dimension.

For example, they suggest that the North-South cleavage which was clearly relevant in 1860 had, by the 1950s, been transformed to a labour-capital cleavage. Since the 1960s and the policy initiatives of L.B. Johnson, the Southern component of the Democrat coalition has switched to the Republican party, and the cleavage separating the parties has increasingly become a social dimension, defined by attitudes toward race and religion, rather than those defined by class.

At times when a new cleavage becomes relevant, or a quandary becomes generally perceived, political actors like Thomas Jefferson, Abraham Lincoln, F.D. Roosevelt, or L.B. Johnson force the electorate (in a sense) to make a judgement about the validity of their declared policy intentions. One way in which the valence of such actors can be enhanced is by the creation of a new activist coalition, whose members are concerned about issues on the previously suppressed dimension. Such a strategy may lead to the destruction of the old party configuration and to what is often termed 'political realignment' (Schofield, Miller and Martin 2003). While such transformations may lead to the enhancement of the public interest, as Madison argued in *Federalist 10*, they may also lead to the creation of countervailing activist coalitions and the increase of political conflict or disagreement in the polity. Obviously, the consequences of forcing such realignments, in order to resolve deep-seated social or political quandaries, cannot be known in advance. The initiators of such transformations must, therefore, be willing to take great political risks. It seems that the American political system, for reasons not understood, has the capacity to bring such leaders into prominence. This may not be what Madison had in mind, when he wrote *Federalist 10*. It may, however, have been in Jefferson's thoughts when he coined the expression an 'Empire for Liberty' in 1809 (Tucker and Hendrickson 1990). As we are all aware these days, this Empire of Liberty may appear to those outside it to be a Empire of Tyranny. It was Madison's belief that, in moments of great uncertainty, the electorate should be called on to render a judgement.

5 Contractarian theory, deliberative democracy and general agreement

Albert Weale

The idea that only government by consent is legitimate government is a long-standing principle of liberal political theory. The claim is often advanced in terms of the idea of a social contract. Only those political arrangements, it is argued, that could be endorsed by parties to a social contract are to be thought of as justifiable. The principle of government by consent is thus rendered in terms of the idiom of hypothetical general agreement to a social contract, the terms of which define a just basic structure of society. Recently, theorists of democracy have taken a deliberative turn, and have argued that democracy is to be understood as a system of public discussion in which general agreement is sought on political principles and public policies. Setting the deliberative claim alongside that of social contract theory highlights the extent to which the principle of general agreement has become a touchstone of contemporary political theory.

Contemporary social contract theory is of course diverse in character. Barry (1995), Gauthier (1986), Harsanyi (1976), Rawls (1996; 1999) and Scanlon (1982), as well as those whom they have inspired, hold to various versions of the theory of the social contract, making different assumptions about the nature of the parties, their reasoning and the function that an appeal to the social contract is supposed to serve. This diversity is nevertheless quite compatible with saying that the appeal to contractual reasoning will characteristically impose constraints on the theory of political principles that can be adopted. Moreover, the diversity is contained within what must be a general form of argument. Here it is useful to invoke the distinction between concept and conception. We

Earlier versions of this chapter have been given at a number of seminars, including University College London, London School of Economics, University of Manchester MANCEPT Conference and Oxford Political Thought Conference. I am grateful to participants on all occasions for their comments, especially Keith Dowding, Cécil Fabre, John Gray, Paul Kelly, Shane O'Neill and Fred Rosen. I am especially grateful to my Essex colleagues in the Political Theory Workshop for repeated testing of these ideas: Richard Bellamy, Michael Freeman, Jason Glynos, David Howarth, Sheldon Leader and Aletta Norval. Bob Goodin provided challenging comments on the penultimate version.

can have a general concept of social contract theory according to which political principles are to be thought of by reference to an agreement among individuals seeking to determine the general rules of their society. Different conceptions of social contract theory will fill out the details of this concept in different ways, including whether the contract is hypothetical or implicit, whether the parties are assumed to know their own circumstances and abilities or not and whether the parties are motivated purely by self-interest or some other set of motivations.

As with social contract theory, we cannot speak of one version of deliberative democratic theory but a variety of approaches, with subtle but important differences among them. One leading view is, of course, that of Habermas (1996). Other, distinct arguments have been advanced by John Dryzek (1990; 2000), David Miller (1993) and Joshua Cohen (1989). An important strand of thinking with which I shall be concerned in this chapter derives from Rawls' (1996: lecture vi) conception of public reason, which has been seen as having implications for deliberative conceptions of democracy (Bohman and Rehg 1997). Gutmann and Thompson develop this idea through the principle of reciprocity which they stipulate as requiring that in political deliberation citizens appeal to reasons that are shared or could come to be shared by fellow citizens (Gutmann and Thompson 1996: 14). On this view, public reason is the ground of general agreement. Hence, a central question for both social contract theory and deliberative democracy is the extent to which the notion of general agreement guided by a principle of reasonableness can do the work that is expected of it.

The relationship of democracy to liberalism is complex and the two bodies of theory are often seen to stand in an uneasy tension with one another. However, the line of argument that I am considering here sees them as complementary rather than competing in offering a critique of a certain conception of politics. For some, the attraction of deliberative democracy is often associated with a critique of what is taken to be the orthodox liberal democratic account of democracy in terms of preference aggregation – the view that politics is about who gets what, when, where and how and in which the pulling and hauling of contesting forces decides the outcome. The trouble here, it is alleged, is that politics as preference aggregation cannot deliver just outcomes. As Joshua Cohen has put it, echoing Rawls, even 'an ideal pluralist scheme, with equal bargaining power and no barriers to entry, cannot be reasonably expected to advance the common good as defined by the difference principle' (Cohen 1989: 20). On the deliberative conception of democracy, by contrast, politics may necessarily involve the aggregation of preferences but only insofar as those preferences are not taken to be given and fixed but are instead seen to be a product of the political process itself arising through reflection and argument.

The conditions of political life that deliberative democrats advance is presupposed by Rawls' stipulation that the parties in the original position recognize that as citizens they will have higher-order interests. These higher-order interests are supposed to be the counterparts in the original position to the two moral powers that Rawls ascribes to citizens: a sense of a conception of the good and a sense of justice (Rawls 1996: 74). In the original position, the representatives of citizens know that they have to legislate for a world in which citizens will wish to develop these moral powers and their deliberation has to be regulated by this knowledge. The 'reasonable' enters therefore as a side-constraint on their deliberations. But this at least means that the upshot of the deliberations must be a subset of the principles that citizens reasonably could regard as consistent with their sense of justice. The outcome of contractual deliberation is not given purely by rational negotiation in circumstances that model conditions of reasonableness. The requirements of the reasonable are a background belief in the reasoning of the contractual parties, and the principles arrived at must be a subset of what could be called reasonable principles.

Thus, the notion that democracy is a political system in which citizens offer reasons for collective choices that are in principle acceptable to all other citizens, so that public policy is based upon consent, can be regarded as a form of political life in which the moral power associated with the sense of justice could be developed. It might even be the case that only a deliberative democracy, founded on the idea of reciprocity in offering public reasons for action, could provide a setting in which the sense of justice could be satisfied. It is not, therefore, surprising to see, as Dryzek (2000: 14) has noted, that Rawls has pursued this logic and concluded that his form of constitutional democracy should be understood as a deliberative democracy (Rawls 1997: 771–2).

I began by saying that the principle of government by consent has often been rendered in liberal theory in the idiom of the social contract, and I shall be investigating the notion of general agreement principally through a discussion of social contract theory. The reason for this is simple. Social contract theory stipulates hypothetical conditions under which general agreement is supposed to emerge. Since I shall express scepticism about this possibility, it follows that general agreement under the conditions of practical politics guided by deliberative principles is even more of a chimera, since social contract theory offers the most favourable conditions under which we should expect agreement to emerge. In what follows I argue that in terms of a test of plausibility for the content of a hypothetical negotiation, there is no reason to expect that social contract theory will provide a clear account of the content of political morality.

In its modern guise the contractual approach has been directed to two interrelated, but distinct, questions. The first is motivational and can be expressed as a demand of political agents as to why they should follow certain political principles or subscribe to certain political practices. Here, the putative contractarian answer is that the principles or practices in question are those that would form the conclusion to a social contract. The second sort of question to which contractarians have sought to give an answer is a question of content: what are the principles of justice or, more generally, what are the principles that ought to define the legitimate terms of political association? This question can be asked independently of any view about what motivates political agents to act in the way that they do.

In this chapter I wish to focus primarily on the second aspect of contractarianism and to ask how adequate a theory it is when considered as an attempt to answer the question of the content of political morality, especially in the light of there being plural intuitions. What, then, is the problem of content?

Contractarianism as a theory of content

One way of understanding the problem of content is to see it as arising from a conjunction of some general features of political morality. One such feature is that there is such a thing as 'common-sense' political morality. The basis for this claim begins with the observation that in large measure people can conduct their political affairs according to well understood political principles. People will thus know when they are committing an injustice or failing in an obligation of citizenship. In other words, the claim is that within human discourse certain notions are passed on, such that these notions form the common stock of principles that govern the evaluation of political decisions and institutions. The exact content of this stock may be large or small, but that there is such a stock is the starting point for the problem.

Another general feature is that this stock of common-sense morality suffers from two defects: first, some central terms are unclear; and, secondly, *prima facie* reasonable principles conflict. To take the question of indefiniteness first. Everyday convictions typically have a formlessness and incoherence to them that means that some analysis and selection is necessary even to supply the data for the moral theory. You only have to think of the wide variety of uses of terms like 'desert' or 'equality' in order to understand what is involved. Here, we have the first reason why a method of ethics is needed. Common-sense principles of political morality are simply too indefinite as they stand to function as a viable currency of political argument.

Moreover, and this is the second defect, there are conflicting political principles at the level of common sense and, without some method for dealing with this problem, it is impossible to decide which of two or more principles in conflict should have priority. Thus, from one point of view, the principle of equality might argue for intervention in the market to correct for distributional faults, whereas from another point of view the principle of freedom might argue for a more *laissez-faire* attitude. Without some method of political ethics, it is argued, we shall not be able to solve these problems of priority.

These two problems might appear to be unrelated to one another, but in fact they share much in common. The problem of indefiniteness can be understood as a problem of which principle should apply in situations in which possible principles conflict with one another. Consider, as an example, Henry Sidgwick's illustration of the indefiniteness of the idea of contractual exchange free from force and fraud. Sidgwick (1891: 84) makes one of the conditions of an individualistic theory of contract the requirement that there be no wilful or negligent misrepresentation of material facts by those participating in the contract. But what does wilful or negligent misrepresentation imply? This seems to be a question of clarification. But it can become a question of choice of conflicting principles, once we realize that one way of reducing the ambiguity is to say that the principle which should apply is that sellers should divulge all they know to a purchaser whereas another way of reducing the ambiguity is to say that each party to a contract is entitled to take advantage of such knowledge as they have lawfully acquired. By choosing one of these principles we have thereby clarified the meaning of wrongful misrepresentation.

Given these problems of indefiniteness and priority, the task for a political theory, according to the contractarian, is to construct a method of political ethics that will enable these problems to be reduced or dissolved. The first stage in this task is to compile a catalogue of those political principles that form the stock of common-sense political morality. Once the catalogue of principles and considerations is constructed, the theorist then has to propose a logical structure that will provide a rationalization of at least a subset of the principles so identified. A good example of how this might work is provided by Rawls' difference principle. The difference principle can be regarded as a justifiable reconciliation between the competing claims of economic efficiency and the claims of economic equality. If it could be shown that the difference principle is the reconciliation that would be favoured by contracting parties, then this would add to its plausibility.

One obvious problem at this point is how we might know whether the method being proposed is the right one. The test of reflective equilibrium is the most commonly employed technique here. According to this test, any method we use to solve the problems of indefiniteness and priority must yield principles that accord with our most deeply held convictions at the common-sense level. Thus, the proposition that slavery is wrong is, according to the method of reflective equilibrium suggested by Rawls (1996: 122–5), one touchstone against which we assess our moral theories. If we had a moral theory that licensed slavery, this conclusion would in itself be a reason for rejecting the method. Moreover, one reason why the test of reflective equilibrium seems appealing is that it resolves one central methodological dilemma. This is how to find a middle way between interpretativism on the one hand and an abstract theory-driven morality on the other. Positive morality needs to be reconstructed in the light of the critical morality derived from theoretical reflection, but in a way that does justice to the central moral requirements of positive morality as it has developed historically.

Notice incidentally that this approach is independent of any view that we might take about the epistemological status of political principles. Thus, it is logically possible for someone to hold that valid political principles are best rationalized within a particular framework, but also hold that such principles are no more than utterances expressive of a certain set of attitudes or emotions. Such a person would be implicitly saying that such attitudes or emotions are structured according to a certain pattern, without making any claims about their epistemological status. Conversely, it is possible to hold that there is a lack of structure to political principles, but that valid principles refer nevertheless to a realm of mind-independent truths.

In this context, contractarianism presents itself as a method of political ethics. That is to say, it is supposed to provide an intellectual device for enabling us to reconcile otherwise conflicting judgements and principles. There are two main alternative views with which contractarianism can be contrasted. The first is utilitarianism. Although this is often presented as a substantive doctrine of political morality, it can also, as philosophical utilitarianism, be thought of as a method of political ethics that rests upon the claim that our stock of common-sense political morality is best accounted for in terms of the tendency of institutions that conform to such principles to produce outcomes that are to the maximum general advantage. Demonstration of this claim was of course the great enterprise on which Sidgwick embarked in *The Methods of Ethics*. I think it fair to say that utilitarianism is normally taken to be the primary target of contractarian theories of justice both as a substantive doctrine and in its philosophical form. Certainly this is so in the writings of Rawls, Barry and Scanlon.

However, utilitarianism is not the only enemy that contractarianism has to beat. The alternative view is intuitionism. Now in some ways it is rather perverse to call intuitionism an answer to the problem of how to formulate a method of ethics, since one of its characteristic claims is that there is no general theory in terms of which principles of political morality are to be accounted for. In this sense it is a 'no-theory' theory. However, it is not vacuous for being such, not least because it denies what contractarianism affirms.

Thus, Rawls made it quite clear in *A Theory of Justice* that intuitionism was a doctrine that had to be defeated as well as utilitarianism, when he wrote:

> The intuitionist believes . . . that the complexity of moral facts defies our efforts to give a full account of our judgments and necessitates a plurality of competing principles. He contends that attempts to go beyond these principles either reduce to triviality, as when it is said that social justice is to give every man his due, or else leads to falsehood and oversimplification, as when one settles everything by the principle of utility. The only way therefore to dispute intuitionism is to set forth the recognizably ethical criteria that account for the weights which, in our considered judgments, we think appropriate to give to the plurality of principles. A refutation of intuitionism consists in presenting the sort of constructive criteria that are said not to exist. (Rawls 1999: 35)

By the time of *Political Liberalism* the notion of 'the sort of constructive criteria' has become the criteria that derive from a form of construction or device of representation within which a theory of principles can be derived, and it is this idea that needs to be explored, which I do in the next section.

Constructivism and models

The notion that contractarianism is a form of constructivist ethics is widespread. One example is Barry who regards his contractarian approach as being a species of constructivism. On this view, constructivist theories are those which seek to characterize justice by reference to the features of some choice situation for putatively rational agents. Barry defines constructivism by reference to two conditions: first, that what comes out of a certain situation is to be counted as just and, secondly, that the construction is by the theorist and not by the people in the situation themselves (Barry 1989b: 266) On this definition, Rawls' own theory is clearly constructivist in seeking to give an account of justice by reference to the hypothetical choices of a set of individuals in his original position. Barry takes this idea and generalizes it to cover all those approaches to the theory of justice that seek to account for justice in terms of the choices that free and rational individuals would make in some specified situation of choice.

Rawls characterizes this constructivist feature of his theory as follows:

> Political constructivism is a view about the structure and content of a political conception. It says that once, if ever, reflective equilibrium is attained, the principle of political justice (content) may be represented as the outcome of a certain procedure of construction (structure). In this procedure, as modeled in the original position . . . , rational agents, as representatives of citizens and subject to reasonable conditions, select the public principles of justice to regulate the basic structure of society. (Rawls 1996: 89–90)

Elsewhere Rawls develops the idea that the original position models the requirements of freedom and equality within the theory, such that 'it becomes perfectly evident which agreement would be made by the parties as citizens' representatives' (Rawls 1996: 26).

In assessing how far political constructivism of this sort can form a method of political ethics, I suggest that we take seriously this notion of the construction as *modelling* the principles of justice. Unfortunately, the notion that the original position is a model opens up a can of worms, because after the word 'parameter', the term 'model' must be one of the most misused words in the English language. We therefore need to understand with some circumspection the sense in which the original position can be said to provide a model.

One sense of the term model that is most frequently used is that one system models another when is stands as a replica or miniature of the system that is being modelled. Mary Hesse (1967) refers to devices understood in this sense of model as 'analogue machines' and notes that though such machines may resemble in many respects the things they are supposed to be modelling (as when a scale model in a wind tunnel resembles the plane design that is being tested), there is no reason in principle why this degree of similarity needs to be maintained (an example, I suggest, being Phillip's hydraulic model of the economy in which a system of pipes containing fluid are supposed to model flows of income in the economy). An alternative sense of model is typically furthest from this familiar analogue machine case and this is model in the logical sense. In the logician's sense of model, a model is simply one way of representing a set of axioms within a formalized system, and to understand the significance of this in the present context we need to understand the notion of the implicit definition of primitive terms within an axiomatized system.

Formalized systems are typical within mathematics and have one feature which is most important: the primitive terms that are used within the axioms of the system have no definition independently of their use within those axioms. Thus, in a formalized system of geometry, for example, the axiom 'Any two points lie on one and only one straight line' will not take its sense from familiar points and lines that are observed in the world. The notions will, instead, be defined implicitly, that is to say in terms of the implications to which they give rise within the formal system. It is this feature of axiomatized systems that gave rise to Bertrand Russell's famous epigram that pure mathematics is a subject in which we do not know what we are talking about, or whether what we are saying is true (cited in Nagel and Newman 1958: 13).

It follows from the notion of implicit definition that we cannot check directly whether any set of formalized axioms are consistent or not. However, it is possible to construct an interpretation of the axiomatized system, or what a logician would call a model. Such models may be constructed in order to test for the consistency of a set of axioms, for if to the counterparts of the formal system within the model there corresponds a set of true statements about the elements of the model, we can say that the axioms are at least consistent, since a set of inconsistent statements about the model will indicate that at least one axiom is false.

The notion of a model in the constructivist interpetation of contract theory hovers rather uneasily between these two quite distinct senses of the term. One reason for taking the term in the analogue sense is that we can understand political principles like equality and freedom through our reflection on political practice. We are not in the position of having no idea what these terms mean, as would be the case if we were solely dependent on implicit definition. Indeed, in some sense, we have a clearer understanding of our political ideals in practice than we do of what the results would be of a model. This is implied, for instance, by the test of reflective equilibrium.

In the logical sense of model, we can say that we learn something about political principles by seeing how putative contracting parties would decide, just as we understand the axioms of geometry by constructing a suitable model. I suggest that this logical notion of a model has one important implication for our evaluation of contractarian theory. Just as we test the consistency of a set of axioms by constructing a model, so we might be said to understand the terms of political discourse by the contract model. In the logical sense, it is the model that provides the content of a justifiable political morality, and we depend upon the results of the model to provide us with that content. We may derive one requirement for the adequacy of a contract theory of political morality as being that its model should provide a self-sufficient way of generating content, in the sense that it should meet Rawls' condition that it is clear which agreement would be made by the parties. The model should thus be capable of generating political principles as conclusions that flow entirely from the terms of the model itself, without tacitly importing the principles that are being argued for. It is this test that existing contractarian theories fail in my view. That is to say, conceived of as models, in this rather precise sense, contractarian political theories fail to provide us with a way of knowing what conclusions would be agreed to in the original position.

In order to see the force of this criticism, it is useful to take two versions of contract theory both of which are aimed at the goal of providing the content of political morality: in the first the agreement of the parties in the original position is seen to be motivated by rational choice; in the second the agreement is motivated by reasonable choice. The first version, in which the agreement derives from hypothetical rational choices, is often discussed in rather discredited terms these days, but I shall argue that it at least has the merit of giving us a definite answer, even if it is the wrong one. The version of contract theory that couches the problem in terms of reasonable agreement by contrast may get the right answers – the answers that may pass the test of reflective equilibrium – but only because the hypothetical process of agreement is too indefinite. So contractarians are stuck in a dilemma: they either get the right answer but for unclear reasons, or they have a clear structure of argument but they get the wrong answer. If the parallels between contract theory and deliberative democracy hold, this conclusion will also be bad news for theories of deliberative democracy.

The idea of rational agreement

Let us begin by considering that version of contract theory that rests upon the idea that the agreement of the contracting parties is founded on a rational choice. One has to be careful here to pick versions that are concerned with the content question and not with the motivational question. So the version that I shall consider under this head is exemplified in the work of Harsanyi (1976), who thought that the content of a defensible political doctrine could be obtained by asking what would be a rational choice for contracting parties behind a thick veil of ignorance.

The pluses and minuses of this approach are pretty well appreciated by now, but in order to bring out the constructivist feature in which I am interested I shall consider its main points. Its crucial elements are that the parties behind the veil of ignorance do not know their own circumstances or conception of the good. It is also assumed that there is a theory of rational choice that holds for all agents, such that it can be assumed that any decision-maker will act in accordance with the conditions of that theory. Harsanyi himself is quite clear that he takes himself to be applying the von Neumann-Morgenstern axioms of choice (or their logical equivalents), which he regards as 'essential requirements of rational behaviour' (Harsanyi 1976: 10), and is plugging them into an account of impersonal preferences, which are the preferences that individuals would have if they did not know their own personal situation in the hypothetical situation of choice. Harsanyi showed that these axioms of choice behind a thick veil of ignorance would yield a generalized average utilitarianism.

So far as I am aware, no one has ever challenged the validity of Harsanyi's argument, and it is easy to see at an intuitive level how a maximizing account of rationality aggregated over persons regarded as mere ciphers of utility would lead to average utilitarianism. So, if there is no questioning the validity of the argument, there must be some problem with the premises. Somehow, these have not captured the salient features of the political morality we are interested in exploring. At this point someone is bound to intervene and to say that the culprit here is the thick veil of ignorance, which has the effect of depriving the individuals in the original position of the knowledge of their own identities. The usual way in which this condition is defective, supposedly, is that the parties to the original contract may as well simply be regarded as one individual. In this situation, so it is said, we do not have a genuine process of bargaining at all, and the absence of such a process is sufficient, it is supposed, to render the construction defective.

It is difficult to know how far this is a decisive objection, however, particularly if we take the modelling requirement in the logical sense. After all, a model in the logical sense need only be one representation of a set of axioms; it does not have to be the only representation. If the thick veil of ignorance with the single decision-maker yielded a set of principles that were in accord with our deepest considered judgements and clarified otherwise indeterminate principles and provided priority rules between disputed principles, then it is difficult to see what the objection might be. Thus, I suspect that the objection is not one of principle, but rather starts from the assumption that the thick veil of ignorance does not provide results that pass the test of reflective equilibrium. That still leaves open the question of where the problem really does lie.

One point to notice in the present context is that, if a constructivist interpretation of the original position is to be taken seriously, the version that relies upon a doctrine of rational choice, understood as axiomatized in a certain way, makes a great deal of sense. So long as the principles upon which the contracting parties choose are thought to be the principles that any rational agent would adopt when confronted by any choice, we can use the original position as a model, in the logician's sense, for a theory of political morality. Here, I suggest, is the problem, however. It is simply implausible to believe that there is just one way of defining rationality, such that any choice that is deemed rational satisfies just one set of conditions. For many theorists of choice the Allais paradox has provided a challenge to standard axiomatizations. The argument is that expected utility theory provides only one way of thinking about choice, and moreover a way that is developed without reference to the manner in which people actually make choices (Sugden 1992). In the face of this challenge, there are now many alternative axiomatizations of individual choice apart from that of expected utility. The thought that one might be able to construct a situation of choice, like that of an original position with a thick veil of ignorance, and then plug in some very general strategies of choice for the contracting parties, is not of itself mistaken. The problem is that there are too many alternative formulations of the notion of rational choice for the answer to be determinate. The problem of plural intuitions at the first-order level has merely been transposed into a problem of alternative axiomatizations of rationality at the level of the model.

So the point at which we arrive is this. In principle, the model of rational choice in accordance with von Neumann-Morgenstern axioms behind the thick veil of ignorance could be a valid device of representation, but such a device does not yield results that are in accordance with a test of reflective equilibrium of at least some people. (It is in accord with the intuitions of someone like Harsanyi, but obviously average utilitarianism is not a widely held principle.) Determinate results seem to be bought at the price of plausibility. So the next obvious question to ask is whether plausible results have to be bought at the price of determinateness. To answer this question we have to consider the move from the rational to the reasonable.

From the rational to the reasonable?

The move from the rational to the reasonable in contract theory seems to have been heavily influenced by Scanlon's 1982 paper, so it will be convenient to have his statement in that paper of the contractual criterion:

> An act is wrong if its performance under the circumstances would be disallowed by any system of rules for the general regulation of behaviour which no one could reasonably reject as a basis for informed, unforced general agreement. (Scanlon 1982: 110)

Here the concept of reasonable rejection is central, and it will convenient to consider the way in which this test might work in the political context. Fortunately, we can do this quite simply, since Brian Barry has taken the trouble to work out the implications of this view in *Justice as Impartiality*.

Developing this view, Barry points out two differences from the theory of rational contractarianism of the sort that Harsanyi advanced. The first is that the parties to the contract are not behind a Rawlsian veil of ignorance. Instead, they are to be thought of as knowing their own circumstances and position in the world, and in particular to know their own conception of the good. The second feature is that the crucial motive for negotiating agreement is that of reasonableness. It is thus built into the Scanlon/Barry original position that one important motive in the contractual negotiation is the desire to put forward principles that everyone can accept. (The motivational problem is thus neatly finessed in the assumption of an agreement motive.) On the Scanlon/Barry original position test, each person or group proposing a principle is supposed to say: is this something that is acceptable to others on reasonable terms?

It is at this point that the contractarian argument and the theory of deliberative democracy converge, at least in some influential versions of the latter. Thus, in motivating their concept of reciprocity, Gutmann and Thompson write: 'Deliberative democracy asks citizens and officials to justify public policy by giving reasons that can be accepted by those who are bound by it. This disposition to seek mutually justifiable reasons expresses the core of the process of deliberation' (Gutmann and Thompson 1996: 52). Many similar quotations from the same work could have been given, but the key idea is plain. Within the theory of deliberative democracy, the test of a justifiable public policy is that reasons can be advanced by each party to a dispute that can in principle be shared by all other parties. So, in both the contractarian theory of justice and deliberative accounts of democracy, the notion of 'acceptability' is central to the logical structure of the theory.

What then can it mean when we say that proposals are acceptable? Clearly, 'acceptable' cannot simply mean 'likely to be accepted' since that would merely be to commit a version of the naturalistic fallacy. Moreover, if it did mean that, the contractarian method would merely reduce to one form of Paretianism, and though there are some versions of contract theory, like those of Buchanan and Tullock (1962), in which this is true, this is a long way from the mainstream. The notion of 'acceptable' has at least to include an element of 'meriting acceptance' and not simply likely to be accepted. Indeed, at one point, Gutmann and Thompson (1996: 64) more or less admit as much when they say, in a critique of solutions to public policy problems that rest on relative bargaining power, that the problem with such approaches is that they rule out any consideration of the merits of each side's claims.

In an earlier paper on the way in which Barry developed the contract argument, I suggested that for Barry the arguments that would merit acceptance in the original position would fall into three categories (Weale 1998: 21–2). The first type of argument that would be regarded as a valid reason in the original position is any argument that sought to protect individuals from an assault on their vital interests, or in other words protect them from absolute deprivation. For example, one agreement that would emerge in the original position would be the need for institutions to protect people from economic destitution. The second type of admissible argument would be one that pointed to the unfairness arising from relative deprivation, for example of the sort that would involve one religion having a privileged status in the political community over others. The third type of admissible arguments would be those concerned with the protection and promotion of public goods, especially those that could only be provided through schemes of taxation. None of these arguments requires a naturalistic interpretation in the sense that their force is made to depend upon a conjecture about what people might in practice be able to accept.

However, one can argue that it is a mistake to seek to drive too sharp a distinction between naturalistic interpretations and ethical interpretations of 'acceptable'. One possible interpretation is that it means something like involving only modest compromises relative to prevailing views or practices. This interpretation would address one issue that has been central in the development of contract theory, namely how to deal with the problem of the so-called 'strain of commitment', the requirement that a set of justifiable political principles should not detach persons too much from what they could legitimately regard as their fair entitlements or personal projects. If we made the concept of the 'acceptable' one which did only involve modest changes from prevailing expectations, it would seem at least to meet this requirement.

In my earlier discussion I dismissed this as a possible formulation of the principles that would emerge from the original position on the grounds that this would enable the beneficiaries of privileges to defend those privileges in a way that would be inconsistent with the demands of justice (Weale 1998: 23–4). However, on further thought, this seems to me to be too quick an argument, especially given that privileged positions might have been legitimately acquired. For one thing, it relies upon taking the domain of the theory of justice to be the comparison of alternative social states, after the pattern of comparative statics in economics, without any application to processes of transition. But to rule out questions of justice from processes of transition from one state to another is arguably to rule out the most difficult and interesting cases. Moreover, as Henry Sidgwick pointed out, the preservation of legitimate expectations does play a role in our thinking about justice, which hovers uneasily between a principle of achieving a just state of affairs and a principle of not disrupting the expectations that individuals have legitimately formed (Sidgwick 1901: 271–3). Indeed, Sidgwick even went so far as to say that this conflict was the chief problem of political justice.

It is difficult to argue that respecting legitimately acquired expectations should not be a part of justice, but such an admission opens up exactly the sort of plural intuitions about values that it was the aspiration of the contractarian approach to resolve. If we simply admit the basic conflict involved in Sidgwick's dilemma, the appeal to reasonableness will not solve Sidgwick's problem of the conflict between an ideal scheme of distribution and meeting the legitimate expectations of those who benefit under some current scheme. At a practical level this need not be a problem, since the conflict of the two principles suggest a reformist political programme using a method involving the cumulative effect of a series of changes, each modest in itself, and designed to accommodate the legitimate expectations of those who would be losers. But to say that there is a perfectly coherent argument of pragmatic reason is not to say that the theoretical construct intended to deal with the problem of plural intuitions is satisfactory.

The problem of persistent pluralism is an embarrassment for any version of contract theory that quite explicitly is intended to provide a method of ethics, but it need not be such a problem for the sort of deliberative democracy advanced by Gutmann and Thompson, which explicitly allows that disagreements may persist and advocates tolerance and mutual understanding in the face of such disagreements. Gutmann and Thompson are quite clear, in contrast to those deliberative democrats who insist upon consensus as a goal of deliberation, that there may be disagreements that cannot be bridged through discussion and public reason. However, it is possible to argue that their insistence on finding mutually acceptable reasons, particularly in the context of decisions about resource allocation, forces reasons to be offered in the public realm that are not demanding enough in terms of the claims that those treated unjustly can make.

Consider one of the running examples that Gutmann and Thompson use, namely claims on behalf of the poor to public support for the cost of organ transplants. Those in need of public subsidy are considered by Gutmann and Thompson (1996: 30) to have a reason that should be publicly acceptable to all, which is that the chance to live a normal life by gaining access to transplants is a basic opportunity, and no one can deny the relevance of the consideration of basic opportunities to the making of such decisions. It may be that Gutmann and Thompson intend this appeal to basic liberties as being a sufficient and not necessary condition for public action. However, it is at least plausible to maintain that contained within the appeal to basic liberties is the thought that anything above the basic liberties is not something that should be guaranteed by public action. If so, this effectively rules out as not being acceptable the social democratic aspiration to establish forms of public service that treat all citizens to a high standard and on the same footing, doing so as an aspect of social justice. And of course this makes sense, since social democrats have always recognized that there was bound to be an element of political conflict in the demands quite distinct from any appeal to a common set of social values.

One source of the problem here is the old conflict, as once formulated by Gallie, between liberal morality and socialist morality, the conflict between seeing justice as a commutative concept or seeing justice as a distributive concept (Gallie 1956: 125). The worry is that the test of mutually acceptable reasons will bias the selection of eligible principles to those that emphasize merely a minimum conception of political morality and which emphasize the commutative aspects of justice. Any theory of political process which rules out one approach from *a priori* arguments of method is surely flawed. This seems to me to be the problem with defining the 'reasonable' in terms of a willingness to seek fair terms of cooperation with other citizens, since the conception of what might be regarded as fair terms is itself the core of the political process.

Another source of the problem, however, is not to recognize that the appeal to shared principles and values, which deliberative democrats often make, is an appeal to a political culture that has been created and shaped by various forms of political action. Consider the example of the Nordic democracies. Barry (1995: 347–8) has offered these as an example of societies that possess the sort of conditions that an egalitarian social contract seeks to embody. In other words, the functioning of the Nordic democracies models the way in which deliberation over a social contract would be conducted. Gutmann and Thompson (1996: 365, n.12) refer to and endorse this parallel of Barry's, suggesting that a hypothetical approach to deliberation needs to be set alongside an empirical approach. Yet, the social democratic culture that forms the basis for such agreement is a culture that is the product of political organization and the institutionalization of certain norms of government by social democratic parties. In such a culture it has become habitual to aspire to high common standards for all in public services, and not simply to acceptable minimum standards for the poor, but the habit is a product of successful political conflict.

It is possible that the bias towards a conception of justice that imposes only minimum standards at a very basic level is even worse than I have presented it here. Consider the example habitually used by Rawls in expounding the method of reflective equilibrium and echoed by others, namely the case of slavery. As I noted earlier, the argument is simple. If any theory of morality endorsed slavery, it would fail the test of reflective equilibrium. But just think what is being said here. Slavery? Can this be a serious example? Surely any political theory that gets even close to endorsing the thought that one human could justifiably be the tool of another – whether in the form of low wages and unhealthy working conditions, domestic drudgery or political manipulation – is to be regarded as failing the test of reflective equilibrium. I do not say that the test of general acceptability will endorse such practices – of course it would not. But neither does it offer the sort of challenge that might lead people to ask whether equal basic liberties, as distinct from equal full liberties, are enough. The theory of justice should offer political aspiration not just protection against the worst that could happen.

Conclusion

I said earlier that contractarianism had to battle on two fronts: against the utilitarian and against the intuitionist. I have no difficulty personally in accepting that utilitarianism cannot be the foundation for a theory of political morality, though I suspect that the deprecation of some forms of utilitarian reasoning has gone too far in some recent discussions. However, that still leaves the alternative of intuitionism. The more the contract doctrine insists on the notion of reasonableness, the happier, I suspect, our intuitionist will be, for the intuitionist can recognize that the appeal to political ideals with their intrinsic merits is plausible, without being committed to the view that there is some method of ethics constructable in social contract terms that will systematize and provide a decision procedure for these different principles.

So far I have pursued a negative argument. Constructions of social contract theory that presuppose rational agents behind a veil of ignorance suffer from there being many ways in which the concept of rationality can be axiomatized. In the absence of a unique (or set of logically equivalent) ways of capturing Harsanyi's essential requirements of rational behaviour, that form of social contract theory is deficient. Similarly, reasonable individuals without a veil of ignorance will have to appeal to substantive political ideals to make their proposals to others acceptable, and this just reintroduces the problem of content that social contract theory was intended to solve.

I conjecture, however, that the negative result is premised on a positive thesis, namely that of the autonomy of ethics. The contractarian programme is in some sense a reductionist programme. It aspires to offer us ethical resolution via some device resting on the notion of practical choice. Suppose, however, that political ideals are emergent properties of reflection and deliberation within a political system. Then we would expect to find any approach that construed them other than in their own terms a failure. But that is a different, and much longer, story.

6 Democracy, justice and impartiality

Robert E. Goodin

Political agitators from Babeuf or even the Gracchi forward have championed democratization of political structures as a means toward democratization of economic holdings. It usually works, to some extent. When it stops working, someone is usually accused of 'betraying the revolution'; and there is rarely any shortage of credible candidates.

But betrayal is not the only reason that scrupulously democratic procedures fail to promote perfect substantive justice. Here I shall explore conceptual sources of the slippage, and discuss some devices by which democracy might be better aligned with justice.

The impartiality connection

Analytically, there is a clear link between the concepts of 'democracy' and 'justice'. The link runs through 'impartiality', which they both manifest and promote. The same 'circumstances of impartiality' are common across both the domain of substantive justice and of procedural democratic fairness: as Brian Barry (1995: 110) says, in passing from the one to the other, 'what defined fairness there will likewise define fairness here'.

Democracy and justice are not interchangeable

The appeal of those other two concepts cannot be *exhaustively* analysed in terms of impartiality, however. If so, justice and democracy would be interchangeable, perfect substitutes for one another. Clearly they are not.

Suppose one politician complains that another's proposals are unjust. Were justice and democracy interchangeable manifestations of impartiality, it would be open to the other to reply: 'No need for us to argue about justice; let's just call a vote and see what wins'. Were democracy and justice interchangeable instruments of impartiality, then that would

I am grateful to Dave Estlund for year-long conversations on these topics, and to Brian Barry for life-long ones.

be a perfectly proper riposte. But surely it is not. Surely the justice of alternative proposals is properly subject to democratic debate.

Were democracy and justice merely alternative manifestations of impartiality, it would not be open to anyone to complain about the injustice of any genuinely democratic outcome. If democracy vouchsafes impartiality, and impartiality is all there is to justice, then no democratic outcome could be unjust. But that is preposterous. Outcomes that are undeniably democratic can be palpably unjust, nonetheless.

That is not merely because democracy or justice or both are merely imperfect manifestations of impartiality (true though that inevitably always is, in practice). Even the purest form of democracy we can imagine could not quell, once and for all, every possible qualm about justice.

Neither do justice and democracy come apart merely because they represent 'impartiality as applied to different objects'. True enough, justice (in its distributive sense, anyway) is ordinarily regarded as an attribute of outcomes, whereas democracy is ordinarily regarded as an attribute of processes. And true enough, it is perfectly possible for an impartial process to yield an outcome that is itself partial, giving everything to one part of the community and nothing to others.[1] And true enough, democracy does sometimes take a 'winner takes all' form that might seem to run that risk.

But that need not be so. Imagine that we voted on distributions directly (rather than on representatives who would subsequently negotiate those distributions). And imagine that each person receives a share of the goods in direct proportion to the number of votes received. In this way it is perfectly possible to envisage the very same standard of impartiality applying to both processes and outcomes.

Nonetheless, outcomes can be impartial in exactly the same way as the democratic process, whilst still being substantively unjust. Counting everyone's vote for one and no one's for more than one is democratically impartial; but giving some people twice as much as others, for no more reason than that they collected twice as many votes, is ordinarily substantively unjust. In cases of majorities tyrannizing over minorities, majority rule is no less democratic for its being tyrannical: it is simply less just.[2]

[1] Suppose we flip a fair coin to decide which of us gets something that we both desire but which, for some reason, cannot be divided or shared: the process (flipping a fair coin) is impartial; the outcome (one of us getting everything, the other nothing) is partial, at least in the sense specified above.

[2] At least that is one perfectly coherent way of conceptualizing the problem of majority tyranny: others, of course, would build non-tyranny constraints into their definition of 'democracy'. Cf. Dahl 1956 and Barry 1979.

Impartiality is necessary, but not sufficient

While impartiality is a necessary condition of both 'democracy' and 'justice', it is a sufficient condition of neither. Tossing a fair coin is paradigmatically impartial.[3] But a flip of a fair coin would never nowadays be regarded as 'democratic'.[4] And it would only rarely (and even then, I argue, wrongly) be thought to be 'just'.

Suppose the results of a free and fair vote are absolutely tied. Suppose we break the tie by flipping a fair coin, declaring the winner of the coin-toss to be elected. Even though the outcome was ultimately determined by the toss of a coin, that outcome nonetheless qualifies as 'democratic' in some fairly strong sense.

Notice, however, that that outcome is democratic by virtue of the votes, not the toss of the coin. The tied vote left both outcomes 'democratically eligible'. The coin toss simply selects which, among democratically equally-eligible outcomes, is the outcome that is actually to be chosen.

Does the other outcome, equally eligible on the basis of the vote, remain the democratic equal of the one that was selected by the toss of the coin? I think so. To be sure, it lacks something that the other possesses – 'authority', call it. But what imparts greater 'authority' to the outcome randomly selected from among those with equal numbers of votes is *not* its greater 'democraticness' but rather its having been selected by procedures displaying some other virtues ('decisiveness', most conspicuously).

Clearly, there may be *un*democratic ways of breaking a tied vote. Prime among those might be procedures manifesting rank favouritism toward one or the other of the contending parties.[5] Random procedures for breaking a tie might be preferred to any alternative way of breaking the tie: they might be 'fairer', they might even be 'less undemocratic'.[6] But again, breaking ties through random procedures does nothing to *increase*

[3] Certainly it 'treats everybody equally' and is impervious to the 'social identity' of parties, and in that way meets the core generic criteria of 'impartiality', even if coin-flipping fails some standards more narrowly applicable to contractualist settings (e.g., 'all those concerned are well informed and have their interests and perspectives expressed with equal force and effectiveness'; 'aim at consensus where possible') (Barry 1995: 110).

[4] Ancients, of course, thought otherwise: 'the appointment of magistrates by lot is thought to be democratic, and the election of them oligarchical' (Aristotle, *Politics* 1294b7–9); below I offer a speculation on that. Notice that modern exponents of 'statistical democracy' seek to make office-holders statistically representative of the electorate, and value random selection as a means to that: randomness itself is not the goal; even Burnheim (1985: 115) would not be content with selecting policies, as opposed to rulers, by lot.

[5] Handing an election to the family of the person who gave you your judgeship, for example.

[6] Maybe this is why ancients thought it uniquely democratic to select rulers by lot: all citizens are equally qualified; distinguishing among them on any other ('oligarchical') criterion is undemocratic; all that is left is to choose among them by lot.

the 'democraticness' of the process. It simply does nothing (in a way that other tie-breaking procedures might) to diminish it.

So too with 'justice'. Certainly the antithesis of justice is favouritism, once again. Precluding favouritism is the central point of all original apparatus of a Rawlsian choice behind the 'veil of ignorance'. But while justice clearly requires impartiality, that alone is not sufficient. That is the upshot of the large literature, also owing largely to Rawls, insisting that justice requires us to efface – not respect – the effects of the 'natural lottery' (the distribution of natural skills, resources, abilities and disabilities).[7]

The outcome of a fair lottery might be just, where that is the best we can do. Imagine an indivisible good that cannot be carved up and shared out without destroying its value. Imagine that there are more people with equally strong claims to such goods than there are indivisible lumps of such goods. Then, as in the case of a tied democratic vote, it might be morally proper to decide by lottery who, among those equally entitled, should get the goods.

Where there are more equally strong claims than can be met from a discrete stock of indivisible goods, that leaves many different distributions of those goods 'justice-eligible'.[8] A random lottery simply picks which, among those outcomes that would be equally just, will be the outcome to be pursued. In so doing, however, the random process does not 'add to the justice' of the outcome it identifies. At best, the lottery merely picks out one, among those that would be equally just, as the authoritative outcome.

Some may say that justice might actually require recourse to random procedures, in such circumstances. Where people have equal claims on something that cannot be divided equally among them, the next-best thing may be giving them equal chances of getting it (Broome 1999: 119–21; cf. Elster 1988).

Still, it is important to recognize that equal chances are always second-best solutions in such situations. If the good *could* be divided equally among everyone with an equal claim to it, then justice requires us to do precisely that. It would not be equally just to single out one person, utterly at random, to receive the entire stock of an in-principle-divisible good. Assuming that process really was random, the latter allocation would (in

[7] The fact that those distributions are 'arbitrary from a moral point of view' counts as criticism, not praise, for Rawls (1971: 511) and many following him (Barry 1989b; cf. Barry 1965: 306).

[8] The 'justice-eligible' set are those distributions that: (a) allocate all those goods to people (and only to people) in the set of people with equally strong claims; and (b) are Pareto-undominated, in the sense that no person in that set could get more of those goods without someone else in the set getting less of those goods.

that sense vouchsafed by randomness and impartiality) be 'fair'. But that simply goes to show that justice is not *just* fairness.

What more is necessary?

The upshot is that, while 'impartiality' is a necessary condition of both 'justice' and 'democracy', it is a sufficient condition of neither. It is tempting to suppose that what differentiates 'justice' from 'democracy' are the differing further conditions that are also necessary for each.

One thought along those lines might be this. Perhaps 'democracy' is supposed to respond impartially to people's *preferences*, whereas 'justice' is not; and 'justice' is supposed to respond impartially to *reasons*, whereas 'democracy' is not. Tempting though that thought may initially seem, ultimately it proves not quite right, either.

By 'preferences' here I mean what philosophers call 'internal reasons': subjective, internally-endorsed evaluations that provide agents with a reason for acting that gets an internal motivational grip on them (Williams 1981). There is no presupposition that preferences are purely egoistic or self-regarding. They are necessarily preferences *of* someone, but the preferences can be *for* the good of another or for some state of the world unconnected to the well-being of any humans at all.

By 'reasons' I shall here mean what philosophers call 'external reasons': evaluations with objective, external validity of some sort or another, which may or may not correspond to agents' own subjective assessments (Williams 1981).

Positive responsiveness to preferences

It is clear enough why we are inclined to suppose that 'democracy' requires not merely 'impartiality' but also something like 'positive responsiveness to people's preferences'.

Suppose we decide what we are going to do by tossing a coin to decide among alternative possible courses of action, without regard to what *anyone* wants. In that way we might end up doing something that *no one* wants. Such a procedure would be utterly impartial among people's preferences. It would impartially ignore the preferences of everyone, equally.

That would be impartial, but not democratic. For a decision procedure to be democratic, there must (it is standardly said) 'be some formal connection between the preferences of the citizens and the outcomes produced' (Barry 1979: 157). Democratic decision procedures must satisfy the criterion of 'positive responsiveness to people's preferences'. Formalized by Arrow and a raft of social choice theorists in his wake, that criterion requires that if one person's preference changes from i to j while everyone else's preferences remain the same, then the social choice should not change from j to i.[9]

The question before us, here, is this: is this further criterion one that is peculiar to 'democracy', not shared by 'justice' – and hence one that can differentiate those two notions from one another?

A case can be made for thinking that 'justice' need not be positively responsive in that way to people's (mere) preferences. Suppose everyone were absolutely identical in every (other) justice-relevant respect, but suppose that some people preferred good A and some people preferred good B. It would be *inefficient* to give them equal shares of A and B, but perhaps not unjust.

Of course, given that initial allocation they might then make agreements among themselves to exchange some A for B, and vice versa, in line with their preferences. A theory of justice may well want, among other things, to respect the agreements people make; hence the distribution that results from fair trades from a fair starting point might be the just distribution, *ex post* of the agreement. But justice does not require – and may not even permit – us to impose that distribution from the start, anticipating in advance and imposing the agreements people would presumably make on the basis of their preferences, rather than merely respecting the results of those agreements after the fact.

Furthermore, justice may dictate that people get things that they also happen to prefer, but for some reason other than merely that they prefer them. People may, for example, prefer things that they also need or deserve; and (depending on one's theory of justice) needs or deserts might underwrite just allocations. But it is arguably positive responsiveness to those other considerations (needs, deserts), rather than positive responsiveness to preferences as such, that justice requires.

[9] 'Positive responsiveness to people's preferences' (May 1952) is the more evocative phrasing of the requirement, although Arrow's (1963: 25–6) formulation ('non-negative responsiveness') is more correct. Where one person's preferences change from i to j while everyone else's remain the same, literal 'positive responsiveness' would require that the social choice change to j (if it was not j already). But suppose the initial vote was 99 for i and 1 for j: surely democracy would not there require the social choice to shift from i to j, just because one voter shifts in that direction (making the revised vote still 98 for i compared to still only 2 for j). All that democracy requires here is 'non–negative responsiveness': that adding more votes in favour of something should not tell *against* it, democratically; if j is the social choice when the vote is 51 for j and 49 for i, then i should not become the social choice when it loses one of its votes to j (and the revised vote becomes 52 for j and 48 for i). Finally, for reasons of aggregatability discussed by Estlund (1990), we ought perhaps to require that these be people's 'judgments about the common good' rather than just their brute 'preferences'; I stick here to the more colloquial phrasing, without intending to prejudice that issue.

Or, again, justice might take account of people's sheer differences in starting points. When distributing the next lot of resource R, justice might require us to give more to those presently holding less R. Again, this might (or might not) be something that is preferred by the people concerned. But, again, justice has us responding positively not to their preferences as such but to certain other attributes of their objective circumstances.

In short, 'democracy' requires (at least) 'impartiality' plus 'positive responsiveness to people's preferences'. 'Justice', we might suppose, requires the former but arguably not (not always, anyway) the latter.

Positive responsiveness to reasons

In searching for some second necessary condition to be added to 'impartiality', for purposes of 'justice', we might naturally be tempted by something like 'positive responsiveness to relevant reasons'.

What 'reasons' would count as relevant depends on one's theory of justice.[10] Alternative theories of justice would offer up notions like 'claims' or 'merits' or 'deserts' or 'needs'.

Which 'reasons' are relevant will also typically vary not only with theories but also with context. It would be clearly unjust to use a lottery to decide whom to award the prize in a violin competition (Broome 1999: 112). So too would it be 'unjust', ordinarily even by the lights of 'needs' theorists of justice, to award such a prize to whichever violinist happens to need the prize money the most.[11]

A standard of 'positive responsiveness to reasons', mimicking the familiar social choice standard discussed above, would be: if one more relevant reason is added in favour of i rather than j, and all other relevant reasons remain the same, then the social choice does not change from i to j.

The hypothesis before us is that positive responsiveness to relevant reasons, rather than to mere preferences, is what distinguishes the impartiality that is characteristic of justice from the impartiality that is characteristic of democracy.

But arguably mere preferences *can* sometimes count as relevant reasons for a just social decision. Indeed, on a preference-utilitarian theory of justice, they are the *only* reasons that ought ultimately to be relevant. Even if we do not want to embrace preference utilitarianism, neither

[10] And the application: justice clearly responds to reasons of a non-distributional sort in cases of non-comparative (e.g., criminal) justice.

[11] Though – taking a leaf from the way courts hearing tort cases sometimes award judgment to a plaintiff to whom they then decline to award any monetary damages – such a theorist might 'award judgment' to the best violinist but then proceed to divide the money according to some standard other than musical merit.

presumably would we want to rule that theory out of the court of justice, purely by definitional fiat. It may be wrong, but it is not incoherent, to say that it would be unjust to opt for the outcome that maximally frustrates people's preferences, where all other justice-relevant considerations are held constant.

The fact that mere preferences might sometimes be justice-relevant reasons implies that the strong form of the hypothesis before us must be wrong. What distinguishes democracy from justice is not that the former takes account of preferences, whereas the latter does not. 'Justice' conceptually *can* count preferences as relevant reasons.[12]

Respecting preferences always and only?

There are two weaker versions of the hypothesis here under consideration that might seem to hold more promise. One version holds that what distinguishes democracy from justice is that democracy *always* takes account of preferences, whereas justice only sometimes does. The other version holds that what distinguishes democracy from justice is that democracy takes account *only* of preferences, whereas justice sometimes takes account of other reasons besides mere preferences.[13] It is tempting (but not necessary: and as we shall see, not advisable) to merge those two options into the conjoint proposition that democracy 'always and only' takes account of people's preferences, whereas justice 'neither always nor only' takes account of mere preferences.

Certainly it is true to say that justice does not always take account of people's preferences, and it is certainly true that justice takes account of things besides people's preferences. (Think of the violin competition, once again.) And it may well be true that democracy always takes (some) account of people's preferences. But it is wrong to say that democracy only (or hence 'always and only') takes account of people's preferences.

To assert otherwise would seem to denigrate as undemocratic (or anyway extra-democratic) any reason-giving designed to *change* people's preferences. But democrats of all stripes suppose that it is democratically right and proper for people to offer and demand from one another reasons for the outcome that they advocate, and in the course of these

[12] Conceptually, it is not incoherent: whether or not it is morally advisable (whether or not that is the correct theory of justice) is a separate issue, not to be adjudicated here.

[13] Notice that, both separately and together, these two hypotheses are different from saying that democracy takes account of *all* preferences: democracy may choose to 'launder' the preferences it will count, and it may do so for reasons that are themselves preference-regarding (Goodin 1986).

exchanges try to persuade one another of the superiority of their own reasons. Democrats would ordinarily regard guillotining of such discussions – forcing the issue to a vote without discussion – as profoundly undemocratic. On the face of it, however, forcing people to subject themselves to attempts to change their preferences cannot ordinarily be justified purely in terms of the preferences of those people themselves.[14]

True, the impact of all this democratic reason-giving is democratically felt only through the reshaping of people's preferences. The deliberative democrat's hope is that people's preferences will be honed in response to good reasons. But at the end of the day, it is people's preferences that democratically count, not disembodied reasons. In that 'at the end of the day' sense, perhaps, democracy is indeed always and only preference-respecting, whereas justice is neither.

But it would be a mistake to define 'democracy' exclusively in terms of what happens 'at end of the day'. There is more to 'democratic procedures' than the impartial aggregating of preferences into social outcomes.

To define 'democracy' purely in terms of the impartial processing of preferences, and consign the impartial weighing of reasons entirely to the realm of justice, would have implausible consequences. One of them would be this: if the way we distinguish 'democracy' from 'justice' is by assigning 'democracy' to the province of preferences and 'justice' to the realm of reasons, then the sense in which the giving of reasons as part of a deliberative democratic process is superior to merely deciding things by a mute show of hands would be that it is more 'just', not 'more democratic'. That cannot be right.

Responding how?

Thus, 'justice' and 'democracy' cannot easily be distinguished by reference to the different *kinds* of things – 'reasons' versus 'preferences' – to which they impartially respond. On certain plausible construals, each can be positively responsive to either, or both.

Perhaps the difference between justice and democracy lies not in the *kinds* of things to which they positively respond but rather in the *manner* in which they respond. Perhaps the difference is not one of 'to what?' but, rather, of 'how?'

[14] Sometimes of course people *do* want to have their preferences challenged and tested, for good Millean reasons; sometimes we can appeal to people's future preferences as warrants for circumventing or contravening their present preferences. The claim in the text refers to the (presumably common) case where neither of those propositions is true.

Democracy is often seen to be a matter of 'counting' (of votes, and the preferences for which they stand).[15] Justice, in contrast, is typically thought to be more a matter of the 'weighing' of reasons. The difference between democracy and justice might thus lie in the difference between 'the weighing of reasons' versus 'the counting of noses' (Barry 1995: 104).[16]

Of course, deliberative democrats would not recognize themselves under that description of 'democracy'. They set themselves up explicitly in opposition to 'aggregative' models of democracy that just add up people's votes (or just aggregate preferences in social welfare functionals). The sorts of deliberations that they insist are democratically required are supposed to be occasions for precisely the weighing of reasons that, on this construal, would be the province of 'justice' rather than of 'democracy'. So this distinction between 'counting' and 'weighing' would have the same odd consequence as above, implying that democratic deliberation makes democracy 'more just' rather than 'more democratic'.

What, in any case, is the real difference between 'counting' and 'weighing' as ways of blending disparate inputs into a decision? 'Reasons' can be 'outweighed' just as citizens can be 'outvoted'. What on balance we ought to do, in a 'weighing' model, is to go with the balance of the reasons. What we ought to do, in a 'counting' model, is to go with the balance of the preferences-cum-votes.

One difference is this. Counting is sometimes thought to be more *decisive* than weighing. Counting yields a determinate result (albeit occasionally a tied result). Weighing involves hazier and more judgmental processes; and its results are inevitably less firm and decisive, in consequence.

One consequence of this difference, in turn, is that there is a certain 'arrogance of aggregation' associated with counting that is absent with weighing (Goodin 2003b: ch. 8). Even if it was a close-run decision – even if opposing considerations were pretty finely balanced – a counting

[15] 'Envisage Democracy in terms of a certain machine', suggests Wollheim (1962: 76) and a raft of social choice aggregators likewise (cf. Miller 1992). 'Into it are fed, at fixed intervals, the choices of the individual citizens. The machine then aggregates them according to the pre-established rule or method, and so comes up with what may be called a "choice" of its own. Democratic rule is said to be achieved if . . . the most recent choice of the machine is acted upon.'

[16] The same contrast is sometimes expressed as one of 'reasoning' versus 'calculating'. These distinctions loom large in discussions of incommensurable values and moral dilemmas, contrasting value-monists who thought there was a common currency in which all competing values could be cashed and hence one 'right answer' determined, and value-pluralists who thought that there was no such common currency, no one 'right answer' (though it was unclear how to understand the nature of the scale in which the 'weighing' was then occurring, either).

procedure confidently yields a unique 'right answer' (or, in the case of a tie, a unique 'set of right answers' from which we must pick). Just as the decisiveness of counting constitutes an invitation to arrogance, the indecisiveness of mere weighing encourages us to be more reticent about asserting any too confidently that we have necessarily reached the 'right result'.

That may well be a true depiction of the phenomenology of counting. Be that phenomenology as it may, it would be just as *inappropriate* in the case of 'counting' as in the case of 'weighing' simply to forget the fact that there were countervailing considerations, once a decision has been reached. If it was a close-run thing, we might want to proceed cautiously even within a 'counting' model, for fear that we have calculated wrongly or for fear that a slight change in circumstances might well tip the balance in the other direction. Likewise in the case of weighing, if we have had to decide against certain valid reasons or certain people's preferences on this occasion, then we might think that this is a reason for leaning the other way on some future occasion. All that can as plausibly be said of one procedure as the other, of counting as of weighing.

Internalizing just reasons

The task of 'making democracy just', thus construed, is to make people internalize justice-relevant reasons, and those alone. Justice-relevant reasons are a subset of all external reasons, and might include some internal reasons as well.

The democratic process fails to track justice insofar as voters' internal reasons (their preferences) fail to track perfectly justice-relevant external reasons (including such consideration of preferences as justice requires). One way that might happen is if there are some justice-relevant external reasons that voters do not internalize. Another is if voters internalize (as preferences) some reasons that correspond to no good justice-relevant reasons. Yet another is if the transformation rules – the ways in which inputs (reasons, internal or external) are transformed into outputs (decisions) – are different in the realm of politics and the realm of justice. The 'task of making democracy just' is thus to ensure that democracy takes account of all right (justice-relevant) reasons, and only right (justice-relevant) reasons, and does so in the right (just) way.

Institutional fixes

One way of pursuing that project is at the level of institutional design. The attempt there is to ensure that the rules of the democratic process somehow are more prone to take account of all right reasons, and only right reasons, in the right way.

Ensuring an expansive franchise is one way of attempting to ensure that more right reasons (anyway, a wider range of internal reasons) are taken into account. Institutionalizing rights guarantees is one way of attempting to ensure that only right reasons are taken into account (or anyway, of blocking implementation of policies manifestly manifesting wrong reasons). One-person-one-vote and one-vote-one-value rules of democratic procedure are ways of attempting to ensure that reasons are taken into account in a right (impartial) way.

But those institutional devices have clear limits. First, they can only help democracy track external reasons that are actually internalized by some political actors (as voters or appellants). External reasons internalized by no one will get no political hearing, however extensive the franchise; they will get no votes, electorally, and hence secure no benefit from one-person-one-vote or one-vote-one-value rules. By the same token, external reasons internalized by no one will issue in no appeals, however broad and robust the rights guarantees; they will be put to no judicial vote, and hence secure no benefit from rights guarantees.

Second, democratic institutions can only weigh reasons as heavily as citizens themselves do, in their own expressed preferences. There are good institutional devices for ensuring that a wider variety of external reasons is internalized, to some extent or another by some political actors or another, and that those external reasons get some representation in the political process in consequence. But there are no good institutional devices for ensuring that proper weight will be attached to each of those external reasons, either by political actors or by the political system as a whole, in consequence.

Third, democratic institutions have only imperfect mechanisms for ignoring or suppressing preferences that run contrary to external reasons. We can require courts to conduct a 'rationality review' of legislation, assuring themselves that there is at least one possible legitimate purpose that the statute serves. We can require legislators (and indeed citizens in general) to provide some reasons for the policies they propose in free and open public fora. But those mechanisms ensure only that there is at least one good reason for the policy in question, when what we really want here is an assurance that good reasons for the policy actually predominate on balance, taking full account of all the reasons there may also be against the policy. Likewise with other strategies. There may for example be good want-regarding grounds for laundering the preferences that enter into the political process (Goodin 1986). Being preference-respecting institutions, however, democracies can incorporate those preference filters only insofar as citizens themselves internalize those good external reasons for that self-denying ordinance.

Motivational prompts

Tempting though it may be to try to 'take humans as they are and institutions as they might be', there are therefore strict limits in the extent to which such attempts at institutional design alone can align internal with justice-relevant external reasons, thereby 'making democracy just'. To complete that task, we need also to work on the 'human' side of that equation.

We need to find ways to encourage democratic agents to internalize a more justice-apt range of external reasons than they might otherwise, and to weigh them more appropriately than they might otherwise in their own (and hence their polity's) decision processes.

One mechanism for doing that is through 'role reminders'. Inspiration for this strategy might be found in Brian Barry's analysis of 'the public interest' as being 'interests that people have in the adoption of a certain policy *qua* "member of the public"' (Barry 1964: 124; Goodin 1996). In that phrase, *qua* – 'in one's capacity as' – serves as a pointed reference to some particular *role* that one occupies.

Everyone occupies many roles, each with an associated set of interests and expectations, many of which will be in conflict with one another on any given occasion. How one balances these competing interests and requirements, and indeed how one interprets and plays them, is subject to individual variability and often to considerable creativity (Dahrendorf 1968).[17]

Roles shape behaviour principally by 'framing' an agent's 'definition of the situation'. Evoking different roles evokes different ways of perceiving the issue, foregrounding some aspects and backgrounding others. Looking at the situation from the perspective of one role rather than another makes different considerations relevant, and different performances appropriate. 'A role', says Herbert Simon (1991: 126–7) in his account of the workings of such heuristics:

[17] As Martin Hollis (1987: 170) describes the process, 'Problems arise within particular role-playing games and their possible solutions are constrained and enabled by this fact. Judgement is the role-player's judgement of how best to satisfy the demands of office, perhaps tempered by a refusal to heed only those demands. The effect is to make rationality less a matter of maximizing the value of a variable and more one of playing a role or a game well'.

> is not a system of prescribed behaviors but a system of prescribed decision premises. Roles tell organization members how to reason about the problem and decisions that face them; where to look for appropriate and legitimate informational premises and goal (evaluative) premises, and what techniques to use in legitimating these premises.

(See further Goodin 1999; 2003a). It is the function of 'role talk' to evoke these different 'logics of appropriateness' (March and Olsen 1995: ch. 2).

Here, then, is my modest proposal for how to 'make democracy just', in the sense of making the preferences upon which people act politically better track the externally right reasons for action. I do not aim to 'change' people, exactly. I merely aim to 'remind' people, when acting politically in their public capacities, that they *are* acting in their public capacities. By situationally sensitizing them to the roles in which they are acting, such 'role reminders' might help to draw political actors' attention to the performances (obligations and expectations) that are appropriate to that role.

On one side, these role reminders might help prompt and motivate people to respond to a broader range of external reasons: reasons pertaining to the common good and shared interests, among all those to whom (and with whom) one is responsible in one's political capacity. On another side, these role reminders might help encourage people to filter the internal reasons upon which they act politically, suppressing preferences that may be perfectly appropriate in their private capacities but that are wholly inappropriate in their public ones. On yet another side, these role reminders might help remind people of the need to respond, in their political capacities, to the right reasons in the right *ways* – attending to the weight of good reasons rather than merely responding to the balance of private preferences, to the justice of outcomes rather than responding to the relative clout of the respective lobbies.

The practical utility of role reminders

Mere 'reminders' (and come to that, the amorphous requirements of 'roles' themselves) might seem flimsy things, incapable of withstanding any staunch attack of blind self-interest. Just as Rawls' (1971: 86) theory of justice can only get a motivational grip on people who already internalize a 'sense of justice', these 'role reminders' will only get a motivational grip on people who already internalize the roles in question (Goodin 1992). How we create and sustain those conditions is a large and complex question of a wholly contingent and empirical nature.

Still, much more often than not, people actually do internalize – however imperfectly – the requisite roles. Voters certainly do. That may be the best (maybe the only) good explanation of why they bother to vote at all (Benn 1979: 304; cf. Barry 1970: ch. 2). And that might be the best explanation of how they vote, once the role requirements of sheer civic duty gets them to the polls (Kiewiet 1983; Rohrschneider 1988).

So too do public officials, both elected and appointed, internalize role requirements. Whatever their private motivations, politicians ordinarily feel obliged to couch their public justifications in terms of role-appropriate references to the 'public interest' – or, at the very least, in terms of the interests of the particular constituencies they were elected to serve (Maass 1983; Fenno 1978).

Bureaucrats, too, ordinarily internalize role responsibilities. They internalize their roles as representative of their bureaux: 'where you stand depends on where you sit' seems to be true, less as a matter of your bureau's (and hence your own) interests, and more as a matter of internalizing the 'bureau philosophy' (Simon, Smithburg and Thompson 1950: 543 *et seq.*; Simon 1991: 37; Hollis 1987: ch. 10). Bureaucrats also internalize their role as servants of the larger public interest. That is why, for example, even toothless reporting requirements can sensitize bureaucrats contemplating environmentally harmful projects to the larger social costs of their schemes, and lead them to back off the proposals in consequence (Taylor 1984).

Of course, all of those roles are by their nature 'partial', in one way or another. Some of them sensitize the role occupant to an electoral or administrative constituency that is very particular and very circumscribed. Even those roles that orient their incumbents toward the 'public at large' tend to sensitize them to a 'public' that is circumscribed substantially more narrowly than the *world* at large, and they thus call to mind external reasons that are equally narrow from that broader perspective of what really impartial reason would require.

Still, reminding people (both masses and elites) of the responsibilities incumbent upon them in their public capacities, in their roles as citizens and officials, might usefully serve to make them more responsive to justice: to right reasons, and only right reasons, in the right way. Gentle role reminders – asking people what are their preferences, *qua* citizen – might work where more mechanical forms of institutional design do not make democracy a more reliable tracker of true justice.

7 Mimicking impartiality

Jon Elster

Introduction

In *Justice as Impartiality* Brian Barry argues that impartiality is two-tiered. First-order impartiality 'means not being motivated by private considerations. This is often cashed out by claiming that to be impartial you must not do for one person what you would not do for anyone else in a similar situation – where your being a friend or relative of one but not the other is excluded from counting as a relevant difference'. Second-order impartiality, which defines 'justice as impartiality', 'calls for . . . principles and rules that are capable of forming the basis of free agreement among people seeking agreement in reasonable terms' (Barry 1995: 11). In some contexts, second-order impartiality mandates first-order impartiality. Parents ought, for instance, to treat their children without favouritism. In other situations, second-order impartiality requires first-order partiality. The second-order principle 'rules out the "the magic of the pronoun 'my'" in this sense: I cannot say "I should rescue my wife and anybody else in a position to rescue one of two people should rescue my wife if she is one of the two". But it does not rule out my saying: "Everybody should rescue his wife in such a situation." For this does not put my wife in a specially privileged position at the second-order level' (Barry 1995: 230).

In this chapter I shall mainly consider first-order impartiality. Specifically, I want to consider how non-moral motivations may simulate or mimic first-order impartiality (henceforward *impartiality*).[1] First, however, I need to extend the notion of first-order impartiality. On Barry's definition, impartiality is a triadic notion: *A* should treat *B* and *C* similarly if their situations are relevantly similar. There is also, however, a simpler notion of dyadic impartiality: *A* should not treat *B* differently from himself if their situations are relevantly similar. Violations of impartiality may take the form of selfishness no less than that of

[1] As readers will note, some of my examples do not fit neatly into the category of impartiality, and are better subsumed under a more general category of disinterested and dispassionate behaviour.

favouritism or prejudice. A father who treats his children with perfect impartiality may think that his interests take precedence over those of his wife. To take a contemporary political example: it would violate impartiality if the European Union accorded Romania fewer voting rights (relative to population) than Poland, and also if they accorded all candidate states fewer voting rights than the existing fifteen Member States. An eighteenth-century precedent of this example will concern us later.

In the cases I shall consider, the threat to impartiality derives from self-interest or group interest. In some cases, the remedy, too, is found in self-interest of a more enlightened variety. Broadly speaking, long-term self-interest is capable of simulating morality. In other cases, the remedy will be found in the love of glory or the fear of shame. In still other cases, self-interest and emotion interact to yield an outcome that approximates what impartiality on its own would require. Some of the arguments in the *catalogue raisonné* I shall offer have clear relevance for institutional design. Others may illuminate moral psychology and the sociology of morality. Their philosophical relevance is less obvious. To the extent, however, that 'strains of commitment' and the 'burden of compliance' can be cited as normatively relevant objections to a particular conception of justice, the convergence of non-moral motivations and moral demands may be pertinent.[2]

Montaigne

In his *Essays*, Montaigne offers several arguments of the general form I am addressing here. A weak argument is that morality can be a tie-breaker in decision-making under uncertainty:

> In the state of indecision and perplexity brought upon us by our inability to see what is most advantageous and to choose it (on account of the difficulties which accompany the divers unforeseeable qualities and circumstances which events bring in their train) the surest way in my opinion, even if no other consideration brought us to do so, is to opt for the course in which is found the more honourable conduct and justice; and since we doubt which is the shorter road, we should keep going straight ahead. (Montaigne 1992: 144)

Later, he makes a stronger argument for virtue: 'Even if I did not follow the right road for its rightness, I would still follow it because I have found from experience that, at the end of the day, it is usually the happiest one and the most useful' (Montaigne 1992: 709–10). Whereas the first argument leaves open that behaving virtuously might be against our self-interest, if only we could know where it lies, the second tends to exclude

[2] For a discussion of the strains of commitment, see Barry (1995: 61–7). For the burden of compliance, see Barry (1995: 205–6).

that possibility. Unlike Descartes (see below), however, Montaigne does not suggest any mechanism that might tend to bring about this happy coincidence between self-interest and virtue.

Another line of argument turns on the difference between intrinsic and extrinsic motivations: acting for the sake of what is right and acting for the sake of what other people think about you. As the former motivation is rare, policy-makers may have to rely on the latter:

> If that false opinion [a concern for what other people think] serves the public good by keeping men to their duty . . . , then let it boldly flourish and may it be fostered among us as much as it is in our power. . . . Since men are not intelligent enough to be adequately paid in good coin let counterfeit coin be used as well. . . . And there is no polity which has not brought in some vain ceremonial honours, or some untruths, to keep the people to their duties. (Montaigne 1992: 715)

If morality is the true coin, then 'approbativeness' (Lovejoy 1961: ch. IV and *passim*) – the desire to be well thought of by others – is the false coin that may have to substitute for it. I return to that idea below. Here, I shall only note that for its success the substitution clearly depends on the actions eliciting praise coinciding or at least overlapping with those that are demanded by impartial morality. In the contemporary USA, this condition is to some extent satisfied with respect to charitable behaviour. In the Art Institute of Chicago, for instance, donors are carefully distinguished by the size of the plaques honouring them, thus creating an emulation for (perceived) goodness. On the night of 4 August 1789, when the French Assemblée Constituante abolished feudal burdens and privileges, many of the delegates were apparently motivated by the desire to sacrifice more than their neighbours.[3] Thus Patrick Kessel (1969: 247) cites a contemporary document that refers to 'the heat of the moment that electrified each individual and made him fear being left behind' in the competition to appear to be generous.

Descartes

Although Descartes did not, strictly speaking, propose a moral philosophy, let alone a theory of justice, several passages from his writings suggest

[3] Some of them were also motivated by spite, that is, by the desire to sacrifice privileges possessed by their neighbours but not by themselves. Thus, after the bishop of Chartres had proposed the abolition of exclusive hunting rights, the Duc du Châtelet said to his neighbours, 'Ah! he takes our hunting, I'll take his tithe', and proposed that the tithe be abolished with compensation (Droz 1860: 308). As Mirabeau wrote in the *Courrier de Provence* (XXIV: 3): 'although one might have proceeded with more method, the results would not have been more advantageous. The kind of mutual challenge of the different orders . . . turned entirely to the general good'.

a prudential perspective on morality along the lines I am discussing here. A famous maxim of 'provisional morality' from the *Discourse on Method* tells us that if one is lost in a forest and wants to get out of it, one should not constantly change direction according to what at any point in time appears to be the best option, but choose to walk in one direction and stick to it (Descartes 1988: 594–5). I do not know if this is a deliberate echo of Montaigne's 'since we doubt which is the shorter road, we should keep going straight ahead'. The concerns in any case are different, since (unlike Montaigne) Descartes is certainly not playing on the double meaning of 'straight' (*droit*). Although (like Montaigne) he is proposing a maxim for decision-making under uncertainty, the problem of getting out of a forest has no moral aspects.

In two letters to Princess Elisabeth, Descartes affirms more explicitly the extensional equivalence of prudence and morality. In the first, he addresses the question of the strains of commitment:

[It] is difficult to determine exactly how far reason ordains that we should devote ourselves to the community [*le public*]. However, it is not a matter on which it is necessary to be very precise; it is enough to satisfy one's conscience, and then leave a lot of room for one's inclination. For God has established the order of things, and has joined men together in so close a community, that even if everyone were to relate everything to himself, and had no charity for others, he would still commonly work for them as much as was in his power, provided he was prudent. (Descartes 1970: 181)

This is little more than a restatement of Montaigne's optimistic view, with the left-hand side of the equation moved to the right hand. Whereas Montaigne said that if you follow the precepts of morality you will end up happy as well, Descartes claims that if you follow the principle of rational prudence, which I interpret as long-term self-interest, you will end up working for the good of others as well. In the second letter, he also offers a mechanism by which this happy coincidence would be brought about:

The reason that makes me think that those who do nothing except for their own private utility must just as much as the rest work for others, and try to please everyone as far as it is in their power, assuming them to be prudent, is that it regularly happens that those who are deemed ready to be of service to others and prompt to please, also receive many services from others, even from those whom they have never obliged in any way, which they would not receive if one believed them to be of a different disposition, and that what it costs them to be of service is usually less than the conveniences they derive from the friendship of those who know them. For others only expect from us the services we can render without inconvenience to ourselves, and we do not expect more from others; but it often happens that what costs them but little benefits us a great deal and may even make the difference between life and death. It is true that sometimes one may lose from doing well, and that conversely one may gain from doing wrong; but that cannot modify the rule of prudence, which only refers to what happens most frequently. As far as I am concerned, the maxim I have followed in all my conduct is to follow only the main road [*le grand chemin*], and to believe that the greatest subtlety of all is never to make use of subtlety. (Descartes 1646: 636)

If we help out a neighbour in a pinch we may benefit him much more, in absolute terms, than what it costs us to help him. If each of two parties to an interaction adopts the strategy of responding to demands for help when helping doesn't cost too much and asking for help when it doesn't cost the other party too much to provide it, both are likely to be better off than if each tried to be self-sufficient. Although the net effect for *A* in his interactions with *B* may turn out be negative, if *B* finds himself in a pinch more frequently than *A*, the net effect of adopting the strategy in all his interactions with *B*, *C*, *D* etc. is sure to be positive. Assuming that agents have a reasonably long time-horizon, enlightened self-interest may indeed mimic morality. The structure of interaction, while not exactly that of an iterated Prisoner's Dilemma, belongs to the same general class of mechanisms. Note how Descartes once again (and again echoing Montaigne) pursues the metaphor of the road.

Shame and glory

If you cannot keep to the straight road by the inner gyroscope of conscience, external pressures to conform or excel may serve as a substitute. This is a central idea of A.O. Lovejoy's surprisingly neglected *Reflections on Human Nature*. He carefully distinguishes between (in my language) shame and glory: 'Those who were keenly aware of the potency of the "love of praise" were rarely equally sensible of the potency of the fear of blame, and *vice versa*' (Lovejoy 1961: 136). Whereas fear of blame is associated with shortcomings with regard to given norms, the desire for praise is linked to superogatory performances. In a given society, one of the motives may be more important than the other. In many small communities, there is both a norm to conform and a norm against excellence. In some societies, such as Athens fifth-century BC, the desire to excel may dominate the norm to conform.

First, consider shame. Whereas guilt is triggered by the violation of a moral norm, shame occurs by the observed violation of a social norm. The causal structure is as shown in Figure 7.1. There seems to be a consensus among psychologists that the burning feeling of shame is more intensely painful than the pang of guilt (Lewis 1992: 77; Tangney 1990: 103). The difference, presumably, is related to the fact that the accusing stare of others is more difficult to ignore or rationalize than the voice of

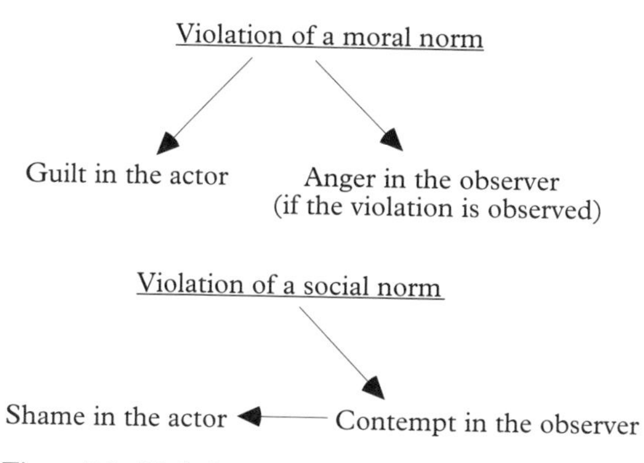

Figure 7.1 Violation of a moral norm/social norm

conscience. If the prescriptions of social norms coincide with the dictates of impartial morality, they may ease the strains of commitment. One instance is the norm of 'everyday Kantianism', summarized in the powerful question 'What if everyone did *that*?'. Norms may also undercut morality, however. A well-known example is the double set of codes regulating duels in early modern France. Louis XIII made laws *against* duels and blamed those who do not respect the laws *of* the duel (Billacois 1986: 123 n. 40; see also 274 n. 118); the same was reported of Louis XIV (Billacois 1986: 305 n. 48).

The fact that my behaviour can be motivated by other people seeing what I do must not be confused with the fact that it can be motivated by what others do. Often, the two go together, and the motivations may then be hard to disentangle from each other. Sometimes, however, it may be possible to distinguish the operation of social norms from what we may call *conditional impartiality*, i.e. the refusal of being a free-rider. Consider some stylized examples of voluntary participation in collective action, and let us assume that we are somehow able to exclude the operation of unconditional impartiality. (i) The city authorities try to reduce water consumption by getting households to use less water. Since others cannot observe how much water I consume, I cannot be shamed into using less. Since I cannot observe how much others use, there is no scope for conditional impartiality. Hence I will not reduce my consumption. (ii) A person walking in the park may abstain from littering because he sees that others don't litter and because others can see him littering. The first observation might trigger conditional impartiality, the second the operation of social norms. (iii) The city authorities try to reduce consumption of electricity by getting people to turn off the lights at 10 p.m.

A person can look out of the window in his high-rise building to see how many others are doing their duty, but cannot himself be observed by anyone who might later identify him as a free-rider (other people in his own building cannot see what he is doing). Conditional impartiality might induce him to turn off the light, but there is no scope for social norms. (iv) Social norms might make a person abstain from walking on the communal lawn with a 'Keep off' sign, if he knows he is being watched by his fellow residents inside their houses. There is no scope for conditional impartiality.

Summarizing a large literature from the seventeenth and eighteenth centuries, Lovejoy writes that 'the craving for admiration or applause . . . was ingeniously implanted in man by his Creator as a substitute for the Reason and Virtue which he does not possess' (Lovejoy 1961: 157). Although the example of Herostratus reminds us that the craving for fame is not logically connected to the desire to be approved for virtuous behaviour (Adair 1998: 15), the two go together often enough. Adair (1998) and Wood (1987: 69–109) have argued that the desire for fame, including the desire for a reputation for disinterestedness, was a central motive for some of the American framers. Among the key figures in the French Revolution, similar claims have been made about Necker, Barnave and Lafayette. On both sides of the Atlantic, there was a widespread perception that this was not the time for politics as usual or business as usual, but a unique occasion to make an impression on posterity.

The desire to be seen as impartial – disinterested and dispassionate – differs from the desire to be impartial. In some societies, and for some writers, *esse* and *percipi* are nevertheless hard to keep apart. In classical Athens, according to Dover (1994: 226) 'goodness divorced from a reputation for goodness was of limited interest'. For Hume (1985a: 86), 'To love the glory of virtuous deeds is a sure proof of the love of virtue'.[4] Montaigne (1992: 1157–8), by contrast, asserted 'The more glittering the deed the more I subtract from its moral worth, because of the suspicion aroused in me that it was exposed more for glitter than for goodness: goods displayed are already halfway to being sold'. At the limit, the only virtuous acts are those that never come to light. Along similar lines, Pascal (*Pensée* 520) wrote that 'the finest things about [fine deeds] was the attempt to keep them secret' and that 'the detail by which they came to light spoils everything'. Among the American framers, Madison

[4] A few lines above he expresses himself with more caution: 'vanity is so closely allied to virtue, and to love the fame of laudable actions approaches so near to the love of laudable actions for their own sake, that these passions are more capable of mixture, than any other kinds of affection'.

seems to stand out in giving priority to getting results over getting credit from getting results.

The Federal Convention

The delegates to the Federal Convention in Philadelphia were much concerned with harnessing interest to socially desirable ends. I shall consider three different arguments from the Convention. The first is a post-constitutional issue. Article 2 Section 1 of the US Constitution says that in choosing the President 'The electors shall meet in their respective States, and vote by ballot for two persons, of whom one at least shall not be an inhabitant of the same State with themselves'. When Gouverneur Morris first made this proposal at the Convention, Madison (Farrand 1966b: 114) 'thought something valuable might be made of the suggestion . . . The second best man in this case would probably be the first, in fact'. Following 'second best', Madison had originally written and then crossed out 'in the partial Judgment of each citizen towards his immediate fellow citizen'. These cryptic statements can be interpreted as saying that the vote cast for the candidate outside the state of the elector would be more likely to reflect an impartial judgement motivated by the general interest. Individuals who were perceived to promote the general interest rather than that of any particular state would be likely to garner sufficient out-of-state votes to beat any in-state candidate. I return to a related idea in the next section.

Second, the framers relied extensively on the argument that long-term self-interest behind a veil of ignorance induced by a long time-horizon would coincide with the dictates of impartiality. George Mason made the best-known argument of this kind when he warned against the danger of overreacting to the abuses and excesses of democracy:

> We ought to attend to the rights of every class of people. He [Mason] had often wondered at the indifference of the superior classes of society to this dictate of humanity & policy, considering that however affluent their circumstances, or elevated their situations, might be, the course of a few years, not only might but certainly would distribute their posteriority through the lowest classes of Society. Every selfish motive therefore, every family attachment, ought to recommend such a system of policy as would provide no less carefully for the rights and happiness of the lowest than of the highest orders of Citizens.[5]

[5] Farrand (1966a: 49). George Mason had ten children. We might ask whether the argument from long-term self-interest of families implies that childless individuals are likely to be less concerned with the public interest. Some years ago I heard a later Nobel-prize winning economist assert that Keynes' disastrous lack of concern for the future ('In the long run we are all dead') had to do with the fact that, as a homosexual, he had no

A similar argument was offered by Gouverneur Morris in the debate over the representation of the states in the Senate:

State attachments and State importance have been the bane of this Country. We cannot annihilate; but we may perhaps take out the teeth of the serpent. He wished our ideas to be enlarged to the true interest of man, instead of being circumscribed within the narrow compass of a particular Spot. And after all how little can be the motive yielded by selfishness for such a policy. Who can say whether he himself, much less whether his children, will the next year be an inhabitant of this or that State. (Farrand 1966a: 531)

On another occasion Gouverneur Morris was on the receiving end of the same argument. In response to Gerry's espousal of Gouverneur Morris's proposal to limit the representation of future Western states, Roger Sherman replied that 'We are providing for our posterity, for our children & our grand Children, who would be as likely to be citizens of new Western States, as of the old States. On this consideration alone, we ought to make no such discrimination as was proposed by the motion' (Farrand 1966b: 3).

The third argument was also made in the context of the terms of accession of future Western states. The question was whether the Western lands that would accede to the Union in the future should be admitted with the same rights as the original thirteen states. When Gouverneur Morris and others proposed that they should be admitted as second-rate states, so that they would never be able to outvote the original states, Mason argued strongly for the opposite view. First, he argued from principle: by admitting the Western states on equal terms, the framers would do 'what we know to be right in itself' (Farrand 1966a: 578). To those who might not accept that argument, he added that the new states would in any case be unlikely to accept a degrading proposal:

If the Western States are to be admitted into the Union, as they arise, they must be treated as equals, and subjected to no degrading discriminations. They will have the same pride & other passions which we have, and will either not unite with or will speedily revolt from the Union, if they are not in all respects placed on an equal footing with their brethren. (Farrand 1966a: 578–9)

Mason refers to the 'pride and passions' of the new states, not to their self-interest. Even if it would in fact be in their interest to accede to the Union on unequal terms rather than remain outside, they might still, out

stake in the welfare of future generations. Apart from the absurdity of the argument when applied to Keynes, who literally gave his life for his country in his war efforts (Skidelsky 2000: 333–4, 426–7 and *passim*), it ignores the fact that family interests can be mediated by other relatives. In the Catholic Church, for instance, prelates often favour the careers of their nephews.

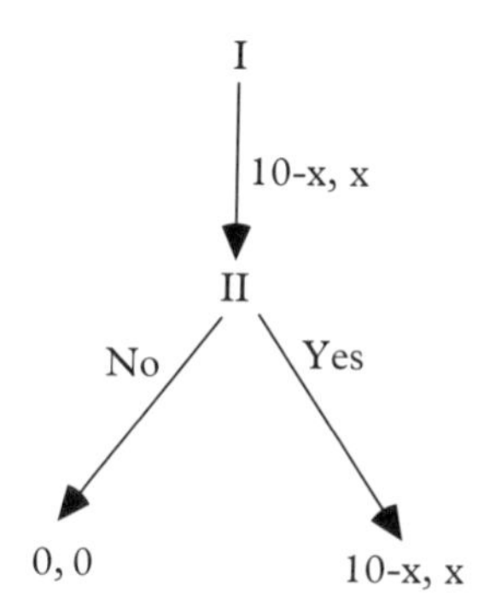

Figure 7.2 Ultimatum game

of resentment, prefer to stay outside. At the same time, he appeals to the self-interest of the old states, not to their sense of justice. Formally, his argument can be modelled as an 'Ultimatum Game' (see Figure 7.2) (see Camerer 2003: ch. 3).

The first player proposes a division of ten dollars between himself and the second player. The second player can reject the proposal, in which case neither player gets anything, or accept it, in which case the proposed division is implemented. Participants interact anonymously through computer terminals in a one-shot interaction that leaves no room for reputation-building. If they are rational, and know each other to be rational, player II will propose nine dollars for himself and one dollar for player II, who will accept the proposal. What happens in experiments is quite different. Player I typically offers something like six or seven dollars for himself, leaving three or four for player II. Player II typically rejects any proposal that gives her less than three dollars.

Consider three interpretations of these findings, in terms of impartiality, envy and resentment. First, we could imagine that those in the position of player I are moved (although not only) by impartial motives when they abstain from making the most self-interested proposal, and that those in the position of player II are moved (although not only) by similar motives when they reject the most unfavourable proposals. Yet in experiments with the 'Dictator Game', in which player II simply has to accept the proposal without the option of rejecting it, player I typically makes a more selfish proposal. This finding suggests that even in the Ultimatum Game player I is motivated mainly by the anticipated rejection by player I of an unfavourable proposal, rather than by what is required by impartiality.

Moreover, it is not really plausible to explain the rejection by imputing the motive of impartiality. If an agent were genuinely moved by this motive, it would animate her in the position of player II as well as in that of player I. Since participants are randomly assigned to the positions of players I and II, there should not be any systematic difference in the sense of impartiality displayed in their behaviour. As those in the position of player I are not (or not strongly) moved by impartiality, it seems plausible to explain the behaviour of those in the position of player II in terms of envy or resentment rather than by a genuine sense of unfairness, and the behaviour of those in the position of player I by their anticipation of such envy or resentment.

Let us now consider the two emotion-based explanations, in terms of envy and resentment. Whereas envy is an outcome-based emotion, resentment is action-based (Hirshleifer 1987). One can imagine that player II, if facing an eight-two proposal, might reject it out of envy. If that is the case, she should also reject the same proposal if player I was constrained to choose, say, between (ten-zero) and (eight-two). Intuition suggests and experiments confirm that player II will be much less likely to reject (eight-two) in this constrained case than in the unconstrained case. The main explanation of the behaviour in the Ultimatum Game must be resentment (and anticipation of resentment) rather than envy. The interaction of emotion and self-interest has the effect of mimicking impartiality. In addition, some genuine impartiality must also be operating, as shown by behaviour in the Dictator Game, where player I can unilaterally impose an allocation and yet does not always choose the one most favourable to himself.

Cross-voting

Cross-voting occurs when each member of each of *n* groups casts *n* votes, one to choose a representative for and from his own group and one in the choice of representatives for and from each of the other *n-1* groups.[6] This system was used in Georgia and Maryland to elect delegates to the First Federal Congress, but later discarded (Zagarri 1987). It was also used in several electoral districts to choose delegates to the French Estates-General in 1789. Here, I give a brief description of the latter procedure and a numerical illustration to show how it can indeed 'mimic impartiality'.

In the elections to the French Assemblée Constituante in 1789, the normal pattern was that members of one estate in a given electoral district

[6] When I first came across this system in American and French voting assemblies in the late eighteenth century, I coined (as I thought) the term 'cross-voting' to denote it. Later I discovered that the term had already been applied to a very similar system adopted in the 1961 Rhodesian Constitution (Palley 1966: 414–16).

chose a representative among themselves to represent them. The electoral rules allowed, however, delegates of all three estates to the electoral assemblies to vote jointly on who should represent a given estate (*Archives Parlementaires* 1867: 623). (This could only happen, however, if each order, voting separately, agreed to this system.) For instance, members of the clergy, the nobility and the third estate would all vote on who should represent the nobility in the National Assembly. A few districts, notably the Dauphiné, took advantage of this possibility. The system could obviously work in peculiar ways. As noted in a memorandum written by dissident clergy and nobles in the Dauphiné some time between the elections there and the opening of the Estates-General, 'it might happen that not a single deputy for the nobility received a single vote from the nobility' (Ilovaïsky 1974: 429).

The idea seems first to have been formulated by the Comte de Virieu in 1787. He proposed that:

> in this new election *all* be elected by *all*, so that there is no deputy from one Order that does not also have the support (*voeu*) of the other two. Although each deputy is destined to communicate the interest of the body to which he belongs, he is nevertheless not its special mandatory, and thus is not obligated to embrace exclusively its particular passions and views, but becomes through this mode of election the representative of all. (cited after J.-P. Joubert, '1788 en Dauphiné', in Chagny 1990: 349)

The system was adopted in the fall of 1788 by an assembly of the three estates convened by the King for the purpose of organizing the meeting of the provincial Estates. Mounier, the leading spirit in the reform movement in the Dauphiné, justified it as follows:

> This form offers a precious advantage: that of having all the Orders contribute to the choice of their respective deputies. They all become the mandatories of the people as a whole (*le peuple en corps*), and this union of the various classes of electors will be a new motive for representatives to consult only the interests they have in common. (cited after Egret 1942: 76)

The new system was implemented at the meeting of the provincial Estates in January 1789, when each elector – 45 from the clergy, 89 from the nobility and 119 from the third estate – established a list of 30 candidates: 5 from the clergy, 10 from the nobility and 15 from the third estate.

The system might simply affect the *attitude* of the chosen deputies, making them more sensible to the common interest, or it could modify the actual *selection* of deputies. The statements by Virieu and Mounier are sufficiently general to be compatible with either. Focusing on the second and more interesting reading, Mounier's claim that the new electoral system would induce a tendency to consider the common interest can be spelled out as follows. A member of the third estate would not have an interest in voting for a member of the privileged orders who would represent and promote only the interests of those orders. He could not, to be sure, expect to find a member of the privileged orders who would represent and promote only the interests of the third estate, but he might find and vote for some members who were willing to consider the general interest. In France in 1789, this meant mainly equality of taxation and abolition of privilege in the access to civil and military office. Correspondingly, members of the privileged orders might vote for members of the third estate who would recognize the importance of property (including feudal dues) and the social utility of distinctions (including noble titles).

Suppose, for a numerical example, that within each estate two-thirds want only to promote the particular interests of that estate and one-third want to promote the general interest. Suppose also that, rather than the numerical proportions in the Dauphiné, we have the more common case of (say) 30 clergy, 30 nobles and 60 from the third estate.[7] Let us also suppose (contrary to what was the case in the Dauphiné) that the candidates are to be chosen from within the electoral assembly, which has to elect 15, 15 and 30 deputies from the three orders. Suppose finally that the candidates elected are those who receive the largest number of votes. Within (say) the clergy, the 10 members who want to promote the general interest will receive 10 votes from the clergy, 30 votes from the nobility and 60 votes from the third estate, 100 votes altogether. These 10 candidates between them will receive 1,000 votes. The total number of votes to be cast is $15 \times (30 + 30 + 60) = 1{,}800$. The remaining 800 votes could in theory be cast for 7 candidates who would each receive more than 100 votes. At worst, therefore, 8 of the 15 deputies from the clergy will represent the general interest. In practice, the votes for those who do not represent the general interest will be so diluted (perhaps for strategic reasons) that all will receive less than 100 votes. In that case, 10 out of 15 deputies from the clergy will represent the general interest. The same reasoning holds for the nobility.

Within the third estate, the 20 members who want to promote the general interest will receive 20 votes from their own estate and 30 votes from each of the other estates, 80 votes altogether. These 20 candidates between them will receive 1,600 votes. The total number of votes to be cast is $30 \times (30 + 30 + 60) = 3600$. The remaining 2,000 votes could

[7] In the assemblies where the third estate had as many deputies as the other orders taken together, the usual pattern was for the clergy and the nobility to have equal numbers of representatives. The Dauphiné was an exception.

in theory be cast for 24 candidates who would each receive more than 80 votes. On that worst-case assumption, only 6 out of 30 deputies from the third estate would represent the general interest. On the best-case assumption, the 2,000 remaining votes would be divided more or less equally among the 40 remaining candidates. All would receive less than 80 votes, and 10 would be elected. In that case, 20 out of 30 deputies from the third estate would represent the general interest. This outcome would in fact be realized as long as the candidate ranked 11 among the 40 candidates received less than 80 votes. It would take considerable coordination to bring the vote of the eleventh-ranked above this threshold.

Needless to say, the numbers are arbitrary. What the exercise shows is that even when two-thirds in each group are concerned only with the interests of that group, cross-voting can produce an assembly in which two-thirds of the members care only about the general interest. As Tocqueville writes in his posthumously published notes to the *Ancien régime*, 'If the practice of voting in common [rather than separately by orders] were to be adopted, it is to be regretted that one did not everywhere follow the practice of the Dauphiné, so that the deputies from each order would have been chosen by all orders; that would have favoured agreement' (Tocqueville 1953: 163; see also 114 for a similar judgement).

Summary

The example from the Dauphiné suggests that institutional design can operate the alchemy of turning bad motives into good. Madison's argument about the double vote to be cast for the President has a similar flavour. The argument (also made at the Convention) that enlightened or long-term self-interest can mimic impartiality also has implications for institutional and constitutional design. By imposing a suitably long delay (one or more years) between the time a new law is proposed and the time it can take effect, one can increase the thickness of the veil of ignorance and force interest to recede into the background. This may indeed be the effect, and perhaps even the intention, of amendment rules that require changes to the constitution to be passed by two successive assemblies (as in Sweden) or proposed during one Parliament and passed in the following (as in Norway).

The Cartesian argument from enlightened self-interest has a different structure. Here, *interaction* rather than *ignorance* provides the mechanism of alchemy. The argument has no implications for institutional design, but might serve to ease the strains of commitment to impartiality, albeit in a severely restricted context. It does not offer any reason why anyone should extend a helping hand to those who, because of disability, are unable to reciprocate.[8] Genuine impartiality imposes a duty to assist others in need that does not depend on the thought that 'my turn may come'.

The argument offered by George Mason that I have modelled as an Ultimatum Game suggests an asymmetry between the desire to act impartially and the resentment caused by *not* being treated impartially. The strength of the latter might induce people to act as if they were swayed by the former. Some of the experimental findings have implications for institutional design. It seems important, for instance, to provide unique focal points for impartiality, to prevent self-serving interpretations.

The arguments from shame and glory depend crucially on the targets of social blame and praise coinciding with those of moral blame and praise. If you believe that morality requires you to turn the other cheek, social norms of revenge will not do much to strengthen your resolve. Social and moral norms seem to agree, though, on the wrongness of free-riding. Although the desire for fame and glory may induce morally neutral or even harmful activities, it can also take the socially beneficial form of wanting to appear to be disinterested.

[8] See also the discussions of 'justice as mutual advantage' and 'justice as reciprocity' in Barry (1995).

8 Justice, democracy and public goods

David Miller

It is a curious fact that in the voluminous literature produced over the last quarter century or so on the topic of social justice, the question what, if anything, justice has to say about the supply of public goods by the state has rarely been asked. Social justice has been understood as a set of principles governing the allocation of private goods to individuals. This is very clear, for example, in the case of John Rawls (1971: 90), whose list of primary goods that constitute the subject matter of justice – 'rights and liberties, opportunities and powers, income and wealth' (and later the more elusive good, 'the bases of self-respect) – is a list of goods that are separately assigned to individuals. For Ronald Dworkin (2000: esp ch. 2), justice is to be understood as requiring equality of (privately-held) resources; for Robert Nozick (1974: esp. ch. 7) it is about protecting (validly-acquired) rights of private property; for Bruce Ackerman (1980: 24) it is about individual shares of 'manna', an all-purpose resource 'which can be transformed into any of the familiar material resources of our own world'. And Brian Barry (1991b) himself, although fully cognizant of the important contribution public goods make to the quality of citizens' lives – his defence of socialism centres on the case for public provision of goods as against market provision – when defining 'justice' again cites principles that apply to the distribution of resources among individuals.[1]

Why do I say that this exclusive concentration on the distribution of privately-held goods is curious? Because the quality of our lives is also greatly affected by our access to *public* goods, by which I shall mean goods that are made available to everyone without charge, and that each person can enjoy without diminishing the opportunity of others to enjoy the same

This chapter has benefited greatly from discussion at the Nuffield Political Theory workshop and from written comments by Tony Atkinson, Avner de-Shalit and Bob Goodin. I am especially grateful to Rebecca Stone for research assistance and for her comments and suggestions on earlier drafts.

[1] The principles he cites are equal rights, responsibility, vital interests, and mutual advantage: see, e.g., Barry (1998; 1999).

good.[2] Since these goods are non-excludable, they are unlikely to be supplied by voluntary contribution or through market mechanisms, and so their provision will depend on political action by the state.[3] That democratic states are indeed in the business of supplying public goods to their citizens is clear on a moment's reflection. Let me quickly list some familiar examples: defence against external aggression, public safety, emergency services, civil law courts, roads and other forms of transport infrastructure, street lighting, sanitation, food safety measures, environmental protection, public parks, public broadcasting, sports facilities, artistic and cultural events, and so forth. (As a further moment's reflection will confirm, the items on this list are very diverse, and this will turn out to be important later in the chapter.) It is certainly true that the biggest items of public expenditure are those that involve providing benefits individually, for instance social security and income support, education and health-care. Nevertheless, public goods provision consumes a significant proportion of government budgets everywhere, and since what is spent in this way must detract either from expenditure on these other items or from the post-tax incomes of citizens, it seems puzzling that the issue has featured so marginally in debates about social justice.

But is there perhaps an obvious reason why public goods have been excluded from theories of social justice? One possible explanation is that since these goods are available equally to everyone, no issue of justice arises. You might reach this conclusion by focusing on a case like national defence: since defence against external attack is a precondition for enjoying almost any of the primary goods used in conventional definitions of justice, and in that sense everyone benefits equally when the state maintains armed forces etc., then although there can certainly be debates about the prevailing level of military expenditure, these debates are hardly going to be debates about social justice. But this line of argument fails

[2] We might call goods that meet these two conditions pure public goods, following the classic treatment in Samuelson (1954). In practice, users may be asked to pay something towards the cost of supplying the good, but less than would be required to cover the whole cost – thus teams using public football pitches may be asked to pay a fee. Equally, goods may be subject to crowding: my consumption of the good may diminish the value of your consumption, as in the case of a park that becomes less pleasant to walk in as the number using it increases. Goods that have either or both of these features might be called impure public goods, but I shall ignore this complication in the discussion that follows. Note also that whether a good is public depends on the conditions upon which it is provided, not on the physical properties of the good. With many goods there is a choice as to whether they are made available to everyone as public goods, or supplied only to those who meet certain requirements, such as paying a fee.

[3] I have explored the conditions under which we might expect public goods to be provided by voluntary means (and especially through 'assurance contracts') in Miller (1993). This is a critical discussion of Schmidtz (1991).

to be plausible even at first glance when we look at other items on the list above: although they are made equally *available* to everyone, they are not going to be equally *used*, nor will they be equally *valued*, by all. Take the road system, for instance; road usage varies very greatly according to a person's occupation, income level, and so forth, so although (almost) everyone can be said to benefit to some extent when the state builds and maintains roads, the benefit is distributed very unequally. When we turn to sports facilities and cultural events, the inequality becomes even greater, ranging as it does between those who have no use at all for these goods and those for whom the chance to play cricket or enjoy high culture forms an essential part of their idea of the good life. How can we fail to see this inequality as an issue that our theories of justice ought to address?

But perhaps this conclusion is too quick. Most of the theories of justice put forward in the standard literature on the topic are non-welfarist theories. Their concern is not with the distribution of happiness or well-being, as such, but with the distribution of the *means* of happiness or well-being, in other words with the resources, broadly construed, that people need in order to lead flourishing and successful lives. The reason for this concern can be understood in terms of a division of responsibility: the political community has a responsibility to ensure that each person gets her fair share of resources – income and so forth – but it is the person's own responsibility to convert those resources into welfare, a conversion which will depend on her preferences as to how she wants to lead her life. If someone is less than satisfied because she has chosen a lifestyle that is beyond her means or for some other reason difficult to pursue successfully, that is no concern of justice. Justice, in other words, involves the distribution of goods whose value we can measure by applying a common standard that is independent of the value a particular good may have for a particular individual. Suppose, for example, that we have to set fair rates of pay for people doing different jobs. We may wish to consider the difficulty of the job, the effort it involves, the risks it carries, and so forth. But we should take no account, as far as justice is concerned, of whether the person holding the job is an ascetic for whom extra money above a certain level is of no value or a *bon viveur* who wants every penny he can get. So why not say the same about public goods? So long as everyone has equal access to these goods, why should justice be concerned about the fact that different people value them differently?

The answer is that, although justice as conventionally understood is at one level about the distribution of goods that are already in existence, at another level it must also consider which goods are going to be made available for distribution. One can see this by thinking about a planned economy in which the state decides to produce only a small range of consumption goods, and decides also to produce goods that are valued much more highly by one section of the community than by others. Although the bundles of goods may be fairly distributed, the make-up of the bundles is in one important sense unfair, because it fails to respond even-handedly to what the eventual recipients want to see included in them. This point has been recognized explicitly by Dworkin in the course of his attempt to define equality of resources, his preferred conception of justice. As is well known, Dworkin (2000: ch. 3) uses the model of a Walrasian auction in which each participant is given equal purchasing power to specify when resource bundles are to be regarded as equal, but he also discusses at some length how the lots to be offered at auction are to be composed, recognizing that different ways of doing this will advantage and disadvantage different people. He favours what he calls 'the principle of abstraction' which requires that lots be divided up into their smallest feasible components, so that bidders have the greatest flexibility in bidding for combinations of items. If we start from the premise that we are to treat each person with equal concern 'it follows that an auction is fairer – that it provides a more genuinely equal distribution – when it offers more discriminating choices and is thus more sensitive to the discrete plans and preferences people in fact have' (Dworkin 2000: 150–1). More generally, Dworkin justifies the economic market on egalitarian grounds as a mechanism that allows people to exchange commodities over time in a way that responds to their ambitions, while at the same time making each person bear the opportunity costs of his or her choices.

In the case of private goods, therefore, justice requires not only that they be distributed in a certain way – whether on the basis of equality or according to some other principle – but also that decisions about which goods are going to be produced in the first place should take citizens' aims and preferences into account in an even-handed way. For many goods, some form of market-based production should meet this requirement. Since, in the case of public goods, it is usually the case that market production is infeasible – no one will pay to have a good that they cannot be excluded from consuming – what justice requires here is a more deliberate attempt on the part of the state to treat citizens even-handedly when deciding which goods to produce, and at what level. This does not require that each person should end up equally happy or equally satisfied, any more than equality of (private) resources entails equality of welfare. Instead the question can be posed in the following way.

Suppose that a society has achieved a just distribution of income and other privately-held or privately consumed resources, but at this point no public goods have been politically supplied. This supposition is in one way hypothetical, since justice of any kind may be unachievable in the absence of certain public goods (national defence, security of person and property, etc.) but we can at least abstractly envisage a regime of pure private justice, as we might call it.[4] If public goods are going to be produced, this must involve retrenching in one way or another on the rights and resources people enjoy under the existing regime. In some cases this might involve limiting individual freedom in a certain respect (for instance when smoke-free zones are created in public places). More often it will involve taking resources through taxation and using these to finance the public good, say, paying people to act as soldiers or firefighters, or investing money in a new sports facility. People's opportunities for private consumption will be diminished a little, and in exchange they will have additional opportunities, or better living conditions. What guidance can justice give when decisions of this kind are being made? To focus our thinking let's consider a simple case when what is being proposed is a public good to be financed by an increase in taxation – say, a national park is to be created, which will conserve wildlife and also provide recreational opportunities for anyone who wants to enjoy them (as indicated earlier I shall ignore problems of crowding). How might we decide whether the good should be provided?

An economist faced with this question would almost certainly suggest one of two answers. The most likely answer he would give is that the park should be created provided everyone benefits from its existence – everyone must be better off (or at least no worse off) with the park plus the tax increase than he was before. This is the principle proposed in a classic paper on public finance by Knut Wicksell, and it might seem at first glance as if would prevent the state from supplying virtually any public goods, since for any public good on the usual list, there are likely to be a few people who regard it as having no value (or even negative value) (Wicksell 1958). However Wicksell's idea was that the public good should be considered along with a range of different tax schedules for financing it, and so long as at least one of these schedules had the property that

[4] For an argument that we need to assume a prior just distribution of private resources in order to tackle the public goods question, see Murphy and Nagel (2002: ch. 4). It might be said in reply that the political provision of public goods is justified in part as a means of offsetting the unfair distribution of private resources – public goods provision being more politically acceptable than income redistribution, for instance. However, this way of justifying public goods strikes me as shaky. For one thing, the distributive impact of many public goods is regressive: they benefit the rich more than the poor (think of roads or support for high culture). For another, even public goods that in general benefit the poor disproportionately may have an uneven impact: many low income families may not use public swimming pools, for instance. The lesson that has been learned in the case of welfare provision – that in the end there is no substitute for straightforward redistribution of income and wealth if your aim is social justice – applies here too. So the question I ask is how to ensure that decisions about the supply of public goods are *justice-preserving* rather than *justice-enhancing*.

everyone gained – which would imply that those who saw no benefit in the good would not be taxed to supply it – the good should be provided. This is equivalent to the rule that any given public good should be supplied by the state up to the point where a proposal to supply more of the good, combined with an appropriate tax schedule to fund it, wins the unanimous support of the members of the political community in question.

Wicksell's proposal has occasionally surfaced in the literature on social justice, and indeed it was endorsed by Rawls (1971: 282–3) himself as an answer to the question whether government expenditure over and above that required by the two principles of justice can be justified. But Rawls also recognizes problems with the proposal, and it is fairly easy to see what these are. Since for any individual or group of individuals, the maximum tax rate that they can be asked to bear depends on the benefit they will receive from the park, each person has an incentive to understate that benefit. So the park may not be created even though, if individual valuations were genuinely revealed, it would be possible to devise a tax schedule that passed the Wicksell test.[5] Second, even if we were able to extract genuine evaluations, it might well turn out that there are many different ways of funding the park. Suppose, for example, that everyone attaches at least a little value to the park's existence, and would be willing to pay 50p per year to maintain it. As it happens this is sufficient to fund the park in the form presently envisaged. But some people value it considerably more, and would be willing to pay different amounts ranging up to, say, £20 per year to have it in existence. Should we impose a flat rate poll tax, or should we graduate the tax on the basis of willingness to pay, and then perhaps enlarge the park or put more money into conservation work? For Wicksell, it appeared to matter little that some might gain more than others under proposals that passed his test:

> Provided the expenditure in question holds out any prospect at all of creating utility exceeding costs, it will always be theoretically possible, and approximately so in practice, to find a distribution of costs such that all parties regard the expenditure as beneficial and may therefore approve it unanimously . . . Whether justice demands any more than this may be left in abeyance for the time being. When it comes to benefits which are so hard to express numerically, each person can ultimately speak only for himself. It is a matter of comparatively little importance if perchance some individual secures a somewhat greater gain than another so long as everyone gains and no one can feel exploited from this very elementary point of view. (Wicksell 1958: 89–90)

[5] There is a literature in economics about tax-allocation mechanisms that would give individuals an incentive to reveal their genuine valuations of public goods. The mechanisms are complex, and they do not guarantee that the overall outcome is efficient. See Myles (1995: ch. 9, sect. 7).

I do not think, however, that this is an issue that can be left in abeyance as far as justice is concerned. What we are considering are gains from cooperation of a particular kind. By banding together and agreeing to be taxed to provide public goods, citizens are able to win an advantage for themselves – everyone is better off. But how the surplus is distributed between them is surely a matter of justice. We can see this immediately by considering different proposals for how the park is going to be managed, some of which share the benefits widely (by providing a range of amenities that between them cater for virtually everyone) and others of which concentrate them more narrowly on a particular group. Suppose that in either case the 50p flat rate tax is unanimously approved, satisfying Wicksell's condition; it still remains the case that the first set of proposals is fairer than the second. We do not, in general, abstain from judging proposed Pareto-improvements in terms of justice – about any proposed improvement we are disposed to ask not only whether it is minimally acceptable but whether there are alternative improvements that do better by, for instance, spreading the gains more equally. So why approach the public goods issue differently?

Satisfying Wicksell's condition does not then seem to be sufficient for justice in the provision of public goods. Is it a necessary condition? It seems not, if it is intended to apply to each public good taken separately. Imagine a society rather rigidly divided between nature lovers and sports fans, neither finding any value in the other's pursuits, and imagine that for practical reasons any feasible tax schedule has to be one that applies uniformly across the two groups – the state cannot partition its citizens in such a way that only the nature lovers are made to pay for the upkeep of national parks and only the sports fans for football pitches and so forth. Then any proposal to spend money on national parks will be vetoed by the sports fans, and any proposal to spend money on sports facilities by the nature lovers. Yet if a Department of Amenities responsible for both operations is created, it can put forward combined proposals – so much expenditure on the natural environment plus so much on sporting facilities, together with an appropriate tax schedule – that can win unanimous support. There is no obvious injustice in a system that requires the two groups to cross-subsidize each other's activities, provided everybody is a net gainer.

As an alternative to Wicksell, an economist might propose using a social welfare function to decide on public goods provision. The simplest such function is straightforwardly utilitarian: public goods should be provided whenever the sum of individual benefits they generate exceeds the sum of individual costs, with all benefits and costs being given equal weight. This would allow public goods to be financed using conventional tax systems, such as income or sales taxes, since there is no longer any requirement that each person must be a net beneficiary, and therefore no need to tailor the tax schedule to avoid scooping in people who do not value the good in question. But from the point of view of justice this is hardly satisfactory, since it takes no account of how costs and benefits are distributed between individuals; in particular, some people may be heavily taxed to provide a basket of goods from which they derive little or no benefit. Since we are considering public goods distribution against the background of an initially just distribution of private goods, the overall effect of implementing this proposal would be to distort this distribution in an arbitrary way.[6]

The problem common to the two economists' proposals I have been considering is that they approach the public goods question primarily in terms of *efficiency*, whereas we are looking for a criterion of *justice* to help us decide when and at what level the state should supply such goods.[7] It is, of course, part of the general rationale for public goods that people are in general better off having them than they would be without them, but there is still a separate issue to consider, namely taking people one at a time, how can we show that a policy that restricts freedom in some respect, or reduces resources available for consumption in order to provide a public good, can be justice-preserving? I want to turn next to Barry's own answer to this question, which is in effect to deny that there can be any substantive criterion of justice that can be applied to public goods decisions. Instead, justice in such cases is simply a matter of following appropriate *procedures* when such decisions are taken.

Barry (1995: ch. 6) gives this answer in the course of his explanation and defence of 'justice as impartiality', and he begins from the premise that, in general, the value of any given public good depends upon the personal conception of the good held by each individual, and there is no reason to expect these conceptions of the good to converge. What is needed, therefore, is a means of reaching decisions that is in a suitable way neutral as between the different conceptions. Barry concedes that a

[6] If the initial distribution is *not* just, then one might try to compensate by specifying a welfare function that gives greater weight to benefits going to individuals, or groups of individuals, who are unfairly disadvantaged (this is apparently common practice when cost-benefit analysis is used to decide on public goods provision). However, this could only be a second-best solution for reasons given in note 5.

[7] Wicksell's unanimity criterion might be said to blend justice and efficiency considerations by virtue of the fact that it rejects any public goods proposal that would leave one or more individuals worse off on balance; however, so long as no one loses, it is indifferent as to how the gains from public goods provision are distributed. As to the second approach, if the social welfare function chosen is utilitarian, then clearly efficiency is the guiding value. If a weighting principle is used – for instance, benefits to worse-off individuals are given greater weight – then we have a criterion that combines efficiency with other values such as equality.

utilitarian approach, which would convert all the individual valuations into want-satisfaction and then aggregate across individuals, delivers neutrality of a kind, but because want-satisfaction is itself a contestable, though second-order, conception of the good, justice as impartiality prefers a more directly procedural solution. Any procedure that could be endorsed by people in circumstances of impartiality is potentially in the frame, but Barry appears to favour majoritarian democracy in which people present arguments to one another in defence of their preferred conceptions of the good before proceeding to a vote. He takes as an example a case where a choice has to be made between two incompatible public goods: building a dam that would supply power and water to the community, and preserving the habitat of an endangered species of fish – the snail darter – that would be destroyed by the dam (Barry 1995: 145–51).[8] Each side tries to persuade the other of its case, appealing to economic and environmental values respectively, and the issue is decided by majority vote. According to Barry, whatever policy is chosen by this procedure is a just policy for the community in question.

Barry does not say explicitly why the procedure he describes is a fair one, once majoritarianism has been uncoupled both from want-satisfaction and from the idea that it is more likely to produce the right answer on some question to which there exists a right answer independently of the process used to discover it. But perhaps what he has in mind is that under this procedure each person and each conception of the good starts out on an equal footing: *a priori*, power-generation and ecological values each stand an equal chance of winning. However, if one thinks of the procedure being used repeatedly, in a community where there is a large majority interested in cheap electricity and a small minority interested in preserving the environment, the appearance of fairness begins to fade. Formally each side stands an equal chance of winning, but in reality the environmentalists will lose every time. So be it, Barry might say: the procedure is a fair one, so one cannot complain about the result.[9] But it seems to me that there *is* an issue of substantive fairness

[8] The snail darter entered political philosophy via Dworkin's essay 'Equality of Welfare' now included as ch. 1 of Dworkin (2000), having been the subject of a legal battle between supporters and opponents of the proposed Tellico Dam on the Tennessee River in the 1970s. Initially classified as an endangered species, Congress later declared the snail darter not endangered and the dam was built.

[9] He might not say this, however. In an earlier essay Barry (1991b: 44) argues that the majority principle would be chosen only for a society in which any group can expect to find itself on the majority side at least half the time. 'Conversely, the more closely a society approximates to the model of a monolithic majority bloc facing a minority which is always on the losing side, the more would reasonably prudent people refuse to accept that, if they found themselves in such a society and in the minority group, they would be bound to respect the laws that had been passed by the majority over minority opposition.'

here: since public resources are being used, it is fairer that some of these at least should be used to support projects of concern to the minority, even if most resources go on building dams and the like.[10] So we cannot entirely side-step the substantive issue. In practice, public goods decisions will need to be made by a political procedure, perhaps by the one that Barry proposes. But that does not exclude considerations of substantive justice from entering into the debate that precedes the decision.[11] The environmental party, in other words, need not confine themselves to arguing about the intrinsic value of preserving the snail darter; it is also perfectly legitimate for them to argue that land use policy should represent a fair compromise between the claims of people with different values and interests, and that since they have lost the last three votes on the dam, it is now time for the other side to make some concessions to them.

This brings us back, therefore, to the question what justice requires, substantively, when public goods provision is at stake. In order to answer it, we need to draw some distinctions. First we need to separate the question of what can justify the state in supplying public goods in the first place from the question how the cost of supplying such goods should be allocated among its citizens. Then we need to distinguish the different justifications that can be offered in answer to the first question. I shall suggest that there are three such justifications, giving rise to three categories of public goods. Having drawn this distinction, I shall turn to the question of costs and ask how goods in each category should be funded if justice is to be preserved.

The first category of public goods I shall consider – category A goods – are public goods whose provision is justified by an appeal to the value of justice itself. These are goods that one might describe as necessary goods: they correspond to basic needs which, I am assuming, the political community has a duty of justice to meet on the part of each member.[12] Obvious examples here would include personal security, basic environmental

[10] For a fuller argument in support of this view, see Jones (1983).

[11] Considerations of substantive justice may also come into play at an earlier point, when the framework for taking decisions is being established. For instance, when deciding whether all decisions should be taken centrally, or some of them delegated to particular constituencies, either on a geographical or one some other basis, a relevant consideration is whether delegation might give minority groups a fairer chance to obtain public goods that would otherwise be denied them. This might apply particularly in the case of language protection or other such cultural goods.

[12] I focus here on what justice requires within the political community, but one should also include here duties of justice owed by the community to people elsewhere, and to future generations. Meeting these duties is a public good in the sense that the state discharges them on everyone's behalf when, for instance, it dispenses part of the budget as foreign aid.

conditions such as clean air, and opportunities for mobility through a transport system. Why must these be provided as public goods? Either because this is the only way in which the corresponding need can be met, or because it is the best way. In the case of physical security, for instance, it would be possible in theory for everyone to hire a personal bodyguard, with those unable to afford any protection at all being subsidized by the state. But this would be both less efficient and less fair than the creation of a public police force whose activities in preventing and detecting crime are intended to create the same level of security for everybody (even if in practice this aim is never fully achieved). In the case of clean air, it is again far more efficient to put pollution controls in place that make this good freely available to everyone than to supply each individual with breathing apparatus. Finally, if mobility can be classed as a basic need, as I am assuming it can, then the creation of a transport system, with road and rail networks, subsidized public transport etc., is a public good which allows people to meet that need in different ways, and again is likely to be both fairer and more efficient than privatized alternatives. In all such cases, then, there is no difficulty in showing why justice requires the state to supply certain public goods. A problem would arise only in cases where resources were scarce, and so decisions had to be made at the margin about which needs were more urgent: should pollution controls be tightened to raise air quality by a couple more notches, or is it more important not to burden firms so that they can pay their employees higher wages? But these are familiar problems that arise in all debates over justice under conditions of scarcity.

The second category of public goods that I wish to distinguish – category B goods – are goods that can be given a public justification within the relevant political community, but not one that makes direct appeal to the value of justice itself. The idea here is that certain public goods may play an essential role in sustaining the community, so that reasons can be given to anyone who is a member to support their provision. The idea of public justification has of course been made familiar chiefly through the work of John Rawls, but in Rawls' hands it is confined to forms of reasoning that can be used to support principles of justice that govern the distribution of privately held resources. This account of public justification seems to me too restrictive. Where it can be shown that the community can be sustained only through the provision of certain public goods, even though there is no *individual* who can claim these goods as a matter of justice, a valid public reason exists to supply the goods.

Many of the examples that belong here have to do with preserving (or enhancing) features of the community that make it distinctive. Language is an obvious case. If the state uses resources in order to promote use of the national language (for instance, commissioning translations of foreign works of literature, sponsoring home-grown television programmes in place of English-language imports, and so forth) this can be justified on the grounds that language is a major characteristic distinguishing this community from its neighbours. The same argument can be used to defend policies that preserve physical elements of the community's cultural heritage – buildings embodying a distinctive architectural style, patterns of landscape, areas of natural beauty that have come to have a symbolic significance in the national culture, etc. Many people will value these things directly, so in their case it is not difficult to justify using public resources in this way. But what of somebody who does not – who has no personal use for the national language, who is oblivious to natural beauty, and so forth? The reason that can be given to such a person is that she benefits from belonging to a political community that is constituted in part by the values in question – in other words what sets the community apart from others and binds its members together is their recognition of the value of features such as the national language. Without this commonality of value, the community could not exist in its present form, and undertake the functions that it now does, including the administering of justice. On the assumption that the dissenting person values these things at least, she has reason to promote the public goods that play a constitutive role in her community.

An analogy may help to drive this point home. Consider someone whose social life centres upon a musical society which meets from time to time to hear its members play, organizes trips to public concerts and so forth. As it happens, this person has no ear for music, so listening to concerts has no value in itself, but he greatly enjoys the company of musicians, likes the trips out, and so on. Suppose now that the society decides to raise its subscription in order to replace some worn-out instruments. Although privately there is no benefit in this to our person, he must still regard 'playing better music' as a valid reason for the subscription increase. For it is only because of the members' shared commitment to playing and enjoying music that the society can exist at all – take that away and the society would dissolve, more or less rapidly.

Of course the analogy presupposes a claim about the nature of political communities: that they can only function effectively if the members share certain values that make each community distinctive and that go beyond a bare commitment to implement principles of justice. This is a controversial claim that I have tried to defend elsewhere (Miller 1995: ch. 4), but if it is true, then we can defend the state's supply of category B public goods on the grounds that everybody has reason to support this even though they derive no direct personal benefit from the good, and even though the good is not required as a matter of justice (it would be implausible to claim that preserving a cultural heritage or a national language are demands of justice as such). Because public reasons can be given for supplying the good, there need be no injustice in the state taxing consumption or restricting freedom to support it.

Barry would not, I think, be much tempted by the defence of public goods I have just sketched – he appears not to be convinced that political communities need a cultural cement to hold them together – but he seems more inclined to accept a parallel argument that appeals to the intrinsic value of at least some cultural goods. This is suggested by some remarks in *Culture and Equality* about the rationale for state funding of the arts. Barry is here attacking the practice of subsidizing minority cultural activities according to how much demand there is for the subsidies, arguing that most cultural production is best left to the market. If there is to be a case for state support of the arts, he claims, this must be made in terms of their 'real excellence' – something that is more than a matter of opinion. 'If it is merely a matter of opinion that Beethoven is better than banjo-playing, then it is a mere matter of opinion that either is better than the monetary equivalent in groceries. And in that case there is no case for earmarking funds at all: let people spend the money on Beethoven, banjo-playing or groceries as they choose' (Barry 2001: 199).[13] Barry's implicit response, then, to someone who objects to state support for symphony orchestras or concert halls on the grounds that he cares nothing for classical music is that music of this kind has intrinsic value – that it is genuinely excellent, whatever the person in question thinks. If market pricing will not work, then public subsidy is justifiable on this ground alone.

The problem with this line of argument is that, given cultural and more generally value pluralism of the kind both Barry and I take for granted, judgements of excellence of the kind needed to make the argument work may be matters of reasonable disagreement. It is not in dispute that Beethoven composed excellent classical symphonies, but that judgement can only be made by standing within a particular cultural tradition and applying the standards of excellence that the tradition supports. Equally, when it comes to Appalachian banjo-playing (Barry's bête noire of the moment), perfectly good, objective judgements can be made to the effect that some performances are excellent and others are poor. But if we try to compare the two musical forms using a single standard of excellence, we shall be forced to conclude that they are simply incommensurable:

[13] This could be read as an argument against *any* state support for the arts, but, given the context, I interpret Barry to be saying that such support can be justified so long as we are prepared to stand by judgements of artistic excellence as more than just personal opinions.

each tradition can judge the other by its own standards, but that is beside the point. So if someone argues for state funding of classical concerts on the grounds of their intrinsic musical excellence, she is liable to be challenged on the ground that the standard of excellence she is invoking is open to reasonable disagreement, and that there are competing claims that could equally well be advanced. Faced with this challenge, there is nothing more that can be said – in contrast to the position that I favour, where category B public goods are defended on the grounds that they promote values that give the community its distinct identity, and bind its members together.

This brings us to category C: public goods whose justification appeals to privately held conceptions of the good, i.e. conceptions of the good over which there can be reasonable disagreement. This category ranges between goods justified very largely in terms of the interests of individuals or groups of individuals (for instance sporting facilities that will only be used by devotees of a particular sport) and goods whose justification is wholly ideal-regarding (for instance, conservation of species or natural habitats, justified purely in terms of the intrinsic value of such conservation). Many goods in this category will have mixed justifications: for instance, arguments in favour of state support for the arts may combine the claim that classical music or opera, say, brings great pleasure to existing fans with the claim that such experiences have intrinsic value and ought to be made widely available in the hope that more people can be brought to share in them. My suggestion is that, despite the different nature of the claims involved, public goods in this category ought to be treated together from the point of view of justice. For what they have in common is that people are being asked to contribute resources for purposes that they do not value, and that do not even benefit them indirectly. Consider the proverbial couch potato, interested only in a life of ease and consumption. He may be asked to pay taxes to build a new swimming pool, which he knows he will never use; or to support a theatre which he knows he will never attend; or to create a new habitat for the snail darter, about whose fate he cares nothing. From his perspective, these three demands, different though they are in other ways, look much the same.

To this it might be objected that, whatever the couch potato thinks, there are real differences between the goods that I am placing together in category C. In the case of the swimming pool, the value of the good is simply the value of the satisfaction it brings to the swimmers (ignoring health benefits etc. for the sake of simplicity). In the case of the wildlife habitat, by contrast, the value of the good is objective: the fact that at present this value is only recognized by a small number of ecologically aware citizens is beside the point. Given enough time, it might be said, we could convince anybody of the importance of saving the snail darter; whereas in the case of the swimming pool, people either enjoy swimming or they don't – persuasion doesn't come into it.

My response, once again, is that there can be reasonable disagreement over the value of the snail darter's refuge.[14] The value in question is the value of the continued existence of a species of small fish; it is not the value of a basic environmental good like clean air or drinkable water. Although we have obligations of justice to future generations to leave them an adequately diverse environment (which will place some environmental goods in category A) this does not extend to the conservation of particular species of animals.[15] Ecologists may care passionately about the fate of the snail darter: but religious believers may care with an equal passion that public resources should be used to promote their faith, and artists that their work should be made freely available for the public to appreciate. In each case what prevents these goods from becoming more than of sectional value is the fact that compelling reasons cannot be given to persuade others to value them.

So what role should the state have in supplying goods in category C? Given reasonable disagreement about the value of these goods, it might seem that those individuals who value any particular good in this category should band together to provide it, using privately-held resources to fund the good. But although this solution may work in some cases, there are clearly many instances in which state provision would be a far more effective means of supplying a particular good, for instance because otherwise the people who value it will be tempted to free-ride on the contributions of others. I may value the preservation of the snail darter, and be willing to vote for a small tax increase to protect its habitat, but if I can see that others are banding together to fund a snail darter refuge, I am more than happy to allow them to proceed without me. So the question becomes: when is state provision of category C goods consistent with justice? Let's be clear that the provision of such goods is not *required* by justice: a state that confined itself to supply goods in categories A and B would not be unjust. But it would nonetheless be responding suboptimally to the values and preferences of its citizens. So we need to turn our attention to the allocation of the costs of public goods. How must these costs be assigned if a socially just distribution of resources is to be preserved?

[14] I have defended this position at greater length in Miller (1999).

[15] For a counter-argument to this, based on the premise that if a species is allowed to become extinct, this imposes an irreversible loss on future generations, see Humphrey (2002).

With goods in categories A and B, there is no separate issue of cost allocation over and above the general issue of just taxation. These are goods, to recall, that can be given a public justification: in the case of category A goods, by direct reference to justice; in the case of category B goods, by reference to the identity and preservation of the community. So these goods have impersonal value. When they are provided, this is done in order to promote justice or other communal goals, and any benefits to particular individuals are incidental. So our only concern is that the resources used to fund them should be raised in whatever way contributes most to distributive justice. This is not the place to debate the relative merits of wealth taxes, income taxes, consumption taxes, etc. Whichever scheme is preferred, the effect of supplying public goods in these two categories should simply be to raise the rate at which the tax is taken.

With goods in category C, by contrast, people will vary in the value that they attach to having them supplied – typically some will attach no value at all to the provision of particular goods – and so the issue of justice is more complex. Let's assume for the moment that for each person we can represent the value of a category C good in monetary terms (I ask later about whether this assumption is justifiable) and assume too that this monetary value can be discovered, setting aside the economists' preference revelation problem. The state proposes to supply a package of category C goods from which every citizen will derive some benefit, although of course the amount of benefit will vary from person to person, depending on their tastes and values. How should the cost of the package be allocated?

One very obvious principle, suggested by our earlier discussion of Wicksell, is that the tax scheme that is applied should leave everyone a net beneficiary. Given that the distribution of resources before the goods are supplied is assumed to be just, it would obviously be unfair if some groups of people are made worse off through having the public goods package provided. But equally it seems unfair if everyone benefits, but to very different degrees. So a plausible stronger principle is that the tax scheme should aim to *equalize* net benefit, so that those who benefit most from the public goods package should contribute most to its production.[16] The intuition behind this is that supplying public goods in category C is a cooperative venture for mutual advantage, and since no one has a better

16 Whether this entails progressive taxation in the conventional sense depends on whether people with higher incomes generally value public goods more highly relative to income. For an analysis see Neill (2000).

claim than anyone else to the net benefit produced in this way, it should if possible be equally distributed. (In the same way, it has been argued that where individuals produce a surplus through bilateral exchange of resources, fairness entails that they should exchange at a price where both gain equally from the transaction.)

The equal net benefit principle has the drawback, however, that it sets a ceiling to public goods supply even though expanding the package would represent a Pareto improvement. Return to the case of the couch potato who has little interest in public goods beyond, say, free daytime television, from which he derives one unit of benefit. Suppose his public goods tax bill is zero; then no one else can enjoy more than one unit of net benefit under the strict equality principle, even though it is perfectly feasible for opera lovers, sports fans etc. to gain more than this without the couch potato losing anything. An alternative approach, therefore, would be to allow the public goods package to be chosen on grounds of efficiency – looking at the size of the gains that can be made by providing goods valued by different groups – and then allocating the costs of the package so as to equalize the gains as far as possible. To illustrate, suppose that public goods providing sixteen units of benefit can be provided at a cost of eight units of benefit, but that the benefits accrue unequally to three different groups as follows:

Group *A*	Group *B*	Group *C*
1	5	10

The taxes needed to finance the goods package would be distributed as follows:

Group *A*	Group *B*	Group *C*
0	1.5	6.5

So that the net benefit derived from the package by each group would be:

Group *A*	Group *B*	Group *C*
1	3.5	3.5

In this case one cannot get closer to strict equality except by taxing group *A* negatively, i.e. giving them a cash hand-out financed by additional taxes on *B* and *C*. If this is excluded, and if the public goods package is optimal from the point of view of the *A*s – they are the couch potatoes who benefit from no form of category *C* provision beyond daytime television – then the argument that can be put to the *A*s is, first, that they are getting the only public good they value for free, and second, that it would be 'dog in the mangerish' on their part to prevent the *B*s and the *C*s from getting their greater net benefits.[17] The *A*s are in one way unlucky as a result of having preferences that limit the benefit they can receive from public goods provision, but in other cases too people can lose out from having the preferences that they do without injustice. For instance, those whose preferences for private consumption involve goods that are intrinsically in short supply – fine wines, Old Masters, and so forth – will in general be less satisfied than those whose tastes are for easily reproducible goods. But this is not unfair.

An alternative proposal for allocating the costs of public goods is made by Murphy and Nagel (2002: 85) who suggest that people should contribute in proportion to the benefit they receive. In the example above, each group would be taxed at a rate equivalent to one-half of the benefit it received from the public goods package, so that net benefit would be as follows:

Group *A*	Group *B*	Group *C*
0.5	2.5	5

What can be said in favour of this less egalitarian principle of cost-allocation? The principle of contribution in proportion to benefit seems the natural one to use in certain contexts, for instance in the case of a joint stock company where investors would expect to share the profit in proportion to the sums they had put in, or a work team where it is generally seen as fair that returns should be in proportion to the effort or sacrifice that each member has made. From this perspective, the earlier egalitarian proposal might seem unfair because group A are benefiting from the public goods package at no cost to themselves. However, this analogy depends on seeing the state as a large productive enterprise, whereas it is more appropriate (in my view) to regard it as a political community whose foundational principle is that each member holds an equal stake. This does not entail that all resources held by individuals within the community must be equally distributed, but it does mean that equality is the default principle: if a benefit is created by no one in particular, it should be shared equally as far as possible. As indicated above, this seems to fit the case of public goods supply, supporting equal net benefit as the ideal principle for assigning costs.

One objection that might be raised to the principle I am proposing for category C public goods is that it overlooks the comparative cost of providing different goods that go into the package. This might be seen as

[17] There are contexts in which an argument can be made for preserving strict equality even though a Pareto improvement can be achieved by permitting inequality, but this does not seem to be one of them. On the rationale for strict egalitarianism, see Miller (1982); Scanlon (2002) and Temkin (2002).

analogous to the 'expensive tastes' problem that is thought to condemn equality of welfare as a principle when what is at issue is the distribution of private resources. In the present context, those who obtain benefit only from public goods that are expensive to produce can ask for them to be included in the package on the grounds that otherwise they will not receive the same net benefit from the package as those with cheaper preferences. This will push the cost of the package up and lower the net level of benefit received by the remaining members, who might then complain that they are being asked to subsidize the expensive tastes of the group in question.

The force of this objection can be diminished to some extent by noting, first, that although I have rejected efficiency as the sole principle for deciding when public goods are going to be supplied, it can still be treated as a necessary condition: that is, no good should be supplied unless the total benefit received by those who value the good exceeds the cost of providing it. This would rule out expensive goods valued by just a few people, unless it could be shown that each of these people received enormous benefits when the good was supplied. Second, although in the case of category C goods people who want them do not have to provide a public justification for the good in the sense of giving reasons that others can be expected to share – my desire to play football or listen to opera is sufficient by itself – there can legitimately be public debate about the means of satisfying that desire. People can be asked to show that cheaper versions of the good are not adequate substitutes, and each person has an incentive to propose such alternatives ('I know you believe that the only thing the community can do for you is build a state-of-the-art Olympic swimming pool, but have you tried a good 25 metre pool recently?'). However, the issue of principle remains: what if there is a group whose tastes and preferences are sufficiently fixed, and these are for a good that is efficient, although relatively expensive, to produce?

I believe the answer to this question must depend on the character of the political community we are considering – in effect, how much of a *community* it actually is. The more communitarian it is, the more people will be willing to allow public good production to be cross-subsidized, subject to the rider that, as noted above, each person should make an effort to demand less expensive rather than more expensive goods. Conversely, the less communitarian it becomes, the more members will demand that each subgroup should pay the costs of the public goods it wishes to see provided, either by devolving provision entirely – inviting subgroups to forms clubs to pay for 'their' public goods[18] – or by adjusting

[18] The classic analysis here remains Buchanan (1965) though Buchanan's analysis assumes that the goods in question are excludable and subject to crowding, hence not 'pure' public goods in the sense used here.

the tax system so that as far as possible each group is charged according to the costs of production of the goods it favours. Think, by way of analogy, of a group of people dining out at a restaurant in which dishes are differentially priced. Among friends it is common to split the cost of the meal equally, on the grounds that if I have a preference for fish and you have a preference for steak (which as it happens costs more) then it is reasonable for me to cross-subsidize your meal on an equal cost/equal benefit principle, subject to the rider that we all have a responsibility not to order lobster thermidor. Among casual acquaintances, by contrast, each is likely to be asked to pay the cost of his or her own meal.

Finally, let me return briefly to the question whether it makes sense to compute the value of all public goods in monetary terms, bearing in mind the heterogeneous range of goods included in category C. It is known to be difficult to persuade people to reveal the amount of money they would be prepared to sacrifice to have environmental goods, especially, provided (see Barry 1995: 154–9; Miller 1999). But is this a practical problem or an issue of principle? Consider again the very simple example of a political community containing an equal number of sports fans and nature lovers, where a proposal to build a football stadium and a wildlife reserve out of tax revenues meets the net benefit condition. The sports fans have no complaint about this, but the nature lovers might think that the other group have been provided with something that benefits them selfishly, whereas their own contribution has gone on something that has impersonal value (they do not expect to get any personal benefit out of the reserve). Put differently, they might believe that the reserve is of value to everybody and should therefore not be counted as a benefit to them in particular. Now, of course, it is open to the environmentalists to try to persuade the sports lovers of the truth of their claim, and if they succeed, the wildlife reserve will be transferred to category B – public goods whose provision can be given a public justification – and they will then be able to claim additional goods under the fairness principle for category C goods. But it is quite likely that the sports fans will treat the environmentalists' project simply as an expression of a particular conception of the good, one that is perfectly legitimate but no more so than their own love of football, in which case the previous conclusion stands, namely that the wildlife reserve has to be treated as a value accruing to the environmentalists, and the problem is simply how that value is to be estimated.

Having now explored the three categories of public goods in some detail, I want to return to democracy as a procedure to be used when decisions about public goods are to be made. Earlier on I challenged the idea that the only issue of justice here was procedural, and I now want to say a bit more about the role that justice should play in democratic deliberation about public goods. So, consider a democratic body assessing a proposal that public funds should be used to provide a new public good, or to expand the provision of an existing good. The first question that has to be decided is whether the good falls into category A, B or C, in my notation. In order to decide the category A question, a substantive conception of justice must be invoked. Suppose the issue is whether a new and safer cycle path should be constructed for commuting cyclists. The issue is whether this falls within the remit of basic mobility rights, or whether it should be seen simply as a (non-essential though valuable) benefit to cyclists. It is fairly easy to see the arguments that might be used to settle this. But in the background there must be a conception of what is owed to each citizen by way of opportunities to travel.

In order to decide the category B question, no direct appeal to justice is needed. The issue here is whether the good being considered is one that is of general benefit, especially on the grounds that it helps to preserve the distinctive character of the community making the decision. So, in this case the argument will move in a different direction, focusing not on how providing the good would affect the rights and opportunities of particular individuals, or groups of individuals, but on the value it has to the community as a whole.

Suppose, however, that the good turns out to belong to category C. Suppose, to continue with the cycle track example, that the track cannot be shown to meet an essential need of cyclists, nor can it be shown to benefit the community as whole, most of whose members neither cycle themselves nor attach any symbolic value to the act of cycling. Nevertheless it provides a real amenity, and a significant number of cyclists are very keen that the track should be constructed. Here the issue of justice is more difficult to decide, and if the approach I am recommending is correct it boils down to this: if we add the costs of constructing the cycle track to existing public goods expenditure, does it remain the case that overall everyone benefits from the pattern of expenditure, and has the extent of net benefit been equalized as far as possible? Obviously this question is very difficult, perhaps impossible, to answer with any precision. But if we assume that transport preferences are independent of preferences for public goods of other kinds, then to get a rough approximation, the decision-making body might look at existing expenditure on roads and other elements in the transport system and ask whether per capita benefits accruing to cyclists are in line with the benefits already enjoyed by other groups (motorists, pedestrians, etc.). If the cyclists are currently losing out relative to these other groups, then fairness will support laying the new cycle track.[19]

It is worth underlining, finally, that the principles of justice I have been proposing for public goods are in no sense principles of equal welfare – indeed they are not welfarist principles at all. We begin with a just distribution of private resources, where resources mean rights, opportunities, income, and so forth, not happiness or utility. We then consider proposals for converting some of these resources into public goods, on the grounds that such conversions are potentially beneficial: everyone can gain from them. Nevertheless, the conversion must be justice-preserving, in the sense that the set of final packages received by each person – private resources plus public goods – respects the distributive pattern initially established. For goods in category C, the value of each person's package is computed as a monetary equivalent. Preferences enter the picture only because we need to be able to establish what any given public good is worth to each person. My proposal, for these goods, is that the tax and expenditure package should be constructed in such a way as to make the net benefit received by each person as nearly equal as possible. But this does not mean that each person's happiness or utility will increase equally when the package is provided. Nor, of course, does it mean that each person will end up equally happy as a result of (justice-preserving) public goods provision.

I have argued as well that the justice of public goods provision cannot be reduced to the justice of the procedure used to decide such policies. I have rejected two positions: one making majority voting a sufficient condition for fairness in the provision of public goods, the other making unanimous consent a necessary condition. Nevertheless, there are good reasons why democratic procedures will contribute to justice in this area. By giving different groups a voice, they help to reveal the extent of the benefit that each group expects to derive from a proposed public good, and they provide the setting in which debate about the nature of the goods themselves can occur. As we have seen, it is important to establish which goods citizens can demand as a matter of justice, and which correspond to communal values that everyone has reason to support. It is only through actual debate that these issues can be decided. Beyond that, when we

[19] Note that the criterion I am applying is not *expenditure* per capita but *benefit* per capita, though the latter will be expressed in terms of money equivalents: how much is it worth to motorists to have the existing road system maintained? How much is it worth to cyclists to have the new cycle track constructed? It is not inherently unfair if cyclists subsidize motorists or motorists subsidize cyclists through the tax system, though see my earlier remarks about the kind of political community in which this kind of cross-subsidization will be seen as acceptable.

reach goods in category C, we have to trust that groups will decide issues of provision in a spirit of fairness. This cannot be guaranteed: seeing that they form a large majority, motorists may simply decide to block expenditure on the proposed new cycle track. But here we face general questions about democracy, public deliberation and social justice that take us well beyond the scope of the present chapter (but see Miller 2000: esp chs 1 and 9).

9 The common good

Philip Pettit

The republican tradition in political theory has long insisted on the centrality of the notion of the common good, arguing that if the state is forced to track the common good then it won't dominate its citizens. Not only can it serve the republican ideal of promoting freedom as non-domination of members of the public against private masters: the state will not itself have the cast of a public master; it will interfere with people in the course of tracking the common good but the interference will not be of the dominating variety (Sellers 1995; Pettit 1997; Skinner 1998; Viroli 2002).

I have two aims in this chapter. One is to look at what 'the common good' has got to mean if this republican axiom is going to be plausible, and the other is to consider how the common good might be identified and empowered in political life, as republican theory suggests that it ought to be. In pursuing these aims – though they relate to my projects rather than his – I will draw freely on Brian Barry's early but still unsurpassed discussion of common or public interests (Barry 1965).

The chapter is in three sections. The first section argues that 'the common good' cannot plausibly refer to people's common net interests but only to the common interests that people have as members of the public. The second maintains that such matters of public interest, while not often agreed on in deliberative discussion, should be theoretically identified as those arrangements that are best supported by the considerations and criteria admitted in such discussion. And the third shows how the institutions associated with electoral-constitutional democracy can function – and can reasonably be assessed – as a fallible means whereby public interests can be identified in practice.

I should mention, finally, that the chapter will abstract altogether from issues of how states should deal with one another or with the citizens of other states, includes states that are poorer and more vulnerable. My

My thanks for helpful criticisms on an earlier draft from Bob Goodin and Nic Southwood. I was also helped by discussion of the chapter when it was presented at La Trobe University, Melbourne and at Georgetown University.

focus is exclusively on the relation between a state and its own citizens, where the category of citizens is itself understood broadly, so as to include at least all adult, competent residents of the country.

People's net interests and their interests as citizens

Under the articulation of republican thought that I have offered elsewhere, someone can interfere in people's affairs and yet not dominate them so far as the interference is forced to track the interests that people are sincerely disposed to avow (whether accurately or not). An agent will not represent an arbitrary power of interference in people's lives, however much interference is involved, so far as he or she is forced to track the avowable interests, in this sense, of the interferees (Pettit 1997; Pettit 2001).

Interference in the sense in play here may involve blocking a person's choice of some option, burdening that choice with costs or penalties, or giving the person to believe that one will block or burden the choice. But no matter what form it takes, there are a number of ways in which the agent can be forced to track the avowable interests of interferees, thereby avoiding arbitrariness. The interferees may be well protected against arbitrary interference or may be capable of retaliation, for example. Or arbitrary interference may be difficult or costly for the agent. Or there may be a third party – say, the state – that is likely to penalize such interference.

Consider the way in which an attorney or accountant may interfere with a client's choices, preempting what the client will be able to do in future. Or consider the way that friends may do this when they have to take a decision on someone's behalf. Or consider the way his sailors interfere with Ulysses when they keep him bound to the mast. In all of these cases, the interference is relatively non-arbitrary; that is, it comes of a relatively non-arbitrary power. The threat of being fired will force the attorney and accountant to take heed of what they know that the client values. The bonds of friendship will have the same effect in the case where friends take a decision on a person's behalf. And the fear of being punished for disobeying instructions presumably inhibits Ulysses' sailors and means that in refusing to listen to him they do not exercise arbitrary, dominating power.

A first reading of 'the common good'

Given this way of understanding non-arbitrary interference, there is one obvious reason why we might be tempted to think that the republican axiom about the common good is sound. Suppose that 'the common good' is just shorthand for people's common avowable interests. Under this assumption, the state which tracks the common good will interfere with citizens only so far as the avowable interest of each is served by that interference. Tracking the common good will mean nothing more or less than tracking avowable interests that people share. And so, by the definitions given, a state that is forced to track the common good will be to that extent a non-arbitrary and undominating presence in the lives of its citizens. There will be little or no mystery about what supports the republican axiom.

But is it plausible that citizens have such common, avowable interests and that in that sense there is a common good that the state can be required to track? The interests envisaged have to be the avowable net interests – the interests, all things considered – that citizens are disposed to avow (Barry 1965: 196). Is it plausible, then, that among the sets of practices and policies that a state might put in place, there is one that is in the avowable net interest of each? I think not. The reason for thinking not is best presented after first looking at two ill-conceived reasons that might be produced in favour of that line.

One ill-conceived reason for favouring a negative answer is this. The state interferes with citizens when it imposes taxes, when it coercively legislates, and when it punishes offenders for breaking the law. But it is extremely unlikely that any one's net interest will be best served by their being coerced or taxed or punished. It will always be better for them if they can benefit from the state's interference with others – the interference associated with establishing some set of practices and policies – while enjoying a free ride themselves. Thus it may seem that no single set of practices and policies could ever be in the avowable net interest of each; for every citizen there will be one, free-riding alternative that does better yet.

This is an irrelevant consideration, because talk of what is in the avowable net interest of each is relative to a given set of options. 'Being in someone's interest is at least a triadic relation between a person and at least two policies' (Barry 1965: 192; cf. 197). The set of options presupposed in this case must be the set of options which it would be feasible for the state to realize and, short of irrelevant extremes, the state's allowing all but one individual to free-ride does not belong to that set. Thus the fact that the free-riding option would serve each better than any set of practices and policies that did not allow them to free-ride is not relevant to the matter in hand. The question is whether, among the feasible, more or less universal practices and policies available to a state, there is one set which is in the avowable net interest of each.

There is a second objection to the possibility of finding such a set of practices and policies that also fails. Think of the person who does relatively badly, as some are bound to do, under a policy that had seemed fine before. Or think of the person who is about to be penalized, as some will surely be penalized, under a law that they had previously approved. The policy or the law is not likely to be in the avowable net interest of that person, given the way things have turned out. But some people are certain to be in that person's position at one or another stage of their lives. And so it seems that no set of practices or policies could ever turn out to be in the avowable net interest of each; it will not be in the avowable net interest of those who do relatively badly, or of those who fail to comply and are consequently punished.

This objection fails, however, because it does not distinguish between what is in someone's *ex ante* interest and what is in their interest *ex post* (cf. Barry 1965: 196–7). Suppose that it is in the avowed net interest of each citizen *ex ante* that the state adopt a certain measure, where everyone knows that this involves a chance element and that, depending on how the chance works out, a given individual will fare better or worse. And now imagine that someone fares worse, and that the measure is not in his or her avowed net interest as that is judged after the event. It would be quite counter-intuitive to say that the fact that the state does not serve the person's *ex post* interest in this way means that it is an arbitrary presence in their life. The relevant question is whether it serves that person's *ex ante* interest well, which by hypothesis it does. Hence, the consideration raised here, like the previous one, is on the wrong track.[1]

And now, finally, to what I see as a sound objection to the idea under discussion. Even given the restriction to feasible alternatives and to *ex ante* interests, it is extremely unlikely that among the different sets of practices and policies available to a state, there is one that will be in the avowable net interest of each. A set of practices and policies will be in a person's net interest, plausibly, if it is one whose expected results are something the agent wants for himself or herself, where that want satisfies conditions that guard it against charges of clear irrationality (Barry 1965; Geuss 1981).[2] The fact that people differ in their capacities and circumstances, their tastes and commitments, means that there is little

[1] Consider in this context Barry's (1965: 198) more or less supportive comment on Rousseau's distinction between laws and decrees: 'Rousseau does not deny that it may be in your interest to break a law which benefits you qua member of the community; all he says is that it is certainly in your interests to vote for it, and that if you have voted in favour of a certain punishment for a certain crime you have no business to complain if your wish for a certain general policy is applied to you in a particular case'.

[2] Worrying about making the question of what a person's interests are into a non-empirical issue – a function of the interpreter's ideals – Barry only considers the irrationality involved

or no chance that among feasible alternatives one and the same set of practices and policies will be in the avowable net interest of each. It is inevitable that different people will want for themselves results associated with rival sets. As someone talented, adventurous and confident, you may want for yourself the results associated with having a *laissez-faire* economy. As someone of modest capacities, I may want for myself the results associated with a welfare state. And so on.

To say that there is no complete set of practices and policies that is in the avowable net interest of each is not to say, of course, that there are no individual practices or policies that are in the avowable net interest of each. And so an alternative may seem to have been neglected. For someone might propose that it would be reasonable for a society to introduce or preserve those individual elements on which people converge, leaving the *status quo* otherwise unchanged (Buchanan and Tullock 1962). I am not moved by this proposal, however, as the complete set of practices and policies it would support – a mix of the new initiatives and the status quo – would not be in the avowable net interest of each (cf. Barry 1965: 274). And that is the point, as I see it, that is relevant in this discussion.

Or is it? Suppose that there is no agreement on changing the status quo in certain respects. Doesn't that mean that the only feasible sets of practices and policies are those that include those elements of the status quo? And doesn't that entail that the proposal mooted points us towards an arrangement that, alone among feasible alternatives, is in the avowable net interest of each? No, it does not.

The set of practices and policies that a state implements has to be characterized in terms of its omissions as well as its commissions: in terms of what it decides not to do as well as in terms of what it decides to do. The decision not to change the status quo in a certain manner, when it is within its power to do so, represents a policy choice – or a choice of practice – just as much as any more positive decision. And it is bound to be noteworthy, therefore, that that decision favours some but not others: that it is in the avowable net interest of some, but not in the avowable net interest of all (see Sunstein 1993).

Barry emphasizes that, *ex ante*, there are various individual policies that are likely to be in the net interest – and, we may presume, the avowable

in an agent's being indifferent to his or her future opportunities of want-satisfaction (Barry 1965: 184–5). I do not share that worry to the same extent. The issue of whether something is in a person's interest will remain empirically tractable to the extent that there is a background consensus on norms of rationality. And there are many norms besides that of temporal neutrality that are a matter of consensus. This is true at least of those norms that spell out conditions for the successful functioning of wants in relation to information and action: say, conditions related to consistency, updating and the like.

net interest – of everyone. But he is pessimistic about 'supposing that the uncertainty of the future is the password to the rehabilitation of common interests in all areas of social life' (Barry 1965: 200). Pessimism about whether there is any one set of practices and policies that will prove to be in the avowable net interest of each, even *ex ante*, has come to dominate contemporary political thought (Goodin 1996).[3]

Let us assume that this sort of pessimism is justified. Whatever 'the common good' refers to, then, the referent cannot be the common avowed net interests of citizens. If there were such a referent for the phrase to pick out – if there were a single set of practices and policies that answered to the avowable net interest of each person in a society – then it would be unmysterious why republicans should claim that so far as a state is forced to track the common good, it is non-arbitrary and undominating. But no such referent is available.

Towards an alternative reading of 'the common good'

If it is to be non-arbitrary and undominating, according to the republican definitions, the state has got to track, and be forced to track, the avowable net interests of those with whom it interferes. We have been discussing the question of how it might be the case, as the republican axiom has it, that the state that is forced to track the common good satisfies this requirement. The resolution we have just explored and rejected starts from the fact that it will certainly do so if the common good is nothing other than the common avowable net interests of those with whom the state interferes: as we assume, its members or citizens. But that resolution, so it transpires, is not the only way in which the republican axiom might turn out to be true.

The resolution rejected starts from the observation that the republican axiom will be made true if 'the common good' is interpetable so that the following formula is satisfied.

In being forced to track the common good, the state is forced to track the common avowable net interests of its citizens But the axiom would also be true in the event of 'the common good' referring to something – something other than people's avowable net interests – that makes the following formula come out true.

[3] It is present, for example, in the background of John Rawls' (1971) theory of justice. It drives him to ask whether there is any single set of practices and policies, or at least any 'basic structure', that will prove to be in the avowable interest of anyone who faces the alternatives, not just *ex ante*, but *ex ignorantia*: that is, from behind a hypothetical veil of ignorance as to their personal properties and prospects.

It is in the avowable net interest of each citizen that there should be a state that is forced to track the common good This formula might be satisfied, without the common good itself coinciding with the common avowable net interests of citizens. What is said to be in the avowable net interest of each is not the common good itself, after all, but the arrangement under which there is a state that is forced to track the common good – for the moment we postpone the question of what 'the common good' now means. Among the feasible sorts of state available, the state that is forced to track the common good is said to answer better than others to people's avowable net interests.

The availability of this formula is supported by some points that Barry himself makes. He remarks that even though certain policies, A, B and C, may not represent common net interests in themselves, still the higher-order policy of implementing policies that satisfy certain criteria may be a common net interest; and this, even though the criteria would select those very policies, A, B and C, for implementation. 'Under favourable conditions it may be that everyone can reasonably expect to gain if a higher-order policy is adopted which specifies some criteria and says that any action or policy which satisfies these criteria is to be put into effect' (Barry 1965: 201).

Is there a plausible interpretation of 'the common good', then, such that the higher-order policy of having a state that is forced to track the common good in that sense is in the avowed net interest of each; and this, even though the common good may not represent something in itself that is in the avowed net interest of each? A plausible interpretation of 'the common good' will have to involve the shared interests of citizens in some sense, of course; otherwise it is hard to see why it might be described as the common good. So what sorts of shared interests might satisfy the condition that it is in the avowable net interest of each that there should be a state that is forced to track them in its practices and policies?

Barry directs us to what is probably the one live candidate. A person's net interests contrast, under his presentation, with the interests that he or she has as the occupant of a certain role. 'As a motorist, tighter enforcement of the speed limit in not in his interest, as a pedestrian it is; as an importer of raw materials it is not in his interests to have higher tariffs all round, as a seller who has to compete with foreign rivals it is; and so on' (Barry 1965: 196). Assuming that 'the common good' refers to matters of common interest, the obvious suggestion is that the phrase refers to the interests that people share in their role as citizens. If the republican axiom is sound, then the reason must be that it is in the avowable net interest of each that there should be a state that is forced to track people's common interests as citizens. To require that a state should be forced to track people's common interests as citizens is to require that what it does should be guided, at whatever level of control, by those interests, and only by those interests. It is to require that the state should be even-handed in seeing no difference between different citizens and that it should be effective in advancing citizens' interests.

I leave for the next two sections the question as to how we should determine what people's common interests as citizens are but the general idea should be clear. When we think of people's common interests as motorists, we consider the interests that they have so far as they share a purpose of using a private car, under the presumptive constraint that there are going to be a number of motorists on the roads and that they each have to be treated equally. When we think of people's common interests as citizens, we presumably take certain goals and constraints to be relevant to the members of any polity, though how we interpret them may vary under different theories. And then we take their common interests as citizens to be the interests they have just in virtue of pursuing those goals under the satisfaction of those constraints.

I shall not be providing an argument for why it is in everyone's avowable net interest that there should be a state that is forced to track their common interests as citizens. But I do think that the claim is quite plausible. What is said to be the case is that, as between the different feasible sorts of political arrangements, it is in the avowable net interest of each person, from an *ex ante* point of view, that there should be a state that is forced to track his or her interests – as it is forced to track the interests of everyone else – as a citizen. And while this is not by any means a self-evident truth, it certainly stands a good chance of being true. If we can institutionalize things so that practices and policies systematically track people's interests as citizens, and only such interests, then that form of arrangement is going to have a powerful claim to be in the avowable net interest of each.[4]

To sum up this discussion, then, we have distinguished two readings of 'the common good'. Each is a plausible reading in the sense of having the

[4] Indeed even this paragraph overstates what has to be claimed under the approach. For a given population, whether in the world as a whole or in a certain territory, there are different ways in which the population may be subdivided into citizenries or peoples. All that is strictly needed for the republican axiom to be sound is that there is a subdivision such that for any people or citizenry identified it is in the interest of each member, from an *ex ante* point of view, that there should be a state established amongst them that is forced to track their common interests as citizens. Nothing like this move, notice, could have been introduced to increase the plausibility of the counterpart claim under the earlier resolution. The reason is that no matter how the population is subdivided into peoples – or at least fairly numerous bands of people – differences in capacities, circumstances and other factors will emerge so as to undermine the idea that a single set of practices and policies might be in the avowable net interest of each member.

phrase refer to shared interests: in the first case, the common avowable net interests of people; in the second, their common interests as citizens. The first reading would make it true, as a matter of analysis, that the state that is forced to track the common good tracks people's common avowable net interests and so is non-arbitrary and undominating. The second reading would make this republican axiom likely to be true but not true for certain, and not true as a matter of analysis; it will be true if, as it seems reasonable to believe, it is in the avowable interest of each that there should be a state that is forced to track people's common interests as citizens.

But this second reading leaves us with two pressing questions. First, how should people's common interest as citizens be defined in theory? And how are they to be identified in practice? I turn to those questions in the two remaining sections of the chapter.

Defining people's interests as citizens

It is plausible that a person might show, just on the basis of choice behaviour, what it is that answers to his or her avowable net interest. If agents are minimally rational and well-informed, and if the context is one where only self-regarding wants are in play, then presumably they will individually choose among different alternatives in a manner that reflects what they are disposed to avow as their net interest. Avowable net interests might amount in this way to revealed interests.

Nothing of the same kind can be true, however, of the interests that a person has in a certain role or capacity, such as his or her interests as a citizen. There is no context of choice in which someone's interest as a citizen, say as between certain alternatives, is bound to be revealed. No doubt the uncertainty of the polling booth, together with the possibility of altruism, means that a person's vote will not necessarily reveal their avowable net interest among possible electoral outcomes (Brennan and Lomasky 1992). But neither will it necessarily reveal their interest as a citizen, or even their image of where that interest lies; there are too many other factors that may affect their decision on how to vote.

This means that there is no escaping the need for people to make judgements, and presumably deliberatively informed judgements, about what their interests as citizens are. But the need for deliberation and judgement is eased somewhat by the fact that whatever a person's interests as a citizen, they will be the same interests as those of anyone else, considered as a citizen. That is part of what is coded into the notion of a role interest as distinct from a net interest. There will be no need for different judgements about the interests of different people as citizens, then, though what those interests require in one person's situation, of course, may differ from what they require in another's (Kymlicka 1995). We might even give up talk of people's common interests as citizens in favour of speaking of public interests, or the interest of the public, or just the public interest. And this, indeed, is what Barry (1965: 190) proposes: 'The definition of the meaning of "the public interest" which I propose makes it equivalent to "those interests which people have in common *qua* members of the public"'.

The fact that their interests as citizens are matters of judgement and deliberation means that if something is a public interest, in the sense of being an interest of the public, it is also going to be public in the further sense of being detectable as a matter of public interest; whether it is a matter of public interest will be determinable by public debate, it will not be a function of how things are in private realms of sentiment that only experts can plumb. This dual resonance makes it attractive to resort to talk of the public interest as distinct from people's common interests as citizens. But if we do talk of the public interest, we should be careful not to suggest that the public interest is the interest of an entity that exists in some way over and beyond members of the public. What is in the public interest will always be so in virtue of the effects that it has on members of the public. Or so at any rate I am happy to assume, embracing in this respect a sort of moral individualism (Kukathas and Pettit 1990: ch. 1).

But what makes it the case with any group that it is in their common interest as members of the group to adopt this or that initiative? In particular, what makes it the case that it is in people's common interest as members of the political public that this or that set of practices and policies be established? What is the truth-maker of a claim about the public interest?

Some false starts

One line might be that what is in the public interest of a group is whatever members collectively say is in the public interest, whether in majority voting or under some other arrangement. This would make members of the group into authorities on the matter. But that is a barely credible approach, since it would mean that there was no sense in the idea of a group coming to the view that members were wrong in the past when they judged that that this or that was in their common interest as members. It would imply that the public interest had changed, not that members had corrected an earlier judgement. But the members of groups do often make that sort of self-corrective judgement and there has to be something missing in a theory that renders self-correction inexplicable.

Another line might be that what is in the public interest of a group is what members would collectively judge to be in their common interest as members were they in the idealized position of having access to all relevant evidence, being each able to make a contribution to the deliberation, not being subject to irrelevant pressures of bias and partiality, and so on. This approach too would make people – but now only idealized people – into authorities on what is in their common interests as members of a group. One interpretation of that line might be to say that what is in the public interest is what people would judge to be in the public interest, were they in the sort of speech situation that answers perfectly to ideals of debate that are immanent, according to Jürgen Habermas (1973; 1984; 1989), in ordinary practice.

This line is no more attractive than the first. For there is no guarantee that what idealized members of the group would find to be in their common interest as members is what is in the common interest of members of the group under actual, distinctly unidealized circumstances (Smith 1994). Imagine that there is a question as to whether it is in the public interest of members of a group to have a body of experts that would review every collective proposal and advise members on its ramifications before putting the proposal to the vote. The idealized members of the group would not find it to be in their interest to consult a body of experts – in their circumstances, such a body would not be needed – but it might well be in the public interest of actual, imperfectly situated members to establish a body of that kind.

The response to this problem might be to propose a third line. Under the third line, the issue of what is in the public interest of the members of a group would be determined by what those members would judge to be in the public interest – the actual public interest, under real-world conditions – were they themselves in the idealized position of having access to all evidence, being able to hear all voices, not being vulnerable to bias and partiality, and so on.

This third line is quite different from the other two. The first two lines make the members of a group, ordinary or idealized, into defining authorities on their common interest as members; what the members say in each case goes, with no possibility of error. But this third line casts idealized members as expert judges on the public interests of ordinary members of the group, not as defining authorities. It presents them as occupying an epistemically favourable position to judge on those interests, rather than making their say-so authoritative in itself.

The *Euthyphro* test marks off this third line from the other two (Pettit 1982; 2002). Socrates asked in Plato's *Euthyphro* whether something is good because the gods love it or whether they love it because it is good.

Under the first reading, the gods would be authorities who dictated what was good by virtue of what they chose to love, under the second they would be experts who could be relied upon to detect the good and love it. Under the first two lines on the public interest of members of a group, something is in the public interest because it is what members – ordinary members or idealized members – say is in the public interest. Under the third line, however, it is not the case that something is in the public interest because idealized judges say it is in the public interest. On the contrary, the idealized judges say it is in the public interest because it is in the public interest; that it is in the public interest reliably guides their judgement, in view of the epistemically favourable position they occupy.

The fact that the third way of identifying the public interest of a group has this character means that we can hardly be satisfied with it as an ultimate standard of the public interest. If we think idealized members would be able to tell what is in the public interest, that must be because we have a notion of the factors that determine whether something is in the public interest, and think that the position of idealized members enables them to detect the presence and the import of those determinants in a reliable manner. But if we do see things like this, then clearly we are committed to thinking that what makes it the case that something is in the public interest of a group is the fact that it answers those determinants appropriately. That idealized members judge it to be in the public interest is a sign that it answers appropriately to those factors; it is not what makes it to be the case that it is in the public interest.

A new beginning

We are back, then, at square one. What are the determinants of the common interests that members of a group have as members of the group? In particular, what are the determinants of the common interests that people have as citizens? We have seen that the question cannot be finessed in favour of identifying authorities or experts who can reliably direct us to such public interests. We have no recourse but to try and approach the question from another angle.

One alternative angle that may appeal to some is to identify people's common interests as citizens with something substantive such as the satisfaction of a privileged list of rights or the maximization of utility in some variant of the utilitarian notion. But this won't serve our purposes, as it is going to be quite implausible that people might each be disposed to avow a net interest in having a state that is constrained to promote such a determinate and controversial end. I propose, therefore, to explore a different line.

Consider any group that is based on the voluntary, deliberative participation of its members. Suppose the members of that group stick together, undertaking now this enterprise, now that, and binding themselves, here to this way of doing things, there to that alternative practice. And suppose further that while those policies and practices are not unanimously endorsed, no one argues that they are illegitimate, being selected in breach of accepted ways of doing things. It seems plausible that the members of such a group would see the modes of group behaviour adopted as answering to their interests as members; otherwise they would presumably protest. So what is it about the way things are done in that paradigm group that makes it the case, by their lights, that the public interest is furthered?

The key to an answer lies in a fact about how the members may be expected to deliberate as they try to identify practices to implement and policies to pursue. When people debate with each other about what they should do as a group, or about how what they do should be determined – when they debate about their decisions or their decision-making – then they invariably produce considerations in support of this or that or the other proposal. Some of those considerations will be rejected by others as reasons that have no hold on them as members of the group. They may be rejected, for example, as representing a sort of special pleading on the part of those who put them forward. Other considerations, however, will be allowed to pass. They will be granted the status of reasons that are relevant to the matter of what the group as a whole should do; different members may give them different weight but all will acknowledge that they deserve a certain weighting.

Considerations that would not pass muster in group debate include self-seeking observations to the effect that such and such an initiative would give one member or subset of members an advantage over others, as well as expressions of what is required by an ideal or cause that is not shared by all. The considerations that are likely to be accepted as relevant on all sides come in two broad categories: first, neutral considerations that concern the general prosperity of the group, or its efficacy in attaining agreed ends, or the assurance available to each that no other members enjoy any particular privilege, and so on; and second, those more personal complaints that members of different groups may raise against various proposals and that secure acceptance as reasonable: 'That's going to make life difficult for those of us who are poor/who belong to an ethnic minority/who live in rural areas . . .'

Not only will the members of any group privilege certain commonly admitted considerations in this fashion, they will also privilege certain criteria of argument bearing on what those considerations are supposed to establish. They will do this, once again, so far as they let certain forms of argument pass, while objecting to others.[5] With one sort of consideration, for example, they may show that they think that its overall satisfaction argues for a certain arrangement, even though a minority may do badly under that arrangement. With another sort of consideration, they may be unwilling to allow aggregate satisfaction to compensate in the same way for individual shortfalls.

The fact that members of our paradigm group will have deliberated in this fashion over different proposals means that in their evolving practice various considerations and criteria of deliberation will have been identified as reasons that are countenanced as relevant to group decisions and group decision-making. They will constitute a fund of reasons such that short of raising novel objections, everyone will be expected to recognize them as relevant to group behaviour, everyone will be expected to expect others to recognize them as having this relevance, and so on.

What constitutes the common interests of the members of a group, then? What determines that this or that decision, or this or that mode of decision-making, is in their common interest as members? The fact, plausibly, that according to publicly admissible criteria of argument, it is best supported among feasible alternatives by publicly admissible considerations; the fact, for short, that it is best supported by the reasons that are publicly admissible within the group. The reasons publicly admitted will presumably approximate to those that are publicly admissible. And so when members of the group see the initiatives taken as ones that the publicly admitted reasons best support – as members presumably do in the case of our paradigm group – they naturally see those initiatives as answering to their common interests as members.

There are different cases, of course, in which members of the group may see initiatives as enjoying the support of publicly admissible reasons. One is the case where the relevant considerations and criteria are aired in the group as a whole and everyone agrees – implausibly – that amongst the available alternatives this or that initiative enjoys the most support. Another is the case where the decision is made by a subgroup that is regarded as a reliable judge of what the relevant considerations and criteria support. And yet another is the case – no doubt the most common of all – where the possibility of reasonable disagreement is acknowledged and the decision is taken among equally supported proposals on a basis

[5] A crucial background assumption here is that the criteria that argument follows – the principles of inference that it respects – may operate without being spelled out as considerations that the argument takes into account. In a classic article, Lewis Carroll (1895) showed that on pain of infinite regress some principles of reason have to operate in this unarticulated manner.

that is itself endorsed by publicly admitted reasons. The basis endorsed may involve a lottery, or the judgement of an impartial panel, or the judgement of a committee or court that is required to follow certain guidelines, or a majority vote among members or representatives.

According to the line of thought emerging from these considerations, an initiative will answer to the public interest of the members of a group precisely when it is supported in some of the ways just rehearsed by the reasons publicly admissible amongst the members; precisely when it answers, directly or indirectly, to publicly admissible, supporting considerations, according to publicly admissible criteria of support.

This line of thought can be easily extended to the case of the polity. The members of a democratic public constitute a group that has to decide on what ends to try and accomplish in a collective manner; in particular, via the agency of a coercive state. As joint agents of that sort, they will discuss among themselves questions bearing on what should be done. Such discussion may take place in assemblies that have decision-making powers but they will occur more routinely in smaller decentralized groups – even just groups of two and three – that have the power, at most, of affecting electoral fortunes. People in these subgroups will discuss what should be done collectively with the same fervour and seriousness as those in positions of power; it is just that their deliberations will be off-line from the point of view of decision-making.

If we think of members of a democratic public as parties to such a plan of joint action, then we can see that like the members of any such group they are bound to privilege certain considerations and certain criteria of reasoning as those that are relevant for their collective purposes. They will generate a fund of public reasons such that everyone in the society will be expected to countenance them, short of producing novel grounds for raising challenges. Part of learning one's way about such a polity will consist in learning what considerations and what criteria pass without saying – pass in every context, not just in this or that particular milieu – as principles of local political argument.

Given this parallelism between the polity and the paradigm group, we can define the political notion of the public interest as follows. A set of practices and policies will be in the public interest in any society just so far as it transpires that by publicly admissible criteria that particular set answers better than feasible alternatives to publicly admissible considerations: the fact that it best satisfies the fund of reasons that are publicly admissible in deliberation about what should be collectively done. This definition is entirely natural with a democratic polity but it applies also in the undemocratic case. Even if there is no deliberation practised amongst citizens as a whole about what the state should do –

even if the state is a private fiefdom – still there is room for asking whether this or that initiative is supported better than alternatives by the reasons that would prove admissible in inclusive political debate.

I propose to go along with the mode of identifying public interests that we have sketched in this discussion. Initiatives that are supported by what members consider to be the reasons relevant to group decision-making have a natural claim to count as being in the group's interest, especially given that such reasons are unlikely to reflect controversial ideals or causes. And in any case, there are no serious rivals available; the proposal explored is the only plausible contender on offer.

Finally, an observation in passing. On the conception of the public interest emerging here, there is an interesting convergence with the version of Rawlsian contractualism espoused by T.M. Scanlon (1982; 1998) and applied to politics by Brian Barry (1995). Under that approach, roughly stated, we seek to establish whether certain principles are just by asking whether anyone could make a reasonable complaint against them as a basis of cooperation with others. On the approach taken here, practices and policies will count as being in the public interest precisely so far as they are immune to reasonable objection, under a particular interpretation of what makes an objection reasonable. The practices and policies that are in the public interest will be immune to the sort of objection that is licensed by the considerations and criteria that are publicly admissible within the society, or they will be selected on a basis that is immune to such objection. Thus they are practices and policies that might count, under a broadly contractualist approach, as arrangements required by justice.

Identifying in practice people's interests as citizens

But it is one thing to have a theoretical account of how in principle people's common interests as citizens are to be defined. It is quite another to give an account of how in day-to-day politics they might be picked out and empowered: that is, given an exclusive role in determining the state's practices and policies. I make some general remarks on that issue in this final part of the chapter.[6]

Suppose we are given the problem of designing a polity so that people's common interests as citizens are reliably identified and empowered. What steps would we need to take in order to ensure this result? What are the main dangers against which we should look for institutional safeguards?

[6] For some further work on related issues see (Pettit 2000; 2002b; 2003).

There are two sorts of danger that stand out at the most abstract level. The first is that the system might fail to identify and empower all the public interests relevant to the polity. And the other is that it might misidentify or misrepresent certain private interests as public interests and proceed to empower them. The first danger is that of a false negative, the second that of a false positive. The false negative would consist in missing out on certain public interests, or on what public interests support; the false positive would consist in mistaking other interests for public interests or in mistaking an outcome supported by other interests for a public-interest outcome. The first involves an ignorance of certain public interests, the second an error about what those interests are.

The false negative danger

How might the false negative occur and what might be done to guard against it in the ordinary practice of politics? It might occur in one of two ways: either because there are publicly admissible reasons that have not surfaced yet within discussions in the polity, or because there are many feasible variations in practice and policy that have not been canvassed, including variations that might prove to have the support of publicly admissible reasons and so to count as being in the public interest. What political institutions would we need to establish with a view to guarding against these problems? Clearly, there has got to be widespread public discussion of what the state should do in order for the fund of publicly admissible reasons to be extended and developed. And, equally clearly, there has got to be an opportunity for members of the polity to propose and canvass any number of variations in political practice and policy.

The electoral institutions that are familiar from current democracies look capable, at least in principle, of playing the role envisaged. Let those institutions facilitate and further deliberative discussion in the electorate, among candidates who stand for election, and in the various forums to which authorities are elected and appointed, and there will be a good chance that a rich fund of reasons will be established as publicly admissible in common currency and consciousness. At least, this will be so, if public discussion is not distorted by the shortcuts of electronic advertising, by resort to personal or party abuse, by the exclusion of certain sectors of the population, by divisions of paralyzing distrust, or by other such melancholy realities.

Not only can the institutions of electoral democracy serve to enrich the fund of publicly admitted reasons. They are also capable, at least in principle, of increasing the likelihood that a maximum of possible variations in political practice and policy will be aired in public. If there are a number of parties competing for election, if candidates increase their chance of election by embracing attractive, distinguishing proposals, and if proposals are going to seem attractive to the extent that they are supported by publicly admissible reasons, then electoral competition should help to counter shortfalls of imagination – wilful or innocent – on this front. Again, of course, the efficacy of electoral institutions here will often be diminished under the influence of familiar, melancholy realities. It will be reduced, for example, if electoral business is so expensive that smaller parties or political groups have no chance of getting a hearing, or if politics is dominated and shaped to their own purposes by two or three major parties.[7]

The false positive danger

Suppose that we have established electoral institutions of the required stamp in the society for which we are designing a political system. And suppose that there is some reason to think that the problem of the false negative that we have been discussing is thereby mitigated. What is this likely to mean for the problem of the false positive?

There are two dangers created by ordinary electoral institutions that are relevant to this problem. The first is the danger of a tyranny of the majority, the second the danger of a tyranny of the elite: the elite, in this picture, are those who are elected and appointed to positions of power, whether within the administration, the legislature or the judiciary. The first danger is that the interests of a majority get to be misrepresented as genuinely public interests, with a minority – a stable or one-issue minority – not being properly taken into account. The second danger is that, as broad electoral platforms get translated into detailed policies, or get to be implemented or interpreted in real-world contexts, they will be shaped by pressures that emanate from sectional or factional sources and that have no connection with the public interest as such.

What institutions might complement electoral institutions, and serve to deal in some measure with the problem of the false positive, in particular with that problem as it arises in an electoral context: in effect, with the danger of majoritarian and elitist tyranny? The best hope, as I have tried to argue elsewhere, is to look to contestatory institutions that

[7] Why not resort to referenda in greater measure, making democracy more and more plebiscitary? Apart from considerations of feasibility, an important argument against allowing the electorate as a whole to dictate policy is that even well-informed, rational electors can make judgements on public policy that aggregate, under majoritiarian arrangements, into inconsistent judgements and policies. The point is made in Pettit (2003), drawing on the impossibility result in List and Pettit (2002).

can allow minorities to challenge majoritarian proposals on the ground of not answering to genuinely common interests, and allow the public as a whole to challenge the objectionably sectarian forms that even public-interest measures can take in the backrooms of special interest and in the corridors of power.

I see contestatory institutions as being democratic in character so far as they serve like electoral institutions, to empower members of the public – in particular, to give power to the interests that they countenance in common as citizens. Those contestatory institutions come in two forms, depending on whether they facilitate or forestall contestation, and both are represented in most regimes that we would be happy to count as democracies.

Facilitating institutions allow contestations to be brought against government decisions in contexts where, ideally, the majoritarian or elitist pressures that may originally have caused a problem are absent or reduced. In extant democracies, the facilitating institutions will include courts of law, administrative appeals tribunals and ombudsman arrangements, as well as those arrangements whereby rights of parliamentary appeal and public demonstration are protected or even facilitated.

Forestalling institutions are those arrangements that serve to reduce likely contestatory burdens without undermining the rationale for contestation. They will include constitutional provisions whereby it is made difficult for government to legislate in potentially contestable ways. They will include depoliticizing measures whereby government decisions are put at arm's length from elected officials; these will be useful in areas where decisions might be influenced by short-term electoral considerations – say, in determining interest rates or electoral boundaries – rather than by the long-term public interest. And they will include consultative measures that require government to consult public opinion, soliciting the reactions of different groups, before going ahead with various legislative or administrative reforms.

I do not suggest that the contestatory institutions reviewed, whether facilitating or forestalling in character, always work well in existing democracies. Their influence is frequently damped or warped so that they may do little good, or even do more harm than good. But in principle I think that something along the lines of those institutions is needed in order to complement the role of electoral institutions and ensure that false positives are not a major problem.

This is not the context to look at ways in which the institutions of an electoral-contestatory democracy can be improved in order to facilitate the systematic identification and empowerment of public interests, as they are conceived in this chapter. In any case, such an examination would require the resources, not just of philosophical analysis and theory, but also of empirical modelling and investigation. But I hope I have said enough to make it plausible that the task of identifying the public interest in the ordinary practice of politics is not necessarily an impossible one.

Conclusion

I looked in the first section at the most plausible way of construing the common good, arguing that it should be identified with the common interests that people have as citizens – with public interests – not with the avowable net interests that they have in common; this construal promises to save the republican axiom linking non-arbitrary government with government in the name of the common good. But government in the name of the public interest will mean nothing unless we can give a theoretical account of what constitutes the public interest and unless we can point towards political institutions that might serve to identify and empower the public interest in practice. I argued in the second section of the chapter that the public interest should be identified with those measures – those practices and policies – that by publicly admissible criteria answer better than feasible alternatives to publicly admissible considerations. And then I argued in the final section that the institutions of an electoral-contestatory democracy hold out the prospect that the public interest, so conceived, can rule in the political life of a society. That prospect needs a lot of further scrutiny but I hope enough has been said to show that it need not be an illusion.

10 Individual choice and social exclusion

Julian Le Grand

Why is social exclusion a problem? Why should we care about an individual 'who does not participate in key activities of the society in which he or she lives' – one definition of the socially excluded (Burchardt, Le Grand and Piachaud 2002: 30)? Does our concern arise from some kind of simple utilitarian or welfarist calculus: the excluded are miserable, and therefore we need to include them in society so as raise their welfare and thereby promote the greatest happiness for the greatest number? But what if the socially excluded are not in fact miserable? After all, not everyone necessarily wishes to participate in the 'key activities of society', whatever these may be. In particular, what if an individual or a group of individuals have voluntarily chosen to exclude themselves? What of the recluse who prefers solitude to human company, the religious sect that values its exclusivity, the young men on a run-down public housing estate who prefer to join a criminal gang rather than go to university? At the other end of the social scale, what of the rich who lock themselves away in gated communities? All of these individuals and groups may not be participating in the key activities of society; but do they all constitute a social problem? If so, is it the same kind of social problem as those who are socially excluded for reasons beyond their control, and what kind of problem is that?

Brian Barry has addressed some of these questions in an important recent paper (Barry 2002a). In doing so, he related social exclusion to two issues of direct interest for this book: justice and democracy. But the questions are also of more general concern. The problem of the relationship between choice, poverty and social exclusion has bedevilled academic political and popular debate on the issue for (literally) millennia. As far back as the Roman Empire politicians and policy-makers have wanted to distinguish between the 'undeserving poor' (those poor from choice) from the 'deserving' poor (those who are poor through no fault of their own). With the current resurgence of belief in individual agency and responsibility (Deacon and Mann 1999), the political interest in attaching notions of responsibilities to rights, and the contributions of Amartya Sen (1994; 1995) and others emphasizing the importance of the distribution of 'capabilities' rather than actual incomes, the debate concerning the importance of choice and its relationship to distributional outcomes has re-ignited.

So in this chapter I want to pursue the general question as to the relationship between individual choice and social exclusion, and in doing so to shed light on the question as to why social exclusion is a problem worthy of concern. I begin with Barry's arguments as to why social exclusion is wrong from the points of view of justice and democracy, and relate these to the question of choice. I conclude that these arguments do not provide a strong argument for treating voluntary social exclusion as a problem. I then demonstrate that, perhaps surprisingly, a better case can be made on welfarist grounds for viewing some forms of voluntary social exclusion as a proper subject of social concern, especially that with long-term implications for individuals' futures. There is a brief concluding section.

Exclusion, democracy and justice

Brian Barry begins his discussion of why social exclusion is wrong with a definition of social exclusion originally put forward by the present author, as follows: 'An individual is socially excluded if (a) he or she is geographically resident in a society, (b) he or she cannot participate in the normal activities of citizens in that society, and (c) he or she would like to so participate, but is prevented from doing so by factors beyond his or her control' (Burchardt, Le Grand and Piachaud 1999: 229). Under this interpretation, voluntary social exclusion is excluded (so to speak), because of condition (c). Barry accepts this definition; but he also points out that it is important to distinguish conceptually between voluntary and involuntary social exclusion, and draws out the implications for both types of social exclusion in his subsequent argument.

Barry puts forward two reasons why social exclusion is wrong. The first is because exclusion dilutes social solidarity, defined by Barry as a sense of fellow feeling that extends beyond people with whom one is in personal contact. Social exclusionary processes do this because they prevent the excluded from sharing in the commonality of experience that is the foundation of social solidarity. And this in turn is a bad thing, partly because social solidarity is 'intrinsically valuable', and partly because an absence of social solidarity creates a problem for democratic politics. It is intrinsically valuable because 'human lives tend to go better in a society whose members share some kind of existence' (Barry 2002a: 24).[1] It affects democratic politics, because in democratic societies, majority interests dominate. In a society without social solidarity, there is no reason to suppose those interests will coincide with those of the socially excluded; indeed, depending on the reason for the exclusion, the interests of the majority and the excluded are likely to diverge. Hence, democratic procedures will result in majorities having both the means and – due to the absence of solidarity – the inclination to oppress socially excluded minorities.

However, in Barry's view, social exclusion is not only wrong because it violates social solidarity and thereby harms democracy. It is also unjust. The injustice arises because social exclusion can create inequality of opportunity, especially with respect to education and work. Obviously, the poverty associated with most forms of social exclusion creates educational barriers: hunger and malnutrition, crowded conditions at home, family pressures to go out and earn money, all make it difficult for children in poor families to make the most of their educational opportunities. But also the social homogeneity of socially excluded communities creates educational problems of its own. So, for instance, children going to local schools with a large number of pupils in socially deprived neighbourhoods will, other things being equal, perform less well than if they had attended schools with a critical mass of middle class pupils.

The problem is not only one of education. To live in social isolation or to live in a socially isolated group cuts the individual concerned off from the networks that are often key to obtaining jobs. Barry (2002a: 20) quotes William Julius Wilson (1987) on inner city isolation, which 'makes it much more difficult for those who are looking for jobs to be tied into the job network': a phenomenon that, as Barry points out, is not confined to the inner city. Further, the lack of job opportunities itself depresses educational aspirations, thus contributing further to inequalities in educational opportunity.

Barry also argues that a further aspect of injustice created by social exclusion concerns political opportunities and hence the workings of democracy. As with education, the deprivation associated with social exclusion can impede people's ability to engage in political activities. And, as with jobs, the absence of contacts with social networks significantly impedes both their knowledge of, and their participation in, politics outside election times. All of this damages democracy.

[1] Actually, this sounds more like a consequentialist justification for social solidarity (and a utilitarian one at that) than an 'intrinsic' one; but let that pass.

This emphasis on social justice as equality of opportunity is very welcome to those of us who have argued for some time that social injustice or inequity was best interpreted in terms of inequalities in opportunities or choice sets (Le Grand 1984; 1991; Arneson 1989; G.A. Cohen 1989). However, its use in the context of the justification for treating social exclusion as a problem does itself create a difficulty for voluntary social exclusion, for it implies that those who voluntarily exclude themselves are not a social problem. Thus the individual who makes a conscious, properly informed decision not to go to university or to take up a training opportunity, and in consequence ends up unemployed and living on a run-down public housing estate, may be socially excluded. But his or her exclusion is not socially problematic because, as a consequence of his or her own choices, it is not unjust.

Barry is aware of this issue, and indeed draws attention to it (Barry 2002a: 23). He argues that it does not apply to the second pillar of his justificatory edifice: the appeal to social solidarity. For solidarity is clearly violated by social exclusion; whether the exclusion is voluntary or involuntary is irrelevant. However, it has to be said that, even here, the possibility of individual choice presents a problem; for if some individuals have voluntarily decided to exclude themselves from society, any move to include them is going to be against their expressed will. Hence, such moves are likely to involve a measure of coercion; and that is unlikely to foster feelings in the people concerned of social solidarity.

So the possibility that individuals may choose to exclude themselves from normal society creates problems for Barry's two justifications for the overall undesirability of social exclusion. Voluntary social exclusion is not unjust or inequitable, because it arises from choice. And, although voluntary exclusion may indeed violate social solidarity, any attempt to correct the situation is likely to create resentment and thereby dilute solidarity yet further.

Choice and welfare

So if Barry's arguments for the undesirability of social exclusion based on the concerns of social justice and social solidarity do not apply to voluntary exclusion, can any justification for regarding exclusion by choice as problematic be found elsewhere? One possibility is a 'welfarist' one: that is, the impact of social exclusion on the welfare of individuals. Now, it might at first seem curious to consider welfarism as a possible source of such justification; for individuals who choose to exclude themselves are presumably doing it because they want to. Hence, their welfare is raised by voluntary social exclusion and so such exclusion cannot be a problem from a welfarist perspective.

However, there are a number of situations where these arguments might not hold, and indeed where the opposite case could be made. The most obvious of these is what we might term 'externalities': when the act of voluntary social exclusion, although increasing the chooser's own welfare, damages other people's welfare. An example would be young men joining a gang that engaged in crime, vandalism or other anti-social activities. Another might be the wealthy locking themselves away in gated estates, thereby physically depriving others of what could be communal facilities and creating resentment in the rest of the community. Indeed, Barry's appeal to social solidarity could also be justified on externality grounds: if social solidarity contributes to everyone's welfare, then for some people to opt out diminishes that welfare.

It is worth noting that those rather closer to the actual experience of social exclusion than most academics can share this view that exclusion has an externality effect. An in-depth study of the views of thirty residents of poor public housing estates found that these residents felt that any person experiencing exclusion (whether they have had a hand in it or not) also caused wider society a problem in terms of the threat such divisions pose to social solidarity. While the group distinguished between the voluntary withdrawal by better off individuals and the voluntary social exclusion of people facing disadvantage, such as through benefit fraud or criminal activity, they were critical of both types of divisive outcome (Richardson and Le Grand 2002).

So there is a welfarist case for regarding even voluntary social exclusion as undesirable because of the externality effect. But there are also cases where voluntary acts may not necessarily increase the welfare of the individual making the choice him or herself. Barry himself deals with one case where we might observe an apparently voluntary act of self-exclusion but nonetheless regard it as neither furthering the individual's own welfare nor, of more concern to his argument, social justice. This is when the opportunity or choice set is small or when the alternatives it contains are pretty meagre. If an individual only has two unpalatable choices ('your money or your life') and if he or she chooses one of them (such as giving up the money), it would be odd to judge the outcome as promoting individual welfare or even a just one simply because it was the product of a choice. Likewise, if a young black man from a public housing estate encounters hostility and discrimination whenever he ventures into white society, and decides to withdraw from that society and its institutions by, for instance, refusing an opportunity to go to university, it would be hard to describe this as welfare-enhancing or as socially just, simply on the grounds that he had chosen to do it. Rather, it is in the limited size and quality of the choice set open to him that the problem lies. Social exclusion that is the result of decisions made over limited opportunities limits welfare and is also unjust – and therefore socially undesirable. In these situations, simply increasing the particular individual's choice set is likely to reduce social exclusion, increase individual welfare, promote social justice and, through rendering the opportunities open to all society's members more similar, increase social solidarity.

Similar arguments apply when decisions are made with poor information. If the university that offered the young man a place was in fact a haven of non-discrimination but he did not know this, then again it would be hard to describe his situation as welfare-promoting or just. Or, to take a broader case, if some individuals chose not to go to university because they did not know about the likely extra income that they could earn over their lifetimes if they went, then again it is hard to hold them responsible for their decisions. Acts of 'voluntary' social exclusion that result from choice sets that are either small or accompanied by poor information cannot be justified by reference either to social welfare or to social justice.

The public housing residents whose views on social exclusion were explored in the study mentioned above agreed with this view. For instance, those who chose to join a youth gang: 'may not be happy [really] they are bolstering each other – it's mutual support for hardships'. Therefore, such participation cannot be considered an equivalent alternative for participation in mainstream society (Richardson and Le Grand 2002: 500).

More difficult cases arise when properly informed individuals with reasonably-sized choice sets make voluntary decisions. Are there reasons for, in some circumstances, not accepting that the individual concerned is happier as a result of those decisions? Is it possible that, even if properly informed individuals judge themselves to be happier living outside the wider society, both they and society would actually be better off if they were brought inside?

Bill New (1999) has identified four possible cases where we might make such a judgement.[2] The first is where there is a technical inability to complete the necessary mental tasks. This inability could arise because the quantity of information is simply too great, relative to mental capacity, or because the technological or causal connections are too difficult to make, again relative to capacity. This appears to be a special problem with respect to long-term decision-making. For this involves assessing the probabilities of benefit or harm from alternative courses of action. And

[2] For a critique of New, see Calcott (2000). For further discussion of individual failure in different contexts, see Le Grand (2003: chs 5 and 6).

experimental evidence suggests that individuals often find it difficult to make rational decisions where weighing up probabilities are concerned (Tversky and Kahneman 1982).

A second source of individual failure identified by New is weakness of the will. This is where individuals know what they prefer in the long term but still make short-term decisions that are not in their long-term interest. Addiction, and more generally substance misuse (a major cause of social exclusion), could be considered an example of this.[3]

A third source of individual failure is emotional decision-making. Becoming attached to certain choices allows emotions to distort decisions. This might arise because of a strong attachment to a particular outcome even though one knows that it is very unlikely to occur; or the decision may be made in a period of stress, such as that following bereavement.

The fourth problem raised by New concerns the relationship between preference and experience. Preference over a set of decisions might be different if the individual had actual experience (as distinct from abstract knowledge or information) of the outcomes of the decision concerned from that if he or she had no such experience. But some experiences it is largely or wholly impossible to repeat. Thus, the decision whether to go to university or not might be different if it were possible for the individual concerned actually to have the experience of having been to university before the decision was taken; but this is not a feasible option. At first sight, this resembles the poor information concern discussed above. But it is not quite the same; for, unlike in the cases considered in that context, no system can supply the relevant information prior to the decision being taken.

How do these potential 'individual failures' (so-called so as to distinguish them from market or other types of system failure) affect the voluntary decision to self-exclude? This will clearly depend upon the situation and the individuals concerned. However, there is an important generalization that can be made. This is that these 'failures' are more likely to be a problem when major decisions with long-term implications are concerned, than when more minor decisions that only have short-term consequences are involved. In part, this is simply a matter of scale: the potential damage done by a mistake in making a big decision that affects one's whole future (such as whether or not to go to university) is obviously greater than that from a mistake involving a smaller short-term decision

[3] The phenomenon of addiction obviously presents problems for any analysis of the status of individual choice. Again, the public housing residents have interesting views on this: they argued that initially the people concerned could be said to be excluding themselves partly out of choice, but after they become addicted, the exclusion/problems they face are more beyond their control (Richardson and Le Grand 2002: 502).

(such as whether to go to an isolated retreat for a week). But also, some of the individual failures above are more likely to involve long-term decision-making. So, for instance, technical incapacity is more problematic when long-term decision-making involving the weighing up of probabilities is concerned; and weakness of the will frequently manifests itself as a way of prioritizing of short-term interests over long-term ones.

Failures in major long-term decision-making may result from another problem: that of myopia. Individuals may make wrong decisions about self-exclusion, because they are too short-sighted to take proper account of the future. Myopia is a common phenomenon. Individuals' time-horizons are limited. They do not always consider the long term; they plan only on the basis of current events, or on their predictions of the very immediate future. In a word, they are myopic.

Now, although this sounds like another form of individual failure, it is actually somewhat different. Here some of the arguments of Derek Parfit (1984) concerning the nature of personal identity have relevance. Parfit's arguments about identity run something like this. We normally invoke the concept of personal identity to link a person in one time period with the 'same' person in another, later period. But what does the concept of personal identity actually mean? It presumably does *not* mean what a possible literal interpretation of the words in the phrase 'personal identity' would mean: that is, the person in the first time period is identical in every respect to the person in the second. The person will have aged physically; external factors (such as income or family status) may have changed; tastes may have changed; aspects of personality may have changed. The extent and magnitude of these changes may be small if the distance between the time periods is small, but they are likely to increase with that distance: compare the physique, income, personal relations, and personality of an eight-year-old with that of the 'same' person eighty years later.

So if it does not mean actual identity, what does personal identity mean? Parfit's answer is a reductionist one: that is, the 'fact' of personal identity can be reduced to some other facts that can be described without using the concept of personal identity. These facts, according to Parfit, are links of a psychological kind, principally those of intention and memory. For instance, a twenty-year-old will have memories of her nineteen-year-old self; and certain features of her current existence will depend on the intentions and actions of that nineteen-year-old. These links are, according to Parfit, what makes the twenty and nineteen-year-old the 'same' person. Similar phenomena would link the eight and eighty-eight-year-old mentioned above; but here the phenomena (and therefore the links) would be much attenuated. Hence, any argument that was based on the continuity of the self would be much weaker for the eighty-year gap than for the one-year gap.

What are the implications of this for the myopia argument? Simply, that a certain degree of myopia may not be 'individual failure'. If people are related to their future selves by links that become progressively attenuated the more distant the future, then it seems quite rational to give those future selves less weight than their present selves. There is no individual failure in the sense of irrational decision-making.

But this in turn means that there *is* a justification for treating long-term decision-making as a social problem. For there is a group of people who have no say in such decisions but who are affected by those who make them: there is an externality. An individual's future self is a person who is directly affected by that individual's current decisions in the marketplace. A sixty-five-year-old may be poor because of myopic decisions taken by her twenty-five-year-old self. Hence, the twenty-five-year-old is imposing costs on the sixty-five-year-old through her decisions; but the sixty-five-year-old has no say in those decisions. There is an externality.

An individual's future self is, of course, someone with whom her current self is linked. But the link is not as strong as that to her present self. Hence, in taking those current decisions she will not give appropriate weight to the interests of her future self, in a similar fashion as if her future self was actually a different person. More specifically, because she is not giving her future self the same weight as that future self would if the latter were present at the point of decision, she will undertake actions relating to the balance of interests between present and future self that are not 'optimal'.

Conclusion

What are the implications of all of this for voluntary social exclusion and the extent to which this is a social problem? It suggests two things. First, voluntary social exclusion may be a problem if we believe there to be a significant degree of individual failure and/or of externality in making the relevant decisions. Second, the problem is more likely to occur with respect to decisions involving voluntary social exclusion that have implications for the long-term future of the individual concerned. For it is here that both individual failure and the myopia externality are more likely.

Of course, one cannot deduce from this directly that government intervention is necessarily required to correct this problem. For there is no guarantee that such intervention will make things better. But that will have to be the subject of another paper.

11 Subnational groups and globalization

Russell Hardin

Far too much of the concern with subnational groups, either long established (and even indigenous) or recently immigrated, is with abstract principles of justice. Far too little of it is about making societies work at all well to give prosperity to everyone and to do so through democratic procedures. Many of the ostensible principles of justice erect barriers between various groups, minority and majority. Assimilationist arguments, pro and con, typically assume assimilation of the minority or new group into the majority or established group. American, Canadian and Australian experience during the twentieth century clearly shows that assimilation goes both ways. Those from Northern European backgrounds in these nations have substantially assimilated with the newly arriving groups of Asians, Latinos and others. There is a substantial shortfall in the assimilation in both directions of blacks in the USA and of indigenous peoples in all three of the former colonial outposts.

Brian Barry (2001) is among the few writers who have forcefully taken on these issues with a main eye out for the workability of contemporary societies, especially liberal societies. It would be easy to read him as merely aggressively supporting liberalism over all-comers. But one of his main concerns is with making the societies he addresses reasonably good places. I wish to take up this problem as it is affected by the massive movement of globalization of the past few decades, a movement that is still on the rise.

It is a seeming anomaly of our time that, just when economic progress seems to work well for remarkably many nations and when advanced nations are increasingly part of a global economy, demands for autonomy of numerous ethnic groups are shrill. There are numerous explanations for the explosion of ethnic conflicts, most of which seem to focus on claims that peoples are motivated by values or group identity. Some argue that globalization, with its supposed imposition of world – or

I wish to thank Casiano Hacker-Cordon, Carolina Curvale, and Huan Wang for their efforts to make this chapter happen and for research assistance.

Western – standards on many nations, stimulates a reaction against uniformity, against the West. Ethnic movements, however, seem to be quite diverse in origin and apparent intent. Indeed, they are at least as diverse as the historical range of nationalist movements.

Except for international radical Islam, most cultural groups appear to focus their hostility on neighbouring or intermingled groups, not on the supposedly hegemonic West. Globalization frees subnational groups from economic dependence on their larger nations while perversely making it less relevant that they gain independence. Indeed, independence is likely to be costly to the individual members of a society because it is apt to focus on issues of linguistic, cultural and religious control of the polity rather than on economic development. It is the perversity of religious and other conflictual issues in the larger societies of which such groups are a part that the groups want autonomy. But globalization pushes nations either to opt out of the global economy or to focus politically on economic opportunities and integration into the larger world economy. Globalizing deflects their attention from social issues that are exacerbated by economic conflict that, without development and growth, is virtually zero-sum. For example, the dreadful conflicts in Burundi and Rwanda are essentially based on zero-sum conflicts over resources, especially the resource of government employment, that can be used to benefit one group over another.

I begin with a thumbnail sketch of nationalism and its origins and later variants and compare these to the commonplace nationalism that is essentially subnationalism in our time. The subnational groups of interest are those that are internally defined; that is, they define themselves as a distinct group. Some of the groups might also be externally defined by others to their detriment, as was true for African-Americans in the days of Jim Crow legal discrimination. But the concern here is with groups that want some degree of group decision over their common fate – a kind of subgroup autonomy in a sense akin to national sovereignty. Nationalism is a political issue only if it is intentionalist for at least many of the relevant group. A national group is, indeed, an imagined community (Anderson 1991). At the extreme, a group may want to be autonomous and to have its own state. In Hugh Seton-Watson's loose definition, there is such a group when 'a significant number of people in a community consider themselves to form a nation, or behave as if they formed one' (Tamir 1993: 65). Unfortunately, this is very loose, because there are few clear indicators of such a desire unless there is a referendum or a very broad struggle. The activities of a small band, such as the Irish Republican Army, is not sufficient evidence to qualify the Catholic population of Northern Ireland as a nation in this sense, although that population might be.[1]

It is sometimes supposed that the political and national or cultural unit should be congruent (Hobsbawm 1990: 9). The USA, France and Italy, among others, attempted to bring about such congruence by making Americans, Frenchmen and Italians out of varied stocks within the national boundaries of these political states. Later movements, and especially many of the contemporary subnationalist movements, strive to make a political unit that matches some supposedly already extant cultural or national unit. In part, this has been the programme since Woodrow Wilson's proposal for self-determination of former colonial peoples after the First World War. In the earlier cases, the view was that it is the state that makes the nation, as Colonel Pilsudski said of Poland. As Massimo d'Azeglio proclaimed upon the success of the Risorgimento, 'We have made Italy; now we have to make Italians' (Hobsbawn 1990: 44). In the later view from Wilson forward, it is the nation that should make the state, as in the programmes of many subnationalist movements. The early movements for nationalism were inclusive; the later movements have more commonly been exclusive. Indeed, later national movements have, because of the exigencies of geography, sometimes encompassed groups that were not welcome as citizens of the new nation.

Original nationalisms and contemporary subnationalisms

In an earlier age in Europe, the idea of the nation was associated with monarchical families, not with peoples. The French nation 'resided wholly in the person of the King.' International relations were relations between kings and princes. The doctrine of sovereignty, which often seems confused today, makes sense as a reference to the sovereign monarch. International law was a set of rules governing relations of rulers and a treaty was a contract between sovereigns that was based on personal good faith. Economic policy was commonly mercantilist because its purpose was to augment the power of the state, because the interest of the nation was identified with the interest of its ruler. There was a common misconception of trade as a zero-sum matter; our trade could increase only if yours decreased. Hence, rulers fought over markets (Carr 1945: 2–6; Morris 2000).

[1] There have been an estimated 500–600 active IRA members in Northern Ireland (Taylor 1999: 363).

With the rise of industrialism in England and of large-scale international war in the era of Napoleon, states needed people as workers and soldiers. Napoleon was therefore the first advocate and missionary of popular nationalism. Ernest Gellner's (1987) theory of nationalism is about nationalism during a stage of expansive economic development in England and then in the USA, France, Germany and Italy. Gellner supposed that the core of all of these was the need for a national language to make factories work (especially in England) or to make armies more effective (especially in France). His argument for England is that nationalism was a more or less unintended by-product of the industrial revolution and the creation of a factory workforce.

Gellner's explanation is functional in the following sense. *An institution or a behavioural pattern X is explained by its function F for group* G if and only if:

1. F is an *effect* of X;
2. F is *beneficial* for G;
3. F maintains X by a causal *feedback* loop passing through G.

The pattern X is linguistic homogenization; its function F is productivity for the society under industrialism; G is the industrial society (or the society moving toward industrialization).

1. Now productivity (F) is an effect of homogenization (X), that is, productivity is enhanced by homogenization.
2. Productivity (F) is good for the members of the society (G).
3. Productivity (F) maintains homogenization (X) by a feedback loop passing through the members of the society (G). This happens because firms seek interchangeable, same-language speaking workers or because workers become same-language speakers on the job.

Hence, Gellner's theory is functional (Elster 1979: 28; Hardin 1980; Hardin 1995: 82–6).[2]

In creating Englishmen and women to fit into the industrial organization of the economy, England created the very possibility of nationalism. The industrial economy sparked and seemingly required growth, which entails constant innovation, which requires mobility, which, in the limit, requires a national language and universal literacy. The result for the individual is to bend one's culture into the national mould. The idiom in which one is trained and within which one is effectively employable is one's ticket to full citizenship and social and political participation.

[2] There is still a seemingly bad (or at least unpacked) functionalist argument in Gellner's claim that the decline of religion contributes to the growth of reverence for the nation (Gellner 1987: 16).

As Gellner (1987: 16) says, culture 'becomes visible' and the 'age of nationalism is born'. Old cultures, if they survive, take on a new, literate underpinning.

The industrial state was virtually required for early nationalism, because it created a far more nearly homogeneous culture. Agrarian societies, with their relative stability and immobility, allow for great cultural and even linguistic diversity. It is the growth of the industrial economy within a state that forced cultural homogeneity and made nationalism plausible. In this account, if industrialism ever starts, it is likely to take off – and nationalism with it. Hence, although it is perhaps correct to say, as Benedict Anderson (1991: 6) does, that nationalism is in a category with kinship and religion rather than with liberalism or fascism, still, nationalism originated in and was fed by liberal, capitalist societies.

Gellner's theory is of the rise of nationalism, even the unintentional rise. In Jon Elster's (1979: 28) view, a functional explanation requires that the nature of the feedback relationship should not be recognized by members of the group that benefits from the functional feedback. But once the idea of nationalism is available and is understood, it can be used, even intentionally. Hence, follower nations or their potential leaders can deliberately seek to make the functional feedback account fit, as was done in Italy, France and Germany. For example, in the latter part of the nineteenth century the national French government successfully replaced a large number of regional languages and dialects with French (Weber 1979). To do this required national control of the schools, widespread education and a couple of generations. The government of France therefore deliberately achieved linguistic homogenization while England had achieved it to some (lesser) degree without deliberate intent. Moreover, the French government pushed for linguistic homogenization for functional reasons, especially for military service, while in the USA arguably it simply happened as polyglot immigrant languages faded from use.

Once productivity is high, we might expect some people could be persuaded that other values now matter enough to trump slight advantages in productivity, as, for example, in the Basque, Welsh, Lombard and other contemporary cases. For successful national *leaders* of these groups, economic benefits of separatism trump those of remaining in a larger nation, although it might be hard to show whether the typical citizen benefits or loses from separation. These leaders in some cases deliberately struggle to reinforce or even reintroduce the languages of various ethnic minorities in order to heighten commitments to the subnational groups.

In the European separatist movements of today, some of the people who are affected are hampered by drawing the boundaries of culture more narrowly while others are made more comfortable. For example, in the very close 50–50 split in a vote on some degree of Welsh autonomy within the United Kingdom,[3] many English-speaking Welsh evidently were bothered by the possibility that an autonomous government would impose the Welsh language on non-Welsh speaking citizens of Wales.

Hence, we might want a theory, such as Gellner's, of the discovery and happenstance creation of nationalism, and also a theory of how nationalism can be put to use. The early nationalisms served the goal of economic advancement and military effectiveness in national defence. Contemporary subnationalisms are very different. Such nationalisms serve the goal of separating groups from their larger nations. They probably often also serve the goal of giving certain nationalist entrepreneurs political offices and power, as in the careers of Franjo Tudjman and Slobodan Milosevic, who led the break-up of Yugoslavia.

Again, the original nationalisms of England, France, Germany, Italy and the USA were programmes for creating a national group or identity, either spontaneously or intentionally. Contemporary nationalism is typically a programme of *internally* defined groups who – or whose leaders – insist on autonomy or separate nationhood for the group. That is, they are defined by membership *ex ante*.

There are two quite different general visions of nationalism. One supposes that there is a transcendental 'right' of a group to enforce its own norms. The other supposes that there is an individual right to participate in a particular culture. Some of the early literature is cast at the group level and is of no interest here. In much of the more recent literature, *including most of the critical literature*, arguments for justification are cast at the individual level. Most of the critical literature is essentially liberal in the individualist liberal tradition. Hence, there is a relatively recent programme of liberal nationalism or group liberalism, which combines the liberal tradition of personal autonomy, reflection and choice with the national tradition of belonging, loyalty and solidarity (Tamir 1993: 6).

In some ways, however, the term liberal nationalism is incoherent. Liberalism has generally been about freeing individuals from various constraints, especially the constraints of government. The group rights implicit in a programme of liberal nationalism must almost always constrain individual members of the group that is being protected. Yael Tamir (1993: 4) therefore takes liberalism as prior, so that her project is to justify nationalist principles as fitted with liberalism, and she does not defend any nationalism that suppresses individuals.

[3] Just 51.3 per cent of the electorate voted and just 50.3 per cent of these voted for devolution: *The Economist*, 27 September 1997, 62.

For example, consider the protection of an immigrant group's use of its language in its dealings with government and in the education of its children. In the USA, such protection probably makes the first generation speakers of Spanish, Korean or Vietnamese better off. But it might partially cripple the next generation because, typically, it means making sure that the next generation is educated in the minority language and plausibly made less able to assume a full role in the larger community or economy. Hence, protecting the supposed group interest requires action against the interest and incentives of some group members. At the very least, this makes group liberalism a very complex version of liberalism. It can hardly be defended either on standard welfarist or autonomy grounds. As a variant of liberalism, group liberalism is very odd in that it somehow elevates the relevant group above its members by protecting the group, commonly *against its own less than fully committed members.*

John Dewey argued in the 1930s for what he called institutional and social liberalisms. These were programmes to protect individuals from the oppressions of big, especially economic, institutions and against crippling social norms and customs (Dewey 1987; Hardin 1999a: 322–8). Group liberalism all too often must work against Dewey's social liberalism. It virtually enforces group norms and customs on group members and, especially, on the young. If the state were asked to enforce religious conformity on the children of various believers, that would clearly be a violation of all traditional senses of liberalism, and yet an analogue of such a policy is the enforcement of the mixture of religious and secular norms of a group on its members. For example, the United States has permitted the Old Order Amish of Wisconsin to enforce its beliefs and norms on future generations in *Wisconsin* v. *Yoder*.

The anthropologist Unni Wikan says that a Moroccan Muslim woman forcibly taken from Norway and married was 'sacrificed on the altar of culture' (Wikan 2000: 74). That woman was allowed by her family to return to Norway later only because she was *de facto* a visa for her forced husband (Wikan 2000: 72). Indeed, in Pakistan, marriageable girls in Norway are called visas; in Morocco they are called gold-edged papers (Wikan 2000: 73). Those who insist that culture is the source of personal autonomy face a difficult task of explaining the way in which such girls are used as a resource for the benefit of others, not as persons. That their treatment is a product of a culture does not seem to rescue it from a charge of enforced prostitution. All that it can do is elevate enforced prostitution to the status of a cultural principle.

Traditional political and economic liberalisms were directed at government intrusions, which were to be blocked. Group liberalism often requires government intrusions to make relevant things happen. It is a saving grace of the demands of the Amish, which were met in the Supreme Court's decision in *Wisconsin* v. *Yoder*, that they were to opt out of the state's provision of education. They were not asking for the state to expend resources or to use its coercive powers on behalf of the Amish, but to spare its resources in allowing Amish children to leave school at age fourteen rather than age sixteen, as was mandated by Wisconsin law.

The Amish are a subnational group that seemingly can survive on its own, just as many religions survive on their own, without substantial support from the state. Some subnational groups and practices may not be able to survive on their own. They pass, just as religious sects sometimes do. It is constitutionally prohibited for the USA to intervene either to oppose or to support a religious group as such. This constraint on the state is at the heart of the American pluralist liberal vision. One might suppose that a similar policy would be right for cultural groups as well. The state should not enforce on, for example, children of a culture that they continue in that culture. The state should allow exit from cultures just as it allows exit from religions.

Will Kymlicka argues that the Inuit of Canada have to expend resources on securing their cultural membership, while non-aboriginal Canadians get their cultural membership for free. He therefore argues that the Inuit should not only be protected through the enforcement of group rights but that they should also be subsidized to help them achieve their cultural values (Kymlicka 1989: 187; see also Tamir 1993: 146–8). For example, to maintain control over their land, they have to outbid non-aborigines just to ensure that their location-dependent cultural structure survives, and that leaves few resources to pursue any other goals (Kymlicka 1989: 189). The historical cultural values of the Inuit included virtually total autarky and subsistence hunting and gathering. Maintaining such values would require no subsidies but would entail poverty and perhaps ill health. Hence, respecting the supposed cultural values of the Inuit would drop them from the Canadian economy as well as from the effects of globalization, which would be of no concern to the Inuit leaders.

Kymlicka further argues that, in fact, it is the situation of aboriginals such as the Inuit that is relevant for understanding issues of protection of minorities in most of the world (Kymlicka 1989: 257). This claim is implausible. Canada's Inuit (1) are a tiny group (2) who are segregated from the rest of Canada, (3) who can be almost autarkic, and (4) who live where few others would want to live. Many important minority groups are not proportionately tiny and cannot be segregated, autarkic, or where others do not wish to live – as in the majority of all states to which Kymlicka refers (1989: 135). The arguments for the Inuit are essentially irrelevant to almost all other cases with the possible exception of aboriginal peoples living in the Australian desert.

To provide the Inuit with the group autonomy that Kymlicka commends could be accomplished by giving Nunavut, the new quasi-province of Canada, full autonomy as a nation completely independent of Canada. In keeping with their long history, that would make the Inuit impoverished or it would lead them to enter the world economy and, from their own incentives, leave much of their past culture behind them. Perversely, they might be able to sustain their historical culture only as a subnational Canadian group dependent on Canadian protection. In that state, they could escape poverty only through subsidies or through abandonment of their historical economic structure of hunting and gathering. But, in any case, escaping poverty is escaping their culture. That is a strange vision of group or subnational autonomy.

Tamir (1993: 146) argues that states should not disbenefit a group just because 'it holds a particular conception of the good'. She calls this principle 'causal neutrality'. It potentially runs aground on cultural practices that involve abuse of group members. This can be a very complicated issue, as is suggested by debates over the female genital mutilation that is practised in some societies (see, e.g., Okin 1999; Shweder 2000; also see Mackie 1996). She also argues for 'outcome neutrality', which rules out policies that result in disbenefit. This principle is plausibly incoherent, because every significant economic policy of a state must result in disbenefit to some. Adopting Adam Smith's market economy can penalize many of those who were doing very well under mercantilist arrangements that gave them monopoly over some provision. If a subnational group is disproportionately involved in some sector to the economy, its fate is tied to policies that affect that sector.

Democracy and nationalism

We are accustomed to thinking democratically in the context of a working democratic constitutional order in which the decisions are generally about marginal issues and are subject to easy reconsideration. For example, we vote on candidates to hold office for the next few years and we decide such issues as the level of taxation or welfare supports or the extent of regulation of some activity – and we can readily change our choices on all of these in the not very distant future.

Many contemporary nationalisms are about taking a whole population in a dramatically different way and then keeping it that way for the indefinite future. Mere democratic majorities may decide such questions. But we should not jump from the fact of such a decision to the conclusion that the relevant nationalist sentiment is definitive for the whole population. In several recent examples (the Welsh vote on devolution, the Quebec vote on autonomy, and the suspended Algerian election of a fundamentalist Islamic regime) the margins of support for a nationalist vision were virtually within the margin of error in democratic counting of votes – and well within the margin of error for Florida. In American elections, 60 per cent is a landslide, but there are still 40 per cent left out of the decision even in such a landslide.

This nationalist vision often involves a fallacy of composition in the meaning of self-determination. The argument for national autonomy is that individuals of a group require collective arrangements of some kind to make the lives of all of them better in some sense. This can be a coherent vision only if all wish simply to coordinate on common purposes or values. Typically, however, even the most adamant nationalist movement has commitment to nationalism as at best a major or foremost goal, not as the only social goal of those who share the nationalist vision. And even the most encompassing of nationalist movements often leaves out cosmopolitans, such as those Irish who are part of the larger economic and other culture of greater Great Britain, or those Algerians, often secular, who are part of the larger French society, in which they formerly might have been citizens.

Once in place, a government has other causal implications that go far beyond mere nationalist coordination. Many people in the twentieth century may have strongly supported the creation of nationalist, fascist and socialist regimes, which then went on to be among the most oppressive governments ever known. Soviet suppression of the arts and dictatorial determination of biological theory, for example, were not entailed by socialism. But strong government was, and such government effectively had licence to do many things other than pursue socialist economic policy. After a burst of remarkable creativity in the 1920s, the Soviet regime, by then under Stalin's rule, was brutal in its attack on the arts (Berlin 2000) and, under Lysenko, on biological science. While Stalin demonstrably had talent for gaining power, he just as demonstrably lacked the intellect to judge the arts or sciences (and, one might add, economics). The commonplace egotism of autocratic rulers that they should decide all such things gives depressing meaning to the claim that absolute power corrupts absolutely.

Finally, even in the best of cases of a group's having some control over its members' choices, there are likely to be severe intergenerational issues, as in the case of *Wisconsin* v. *Yoder*, in which present adults determine what choices their children will even be capable of making.

Towards autonomy and nationhood

There are at least three classes of reasons for seeking group autonomy or separate nationhood:

(1) satisfaction of interests that the group's members have in the ordinary kinds of policy that more or less all persons have interests in;
(2) self-expression of a group or protection of its racial, linguistic, religious or other purity;
(3) capacity to participate reasonably fully in politics, as in the case of some linguistic groups (this is essentially a concern grounded in the nature of democracy).

The first of these reasons makes sense in many contexts because, as minorities, many groups are excluded from, or at least disadvantaged in, the quest for the benefits of national organization of economic rewards. The civil rights movement in the USA was directed at getting equal political treatment and equal economic opportunity for blacks. The programme was merely to gain the status of white citizens. Use of a constitutional, liberal nation state may be the most workable device for achieving welfare even for a minority group. Indeed, the age of liberal individualism has also been the age of nationalism, because liberal practices have required states for their realization (Tamir 1993: 207). Furthermore, the age of ardent nationalism is a product of democracy. Such nationalism was not often an issue before the possibility of a group census vote. A liberal state might be able to take for granted the existence of subnational groups that have their own social orders in many respects, so that such groups are fully included in the polity and the economy. This is clearly done in the perhaps limited context of including diverse religious groups in the USA and many other nations. It would be difficult for broader aspects of cultural differences only if these are essentially illiberal or are organized in ways that block economic integration in the larger society (see further discussion below).

In roughly similar conditions, some groups seek greater independence within their states. By gaining autonomy, such groups might then finally at least participate more fully in the economy and the polity not as individuals but as corporate groups. Note how different seeking group autonomy is from the nationalism of industrializing England. In the latter case, nationalist moves (many of them spontaneous rather than matters of policy or political choice) created individual opportunities to participate more fully in the developing economy and, at the same time, increased the prospects for development by giving that economy a broader base. Increasing the economic base required *inclusion of groups*.

The second reason for seeking autonomy – self-expression of a group or protection of its racial, linguistic, religious or other purity – fits President Wilson's vision of nations at the end of the First World War. This was a vision of homogeneous groups that could be given their own states through self-determination. It is odd that this citizen of a culturally diverse and not at all homogeneous society with its own remarkably successful state put forth such a programme, as though its tenets were a matter of logic. The implicit assumption of his programme was that such groups could not prosper without their own states. If prospering requires cultural stagnation without change, then perhaps separate states were necessary. But even with separate states, the benefits of economic participation in the world economy in our time make the seeming isolation of such groups into independent states virtually impossible without severe economic costs that would be visible to their peoples. The lesson of virtually all of the most prosperous societies in the twentieth century is that homogeneity is not necessary for economic life and may be harmful to the autonomy of individuals who might enjoy dealing with diverse others.

For a subnational group to seek autonomy is arguably contrary to the mere demand for equal treatment. It is, as Tamir (1993: 71) says, likely to be a yearning not for freedom or civil liberties, but for status. But autonomy that includes economic organization, as in the case of the Amish in the USA, may entail economic losses from reducing the base and hence the opportunities for beneficial exchange through division of labour and industry.

Groups that seek protection of their racial, linguistic, religious or other purity or even merely their domination of their societies are often majority groups within nations, as in the case of the majority Sinhalese of Sri Lanka or the 'Aryan' Germans of Nazi Germany. Often, however, they are minorities, such as the Amish of the USA, many native peoples of various settler states, or ethnic enclaves within larger states. Subnationalist movements, whether of minority or majority groups, typically involve exclusions of other groups in order either to keep themselves separate and pure or to control what resources there are for the relevant subnational groups.

One can imagine groups that wish to maintain their culture while their members participate fully in the economy. But many of these groups wish to have partially separate economies, as the Amish do. In such cases, their impact is contrary to what happened in the early nationalisms, which, again, were inclusive. But they impose no noteworthy direct costs on others in the larger society when they are so nearly autarkic, so that their choice of self-abnegation costs only themselves and not others. However, if they receive subsidies to help them sustain their separate cultures, as Kymlicka and others recommend, they do impose costs on others.

Perhaps the strangest case is of groups that wish to bear costs to sustain (or revive) their culture and wish to have others share those costs. The European Union has an office to encourage the preservation and revival of ethnic languages (Tamir 1993: 152) ('Ethnic' here should read 'dying' or 'dead'). It is implausible that children of, say, South-western England wish to be forced to learn Cornish, more than a century after the language died, or that any court appointed agent on behalf of any child there would accept such a requirement on the child. But Europeans generally may be required to subsidize the teaching of a revived Cornish language and the next generations of children in Cornwall may have their prospects in the world diminished by their need to expend a great deal of their educational effort in learning that essentially useless language (useless even for speaking with their own parents at this point).

In such a programme of salvaging a very minor language, the concern with a cultural language may hamper people's participation in the world economy. As E.J. Hobsbawm (1990: 178) remarks, 'the sort of provincial middle classes who once hoped to benefit from linguistic nationalism can rarely expect more than provincial advantages from it today'. In some cases, such as in the Basque and Catalan lands of Spain, the result may be that children learn Basque or Catalan but also learn English, which will then be their currency for entry into the broader world. For previous generations there, Spanish would have been the international currency, as well as, for many, the main or only language. In many of these cases, many children of the next generations will be culturally rescued by the force of globalization, which will give them opportunities for access to the larger world. Globalization will save them from being sacrificed on the altar of culture, in particular, the altar of their parents' culture (see further, Hardin 1995: 65–70).

Finally, consider the third reason for a group's seeking some degree of autonomy within its nation. For some linguistic groups, capacity to participate reasonably fully in politics requires that the state allow the use of their language as an official language. This can be essentially a democratic rather than a nationalist demand. Major linguistic groups in India could hardly be expected to participate in orderly ways at all if they cannot have candidates for public office who campaign in the local language and government officials who can deal with locals in their language. This may be the only credible claim for why government ought, as a matter of liberal democratic principle, expend resources for a subnational group as such rather than through welfare and other programmes directed at individuals (Hardin 1999b).

Globalization and subnational groups

If globalization is genuine, its effect is to mock the earlier nationalism by including more groups in the larger world economy in order to increase its base in order to make it generally more productive to the mutual benefit of all. Globalization is the old nationalism of England and the USA writ large across the globe. Globalization does not strictly work against subnationalism, because a subnational group might participate fully in the larger economy even while gaining autonomy from its national government. But it seems typically to be true that subnationalisms today are focused not on economic issues, but rather on cultural, religious and ethnic issues. Their programmes of separation and autonomy are often inherently contrary to the openness and inclusiveness of economic development.

A subnational group might gain autonomy and then be entirely open in participating in the larger economy. This may be the future of some of the European moves for regional autonomy. But then these moves begin to seem like little more than book-keeping devices to put legislation and administration at a more nearly local level. If they are accompanied by genuine efforts to control culture and other values, they are likely to get in the way of full participation in the global economy and therefore not to be economically as beneficial for their citizens as remaining in their original nations might have been. But that just means that autonomy has little to offer while it runs the risk of diminishing economic prospects. Oddly, therefore, the globalization that finally makes it feasible for subnational groups to opt out of their 'home' nations without loss of economic opportunity also makes it less worthwhile to be autonomous.

In grimmer cases, such nations as Rwanda may be incapable of genuinely participating in the world economy. Their own economic development is very primitive. Indeed, their economies are virtually subsistence economies in which there is very little production for the market. Their economic units are like the peasants described by Marx (1963: 123–4) as so many homologous masses, like potatoes in a sack, all alike and not interacting. The contest between Hutus and Tutsis in both Burundi and Rwanda is a virtually zero-sum conflict over the basic resource of land and over the limited number of jobs in government. Because these jobs can be assigned by whichever group gains political hegemony, politics gets focused on groups and their share of these resources rather than on economic development and individuals in it. For these economies, globalization is an irrelevance. If they cannot even generate internal trade, they are unlikely to have external trade unless they have commodities that can be exploited without much need of local labour or economic institutions.

Edward Said argues that an immigrant group need no longer assimilate in its new nation because its prior world remains readily accessible with relatively cheap international travel, telephone and Internet connections. Indeed, while immigrants earlier in the twentieth century could even forget their past, today's immigrants cannot so readily forget (Tamir 1993: 86). Oddly, therefore, globalization of communications makes the maintenance of national ties after immigration possible and even, perhaps, inescapable, so that globalization may often contribute to maintaining group ties.

Concluding remarks

In some respects, globalization is merely a global version of the earlier English nationalism in response to industrialism. It is unintentional because there is no one in control. It simply happens. The question for many societies that are *de facto* participating in globalization is: how much can economy and culture be kept separate? If fast food is part of culture or an attack on culture, then they cannot be kept entirely separate, but this seems like a trivial consideration despite the volume of commentary on the issue from, especially, French sources. For some relatively undemanding cultures, there might be no deep conflict, so that economic change could happen without concomitant cultural change to fit the mostly Western globalizing forces. Some cultures fit better with a liberal market economy.

For fundamentalist cultures, such as those of the Amish and fundamentalist Islam in much of the Arabic world, Afghanistan and Pakistan, there may be enormous conflict. These societies can only lose economically if their cultures do not yield. For the Amish, this conclusion does not appear to be bothersome because their leaders apparently do not want the benefits of economic change. For some Islamic nations, their roles in international relations will suffer if they do not liberalize and open up their economies. For example, in the conflict between Palestinians and Israelis, secular Israelis are in the forefront of modern economic developments with the result that Israel has a prosperous modern economy. The ultra-orthodox Jews and many of the Palestinian Arabs, however, have stayed out of the modern economy, along with fundamentalists in many other places.

With their women suppressed and blocked from full participation in the economy, many Islamic states must finally be poorer per capita, all else equal, than states with more liberal cultures. Similarly, such subnational groups as the Amish and the ultra-orthodox Jews must be poorer per capita than are the secular citizens who dominate their societies. The ultra-orthodox Jewish males of Israel spend their years studying Talmud rather than working productively. They are a heavy drain on the national economy because they are subsidized in various ways (in keeping with the seeming recommendations of Kymlicka for such minority groups) from the wealth of more productive Israelis. Even with those subsidies, however, they still live in relative poverty.

The conflict between economics and culture is, of course, ancient. In medieval times, the Catholic Church had strictures on usury, which meant merely lending at interest, even very low rates of interest, that were a drag on economic possibilities. The rise of Jewish bankers enabled developments that might otherwise have been blocked. Similar strictures on so-called usury in Islam have spawned numerous subterfuges to enable banking at all. But the transaction costs of borrowing and lending are likely to be higher in such a system and to burden entrepreneurial efforts.

It is relatively common to suppose that globalization bulldozes cultures around the world. In many ways, however, it has heightened attention to subnational cultures that were long moribund. Its consequences for the autonomy of cultures, therefore, are multiple. Its consequences for individual autonomy seem likely to be generally beneficial. It is perhaps especially likely to affect cultures negatively through its positive effects on individuals. And the demand for cultural protection in the face of globalization seems far more to be a demand for strictures on individuals and individual actions within subnational groups than for strictures on outsiders. It is ironic that much of the concern with the supposed consequences of globalization is relatively paternalistic concern by wealthy Westerners for 'protections' of cultural groups, many of them in the Third World or otherwise still outside the main flood of the global economy, and that those protections would generally be strictures on members of those groups, strictures that the proponents of protection would adamantly refuse for themselves.

References

Ackerman, Bruce. 1980. *Social Justice in the Liberal State*. New Haven: Yale University Press.

Adair, Douglass G. 1943. *The Intellectual Origins of Jeffersonian Democracy: Republicanism, the Class Struggle and the Virtuous Farmer*. Ph.D. Thesis: Yale University.

1974. *Fame and the Founding Fathers* (T. Colbourn ed.). New York: Norton.

1998. *Fame and the Founding Fathers*. Indianapolis: Liberty Press.

Aldrich, J. 1993. Rational Choice and Turnout. *American Journal of Political Science* 37: 246–78.

Anderson, Benedict. 1991. *Imagined Communities*. London: Verso (revised edn).

Anscombe, G.E.M. 1981. War and Murder in her *Ethics, Religion and Politics: Collected Papers*, vol. 3. Minneapolis: University of Minnesota Press: 51–61.

Ansolabehere, Stephen and Snyder, James. 2000. Valence Politics and Equilibrium in Spatial Election Models. *Public Choice* 103: 327–36.

Archives Parlementaires. 1867. Série I 1787–1799, vol. I. Paris.

Aristotle. 1984. *The Politics*. (B. Jowett trans.) in Jonathan Barnes ed. *The Complete Works of Aristotle*. Princeton, NJ: Princeton University Press.

Arneson, Richard. 1989. Equality and Equality of Opportunity for Welfare. *Philosphical Studies* 56(1): 77–93.

1993. Democratic Rights at National and Workplace Levels in Copp *et al.* eds 1993: 118–48.

2001. Against Rights. *Philosophical Issues* 11, *Social Political and Legal Philosophy*, supp. to *Nous*: 172–201.

2003. Defending the Purely Instrumental Account of Democracy. *Journal of Political Philosophy* 11: 122–32.

Arrow, Kenneth J. 1963. *Social Choice and Individual Values*. New Haven, CT: Yale University Press (2nd edn).

Astell, Mary. 1706. *Reflections upon Marriage in Political Writings* (Patricia Springborg ed.). Cambridge: Cambridge University Press 1996 (3rd edn).

Austin, J.L. 1962. *Sense and Sensibilia*. Oxford: Oxford University Press.

Bachrach, P. and Baratz, M.S. 1963. Decisions and Non-Decisions: An Analytic Framework. *American Political Science Review* 57: 632–42.

Badinter, Elizabeth and Badinter, Robert. 1988. *Condorcet: Un Intellectuel en Politique*. Paris: Fayard.

Baker, Keith M. 1975. *Condorcet: From Natural Philosophy to Social Mathematics*. Chicago: Chicago University Press.

Banks, Jeff, Duggan, John and le Breton, Michel. 2002. Bounds for Mixed Strategy Equilibria and the Spatial Model of Elections. *Journal of Economic Theory* 103: 88–105.

Barber, Benjamin. 1984. *Strong Democracy: Participatory Politics for a New Age*. Berkeley, CA: University of California Press.

Barry, Brian. 1964. The Public Interest. *Proceedings of the Aristotelian Society* 38: 1–18. Reprinted in Anthony Quinton ed. *Political Philosophy*. Oxford: Oxford University Press. 1967: 112–26.

1965. *Political Argument*. London: Routledge. Reprinted University of California Press. 1990.

1970. *Sociologists, Economists and Democracy*. London: Collier-Macmillan. Reprinted University of Chicago Press. 1978.

1973. *The Liberal Theory of Justice*. Oxford: Clarendon Press.

1975. The Consociational Model and its Dangers. *European Journal of Political Research* 3: 393–412. Reprinted in Barry 1989a.

1979. Is Democracy Special? in Peter Laslett and James S. Fishkin eds *Philosophy, Politics and Society*, 5th series. Oxford: Blackwell.

1989a. *Democracy, Power and Justice*. Oxford: Clarendon Press.

1989b. *Theories of Justice: A Treatise on Social Justice*, vol. 1. London: Harvester-Wheatsheaf; Berkeley, CA: University of California Press.

1989c. Chance, Choice and Justice in his *Democracy, Power and Justice*. Oxford: Oxford University Press.

1991a. The Continuing Relevance of Socialism in his *Liberty and Justice: Essays in Political Theory 2*. Oxford: Clarendon Press.

1991b. Is Democracy Special? in his *Democracy and Power: Essays in Political Theory 1*. Oxford: Clarendon Press.

1991c. Is it Better to be Powerful or Lucky? in his *Democracy and Power: Essays in Political Theory 1*. Oxford: Clarendon Press.

1995. *Justice as Impartiality: A Treatise on Social Justice*, vol 2. Oxford: Oxford University Press.

1998. International Society from a Cosmopolitan Perspective in D.R. Mapel and T. Nardin eds *International Society: Diverse Ethical Perspectives*. Princeton, NJ: Princeton University Press.

1999. Sustainability and Intergenerational Justice in Andrew Dobson ed. *Fairness and Futurity: Essays on Environmental Sustainability and Social Justice*. Oxford: Oxford University Press.

2001. *Culture and Equality: An Egalitarian Critique of Multiculturalism*. Cambridge: Polity.

2002a. Social Exclusion, Social Isolation and the Distribution of Income in Hills, Le Grand and Piachaud, eds. 2002.

2002b. Capitalists Rule OK? Some Puzzles About Power. *Philosophy, Politics and Economics* 1: 155–84.

Barry, Brian. nd. *Wasted Votes and Other Mares' Nests: A View of Electoral Reform*. Unpublished MS.

Barry, Brian and Hardin, Russell, eds. 1982. *Rational Man and Irrational Society?* Beverley Hills, CA: Sage.

Barry, Brian and Rae, Douglas. 1975. Political Evaluation in Fred I. Greenstein and Nelson W. Polsby eds. *Political Science: Scope and Theory: Handbook of Politics*, vol 1. Reading, MA: Addison-Wesley.

Beard, Charles. 1913. *An Economic Interpretation of the Constitution of the United States*. Macmillan: New York.

1915. *Economic Consequences of Jeffersonian Democracy*. Macmillan: New York.

Beitz, Charles. 1989. *Political Equality: An Essay in Democratic Theory*. Princeton: Princeton University Press.

Benn, Stanley I. 1979. The Problematic Rationality of Political Participation in Peter Laslett and James S. Fishkin eds *Philosophy, Politics and Society*, 5th series. Oxford: Blackwell.

Bentham, Jeremy. 1823. *An Introduction to the Principles of Morals and Legislation.* London: Pickering.

Beran, Harry. 1984. A Liberal Theory of Secession. *Political Studies* 32: 21–31.

Berlin, Isaiah. 2000. The Arts in Russia under Stalin. *New York Review of Books* (19 October): 54–63.

Besley, Timothy and Case, Anne. 2003. Political Institutions and Policy Choices: Evidence from the United States. *Journal of Economic Literature*. XL: 7–73.

Billacois, F. 1986. *Le Duel dans la Société Française des XVIe–XVIIe Siècles*. Paris: Editions de l'Ecole des Hautes Etudes en Sciences Sociales.

Binmore, Ken. 1994. *Game Theory and the Social Contract I: Playing Fair.* Cambridge, MA: MIT Press.

1998. *Game Theory and the Social Contract II: Just Playing.* Cambridge, MA: MIT Press.

Black, Duncan. 1958. *The Theory of Committees and Elections*. Cambridge: Cambridge University Press.

Bohman, James. 1998. The Coming of Age of Deliberative Democracy. *Journal of Political Philosophy* 6: 399–423.

Bohman, James and Rehg, William, eds. 1997. *Deliberative Democracy: Essays on Reason and Politics*. Cambridge, MA: MIT Press.

Brecht, Bertolt. 1947. *The Caucasian Chalk Circle* (Eric Bentley trans.). New York: Grove Press.

Brennan, Geoffrey and Hamlin, Alan. 2000. *Democratic Devices and Desires*. Cambridge: Cambridge University Press.

Brennan, Geoffrey and Lomasky, Loren. 1992. *Democracy and Decision.* Cambridge: Cambridge University Press.

Brewer, John. 1976. *Party Ideology and Popular Politics at the Accession of George III.* Cambridge: Cambridge University Press.

1988. *The Sinews of Power*. Cambridge, MA: Harvard University Press.

Brighouse, Harry. 1996. Egalitarianism and Equal Availability of Political Influence. *Journal of Political Philosophy* 4: 118–41.

Broome, John. 1999. *Ethics Out of Economics*. Cambridge: Cambridge University Press.

Buchanan, Allen. 1991. *Secession: The Morality of Political Divorce from Fort Sumter to Lithuania and Quecbec*. Boulder, CO: Westview.

2002. Political Legitimacy and Democracy. *Ethics* 12: 689–719.

Buchanan, James M. 1965. An Economic Theory of Clubs. *Economica* 32: 1–14.

Buchanan, James and Tullock, Gordon. 1962. *The Calculus of Consent*. Ann Arbor: University of Michigan Press.

Burchardt, Tania, Le Grand, Julian and Piachaud, David. 1999. Social Exclusion in Britain 1991–1995. *Social Policy and Administration*. 33(3): 227–44.

2002. Degrees of Exclusion: Developing a Dynamic, Multi-dimensional Measure in Hills, Le Grand and Piachaud 2002.

Burnheim, John. 1985. *Is Democracy Possible?* Berkeley, CA: University of California Press.

Calcott, P. 2000. New on Paternalism. *Economics and Philosophy* 16: 315–21.

Camerer, C. 2003. *Behavioral Game Theory*. Princeton: Princeton University Press.

Carens, Joseph H. 1981. *Equality, Moral Incentives and the Market*. Chicago: University of Chicago Press.

Carling, Alan. 1995. The Paradox of Voting and the Theory of Social Evolution in Keith Dowding and Desmond King eds *Preferences, Institutions and Rational Choice*. Oxford: Clarendon Press: 20–42.

Caro, Robert. 2002. *The Years of Lyndon Johnson: Master of the Senate*. New York: Knopf.

Carr, E.H. 1945. *Nationalism and After*. London: Macmillan.

Carritt, E.F. 1967. Liberty and Equality in Anthony Quinton ed. *Political Philosophy*. Oxford: Oxford University Press: 127–40.

Carroll, Lewis. 1895. What the Tortoise said to Achilles. *Mind* 4: 278–80.

Chagny, R., ed. 1990. *Aux Origines Provinciales de la Révolution*. Grenoble: Presses Universitaires de Grenoble.

Christiano, Thomas. 1996. *The Rule of the Many*. Boulder, CO: Westview Press.

2001. Knowledge and Power in the Justification of Democracy. *Australasian Journal of Philosophy* 79: 197–215.

Clayton, Mathew and Williams, Andrew, eds. 2002. *The Ideal of Equality*. Basingstoke: Palgrave Macmillan.

Cohen, G.A. 1988. Are Disadvantaged Workers who Take Hazardous Jobs Forced to Take Hazardous Jobs? in his *History, Labour and Freedom: Themes from Marx*. Oxford: Clarendon Press: 239–54.

1989. On the Currency of Egalitarian Justice. *Ethics* 99: 906–944.

1995. The Pareto Argument for Inequality. *Social Philosophy and Policy* 12: 160–85.

2000. *If You're An Egalitarian, How Come You're So Rich?* Cambridge, MA: Harvard University Press.

Cohen, Joshua. 1989. Deliberation and Democratic Legitimacy in Alan Hamlin and Philip Pettit. *The Good Polity: Normative Analysis of the State*. Oxford: Basil Blackwell: 17–34.

1997. Procedure and Substance in Deliberative Democracy in James Bohman and William Rehg eds *Deliberative Democracy: Essays on Reason and Politics*. Cambridge, MA: MIT: 407–38.

2003. For a Democratic Society in Samuel Freeman ed. *The Cambridge Companion to Rawls*. Cambridge: Cambridge University Press: 86–138.

Condorcet, N. Marquis de. 1785. *Essai sur l'Application de l'Analyse a la Probabilité des Voix*. Paris: L'imprimerie royale.

1794. *Esquisse d'un Tableau Historique des Progres de l'Esprit Humain*. Paris: Gravier.

Converse, Philip E. 1964. The Nature of Belief Systems in Mass Publics in David Apter ed. *Ideology and Discontent*. New York: Free Press: 206–61.

Copp, David. 1993. Could Truth Be a Hazard for Democracy? in Copp *et al.* 1993: 101–17.

Copp, David, Hampton, Jean and Roemer, John E., eds. 1993. *The Idea of Democracy.* Cambridge: Cambridge University Press.

Crafts, Nick. 1994. The Industrial Revolution in Roderick Floud and Deirdre McCloskey eds *The Economic History of Britain since 1700*, vol. 1. Cambridge: Cambridge University Press.

Dahl, Robert A. 1956. *A Preface to Democratic Theory.* Chicago: University of Chicago Press.

1961. *Who Governs? Democracy and Power in an American City.* New Haven: Yale University Press.

1989. *Democracy and Its Critics.* New Haven: Yale University Press.

1998. *On Democracy.* New Haven: Yale University Press.

2002. *How Democratic is the American Constitution?* Yale University Press: New Haven.

Dahrendorf, Ralf. 1968. *Homo Sociologicus.* London: Routledge and Kegan Paul.

Darnton, Robert. 1997. Condorcet and the Craze for America in France in J. Brown ed. *Franklin and Condorcet.* Philadelphia: American Philosophical Society 27–39.

Deacon, A. and Mann, K. 1999. Agency, Modernity and Social Policy. *Journal of Social Policy* 28(3): 413–36.

Descartes, René. 1646. To Elisabeth, January 1646 in *Oeuvres Philosophiques*, vol. III. (F. Alquié ed.). Paris: Classiques Garnier.

1970. To Elisabeth, 6 November 1645, in *Descartes, Philosophical Letters* (Anthony Kenny trans.). Oxford: Oxford University Press.

1988. *Oeuvres Philosophiques*, vol. 1. (F. Alquié ed.). Paris: Classiques Garnier.

Dewey, John. 1987 [1935]. Liberalism and Social Action in Jo Ann Boydson ed. *The Later Works of John Dewey, 1925–1953*, vol. 11. Carbondale, IL: Southern Illinois University Press: 1–65.

Dover, Kenneth. 1994. *Greek Popular Morality.* Indianapolis: Hackett.

Dowding, Keith. 1991. *Rational Choice and Political Power.* Aldershot: Elgar.

1996. *Power.* Buckingham: Open University Press/Minnesota University Press.

1998. Secession and Isolation in Percy B. Lehning ed. *Theories of Secession.* London: Routledge: 71–91.

1999. Shaping Future Luck. *Journal of Conflict Processes and Change* 4(1): 1–11.

2003. Resources, Power and Systematic Luck: Reply to Barry. *Philosophy, Politics and Economics* 3(2): 305–22.

Dowding, Keith, De Wispelaere, Jurgen and White, Stuart, eds. 2003. *The Ethics of Stakeholding.* Houndmills: Palgrave Macmillan.

Downs, Anthony. 1957. *An Economic Theory of Democracy.* Harper: New York.

Droz, J. 1860. *Histoire du Règne de Louis XVI*, vol. II. Paris: Renouard.

Dryzek, John S. 1990. *Discursive Democracy: Politics, Policy, and Political Science.* Cambridge: Cambridge University Press.

2000. *Deliberative Democracy and Beyond: Liberals, Critics and Contestations.* Oxford: Oxford University Press.

Duflo, Esther and Chattopadhyay, Raghabendra. 2003. Women as Policy Makers: Evidence from a Randomized Experient. BREAD Working Paper 001. Harvard University.

Dull, Jonathan. 1985. *A Diplomatic History of the American Revolution*. New Haven: Yale University Press.

Dworkin, Ronald. 1977. *Taking Rights Seriously*. Cambridge: Harvard University Press.

2000. *Sovereign Virtue: The Theory and Practice of Equality*. Cambridge, MA: Harvard University Press.

Easton, David. 1965. *A Framework for Political Analysis*. Englewood Cliffs, NJ: Prentice-Hall.

Egret, J. 1942. *Les Derniers Etats de Dauphiné*. Grenoble: B. Arthaud.

Eisenstein, Hester. 1996. *Inside Agitators: Australian Femocrats and the State*. Sydney: Allen and Unwin.

Elster, Jon. 1979. *Ulysses and the Sirens: Studies in Rationality and Irrationality*. Cambridge: Cambridge University Press.

1988. Taming Chance: Randomization in Individual and Social Decisions. *Tanner Lectures on Human Values* 9: 105–80. Reprinted in Jon Elster *Solomonic Judgements*. Cambridge: Cambridge University Press. 1989: 36–122.

Elster, Jon, ed. 1996. *The Roundtable Talks and the Breakdown of Communism*. Chicago: University of Chicago Press.

1998. *Deliberative Democracy*. Cambridge: Cambirdge University Press.

Engelstadt, Frederik, Østerud, Øyvind and Selle, Per. 2003. *Maketen og Demokrateit*. Oslo: Gyldendal Akademisk.

Estlund, David. 1989. Democratic Theory and the Public Interest: Condorcet and Rousseau Revisited. *American Political Science Review* 83(4): 1317–22.

1990. Democracy Without Preference. *Philosophical Review* 99: 397–423.

1993. Making Truth Safe for Democracy in Copp *et al.* 1993: 71–100.

1994. Opinion Leaders, Independence and Condorcet's Jury Theorem. *Theory and Decision* 36(2): 131–62.

1997. Beyond Fairness and Deliberation: The Epistemic Dimension of Democratic Authority in James Bohman and William Rehg, eds *Deliberative Democracy: Essays in Reason and Politics*. Cambridge: MIT Press: 173–204.

2000. Waldron on Law and Disagreement. *Philosophical Studies* 99: 111–28.

Farrand, M., ed. 1966a. *Records of the Federal Convention*, vol. I. New Haven: Yale University Press.

1966b. *Records of the Federal Convention*, vol. II. New Haven: Yale University Press.

Feinberg, Joel. 1973. *Social Philosophy*. Englewood Cliffs, NJ: Prentice-Hall.

Felsenthal, Dan S. and Machover, Moshe. 1998. *The Measurement of Voting Power*. Cheltenham: Edward Elgar.

Fenno, Richard. 1978. *Home Style*. Boston: Little, Brown.

Fishkin, James S. 1995. *The Voice of the People: Public Opinion and Democracy*. New Haven, CT: Yale University Press.

Fishkin, James S. and Laslett, Peter, eds. 2003. *Debating Deliberative Democracy: Philosophy, Politics and Society*, 7th series. Oxford: Blackwell.

Freeman, Joanne, ed. 2001. *Hamilton: Writings*. New York: Library of America.

Frey, Bruno S. and Stutzer, Alois. 2002. What Can Economists Learn from Happiness Research? *Journal of Economic Literature* 40(2): 402–35.

Gallie, W.B. 1956. Liberal Morality and Socialist Morality in Peter Laslett ed. *Philosophy, Politics and Society*. Oxford: Basil Blackwell: 116–33.

Gauthier, David. 1986. *Morals by Agreement*. Oxford: Clarendon Press.

Gaventa, J. 1980. *Power and Powerlessness: Quiescence and Rebellion in an Appalachian Valley*. Oxford: Clarendon Press.

Gellner, Ernest. 1987. Nationalism and the Two Forms of Cohesion in Complex Societies in Ernest Gellner *Culture, Identity, and Politics*. Cambridge: Cambridge University Press: 6–28.

Geuss, R. 1981. *The Idea of Critical Theory*. Cambridge: Cambridge University Press.

Giddens, Anthony. 1984. *The Constitution of Society*. Cambridge: Polity.

Gintis, Herbert. 2000. *Game Theory Evolving: A Problem-Centered Introduction to Modeling Strategic Interaction*. Princeton, NJ: Princeton University Press.

Glover, Jonathan. 1999. *Humanity: A Moral History of the Twentieth Century*. New Haven: Yale University Press.

Goodin, Robert E. 1986. Laundering Preferences in Jon Elster and Aanund Hylland eds *Foundations of Social Choice Theory*. Cambridge: Cambridge University Press.

1990. Government House Utilitarianism in Lincoln Allison ed. *The Utilitarian Response: The Contemporary Viability of Utilitarian Political Philosophy*. London: Sage: 140–60.

1992. *Motivating Political Morality*. Oxford: Blackwell.

1995. *Utilitarianism as Public Philosophy*. Cambridge: Cambridge University Press.

1996. Institutionalizing the Public Interest. *American Political Science Review* 90: 331–43.

1999. Rationality Redux: Reflections on Herbert Simon's Vision of Politics in James Alt, Margaret Levi and Elinor Ostrom eds *Competition and Cooperation: Conversations with Nobelists about Economics and Political Science*. New York: Russell Sage Foundation.

2003a. Heuristics of Public Administration in James G. March ed. *Models of a Man: Essays in Honor of Herbert Simon*. Cambridge MA: Cambridge University Press.

2003b. *Reflective Democracy*. Oxford: Oxford University Press.

Griffin, Christopher P. 2003. Democracy as a Non-instrumentally Just Procedure. *Journal of Political Philosophy* 11: 111–21.

Grofman, Bernard, and Feld, Scott L.. 1988. Rousseau's General Will: A Condorcetian Perspective. *American Political Science Review* 82(2): 567–76.

Groseclose, Timothy. 2001. A Model of Candidate Location when One Candidate has a Valence Advantage. *American Journal of Political Science* 45: 862–86.

Gutmann, Amy and Thompson, Dennis. 1996. *Democracy and Disagreement*. Cambridge, MA: Harvard University Press.

Habermas, Jürgen. 1973. *Wahrheitstheorien. Wirchlichkeit und Reflexion: Walter Schulz zum 60 Geburtstag*. Pfullingen: Neske.

1984. *A Theory of Communicative Action*, vol. 1. Cambridge: Polity Press.

1989. *A Theory of Communicative Action*, vol. 2. Cambridge: Polity Press.
1996. *Between Facts and Norms*. Cambridge: Polity Press.

Hadenius, Axel, ed. 1994. *Democracy's Victory and Crisis*. Cambridge: Cambridge University Press.

Hampshire, Stuart. 2000. *Justice Is Conflict*. Princeton, NJ: Princeton University Press.

Hardin, Russell. 1980. Rationality, Irrationality, and Functionalist Explanation, *Social Science Information* 19 (September): 755–72.
1988. *Morality Within the Limits of Reason*. Chicago: University of Chicago Press.
1995. *One for All: The Logic of Group Conflict*. Princeton, NJ: Princeton University Press.
1999a. *Liberalism, Constitutionalism, and Democracy*. Oxford: Oxford University Press.
1999b. Communities and Development: Autarkic Social Groups and the Economy in Mancur Olson, Jr. and Satu Kähkönen eds *A Not-so-Dismal Science: A Broader, Brighter Approach to Economies and Societies*. Oxford: Oxford University Press: 206–27.

Harsanyi, John C. 1953. Cardinal Utility in Welfare Economics and in the Theory of Risk-Taking. *Journal of Political Economy* 61: 434–5.
1955. Cardinal Welfare, Individualistic Ethics and Interpersonal Comparisons of Utility. *Journal of Political Economy* 63: 309–21.
1976. *Essays on Ethics, Social Behavior, and Scientific Explanation*. Dordrecht: D. Reidel.

Hawkesworth, M.E. 1990. *Beyond Oppression: Feminist Theory and Political Strategy*. New York: Continuum.

Heclo, Hugh. 1978. Issue Networks and the Executive Establishment in Anthony King ed. *The New American Political System*. Washington, DC: American Enterprise Institute: 87–124.

Held, David. 1993. *Prospects for Democracy: North, South, East, West*. Oxford: Polity.

Hesse, Mary. 1967. Models and Analogy in Science in Paul Edwards ed. *The Encyclopedia of Philosophy*, vol. 5. London: Macmillan: 354–9.

Hills, John, Le Grand, Julian and Piachaud, David, eds. 2002. *Understanding Social Exclusion*. Oxford: Oxford University Press.

Hinich, Melvin. 1977. Equilibrium in Spatial Voting: the Median Voter Result is an Artifact. *Journal of Economic Theory* 16: 208–19.

Hirshleifer, Jack. 1987. The Emotions as Guarantors of Threats and Promises in John Dupré ed. *The Latest on the Best*. Cambridge, MA: MIT Press: 307–26

Hobsbawm, Eric. 1990. *Nations and Nationalism since 1870*. Cambridge: Cambridge University Press (2nd edn).

Hollis, Martin. 1987. *The Cunning of Reason*. Cambridge: Cambridge University Press.

Hume, David. 1985a. Of the Dignity or Meanness of Human Nature in his *Essays: Moral, Political and Literary*. Indianapolis: Liberty Fund: 80–6.
1985b [1777]. *Essays Moral, Political, and Literary* (E. Miller ed.). Indianapolis: Liberty Fund.

Humphrey, M. 2002. Nonbasic Environmental Goods and Social Justice in D.A. Bell and A. De-Shalit eds. *Forms of Justice*. Lanham: Rowman and Littlefield.
Hunter, Floyd. 1953. *Community Power Structures*. Chapel Hill, NC: University of North Carolina Press.
Ilovaïsky, O., ed. 1974. *Recueil de Documents Relatifs Aux Séances des Etats Généraux*. T.II.i, Paris: CNRS.
Jackman, Robert. 1972. *Politics and Social Equality*. New York: Wiley.
Jones, Peter. 1983. Political Equality and Majority Rule in David Miller and Larry Siedentop eds *The Nature of Political Theory*. Oxford: Clarendon Press: 155–82.
1988. Intense Preferences, Strong Beliefs and Democratic Decision-Making. *Political Studies* 36(1): 7–29.
Kessel, Patrick. 1969. *La Nuit du 4 Août 1789*. Paris: Arthaud.
Ketcham, Ralph. 1971. *James Madison: A Biography*. Charlottesville: University Press of Virginia.
Kiewiet, D. Roderick. 1983. *Micropolitics and Macroeconomics*. Chicago: University of Chicago Press.
Kramnick, Isaac. 1992. *Bolingbroke and his Circle*. Ithaca: Cornell University Press.
Kukathas, Chandran, ed. 2002. *Rawls: Critical Assessments*. 4 vols. New York: Routledge.
Kukathas, Chandran and Pettit, Philip. 1990. *Rawls: A Theory of Justice and its Critics*. Cambridge: Polity Press.
Kymlicka, Will. 1989. *Liberalism, Community, and Culture*. Oxford: Oxford University Press.
1995. *Multicultural Citizenship: A Liberal Theory of Minority Rights*. Oxford: Clarendon Press.
Le Grand, Julian. 1984. Equity as an Economic Objective. *Journal of Applied Philosophy* 1(1): 39–51.
1991. *Equity and Choice: An Essay in Economics and Applied Philosophy*. London: Harper Collins.
2000. From Knight to Knave? Public Policy and Market Incentives in P. Taylor-Goodby ed. *Risk, Trust and Welfare*. Houndmills: Macmillan.
2003. *Agency and Public Policy: Of Knights and Knaves, Pawns and Queens*. Oxford: Oxford University Press.
Lewis, M. 1992. *Shame*. New York: The Free Press.
Lijphart, Arend. 1968/1975. *The Politics of Accommodation: Pluralism and Democracy in the Netherlands*. Berkeley, CA: University of California Press.
1969. Consociational Democracy. *World Politics* 21: 207–25.
1999. *Patterns of Democracy*. New Haven, CT: Yale Univeristy Press.
Linz, Juan J. and Stepan, Alfred. 1996. *Problems of Democratic Transition and Consolidation: Southern Europe, South America and Post-Communist Europe*. Baltimore, MD: Johns Hopkins University Press.
List, Christian, and Goodin, Robert E. 2001. Epistemic Democracy: Generalizing the Condorcet Jury Theorem. *Journal of Political Philosophy* 9: 277–306.
List, Christian and Pettit, Philip. 2002. The Aggregation of Sets of Judgments: An Impossibility Result. *Economics and Philosophy* 18: 89–110.

Little, I.M.D. 1952. Social Choice and Individual Values. *Journal of Political Economy* 60: 422–32.

Locke, John. 1980. *Second Treatise of Government*, (C.B. Macpherson ed.). Indianapolis: Hackett Publishing. (Originally published 1690).

Lopez, Claude-Anne. 1966. *Mon Cher Papa: Franklin and the Ladies of Paris*. New Haven: Yale University Press.

Lovejoy, A.O. 1961. *Reflections on Human Nature*. Baltimore: Johns Hopkins Press.

Lukes, Steven. 1974. *Power: A Radical View*. London: Macmillan.

Lynd, Robert and Lynd, Mary. 1929. *Middletown*. New York: Harcourt, Brace.

Maass, Arthur. 1983. *Congress and the Common Good*. New York: Basic.

Mackie, Gerry. 1996. Ending Footbinding and Infibulation: A Convention Account. *American Sociological Review* 61: 999–1017.

Macpherson, C. B. 1973. *Democratic Theory*. Oxford: Clarendon Press.

1977. *The Life and Times of Liberal Democracy*. Oxford: Clarendon Press.

Madison, James. 1977. *Papers*, vol. 10. (Robert Rutland and Charles Hobson eds). Chicago: University of Chicago Press.

1979. *Papers*, vol. 12. (Charles Hobson, Robert Rutland, William Rachal and Jeanne Sissan eds). Charlottesville, VA: University Press of Virginia.

1985. *Papers*, vol. 15. (Thomas Mason, Robert Rutland and Jeanne Sisson eds). Charlottesville, VA: University Press of Virginia.

McKelvey, Richard D. 1986. Covering, Dominance, and Institution – Free Properties of Social Choice. *American Journal of Political Science* 30: 283–314.

McKelvey, Richard. D. and Schofield, Norman. 1986. Structural Instability of the Core. *Journal of Mathematical Economics* 15: 267–84.

McLean, Iain. 1991. Forms of Representation and Systems of Voting in David Held ed. *Political Theory Today*. Cambridge: Polity.

2001. *Rational Choice and British Politics*. Oxford: Oxford University Press.

McLean, Iain and Hewitt, Fiona. 1994. *Condorcet: Foundations of Social Choice and Political Theory*. Aldershot: Edward Elgar.

McLean, Iain and Urken, Arnold. 1992. Did Jefferson or Madison Understand Condorcet's Theory of Social Choice? *Public Choice* 73: 445–57.

Mansbridge, Jane. 1999. Everyday Talk in the Deliberative System in Stephen Macedo ed. *Deliberative Politics*. New York: Oxford University Press.

2003. Rethinking Representation: Expanding Normative Analysis to the Promissory, Anticipatory, Self-Referential and Surrogate Forms. *American Political Science Review* 97(1): 515–28.

March, James G. and Olsen, Johan P. 1995. *Democratic Governance*. New York: Free Press.

Marx, Karl. 1963 [1852]. *The 18th Brumaire of Louis Bonaparte*. New York: International Publishers.

May, Kenneth O. 1952. A Set of Independent, Necessary and Sufficient Conditions for Simple Majority Decision. *Econometrica* 20: 680–4. Reprinted in Barry and Hardin 1982: 97–304.

Mill, James. 1820. Government in Terence Ball ed. *James Mill: Political Writings*. Cambridge: Cambridge University Press.

Mill, John Stuart. 1869. The Subjection of Women in Richard Wollheim ed. *John Stuart Mill, Three Essays*. Oxford: Clarendon Press. 1975: 425–58.

1977. Considerations on Representative Government in John Stuart Mill, *Collected Works*, vol. 19, (J.M. Robson ed.). Toronto: University of Toronto Press.

Miller, David. 1982. Arguments for Equality in P.A. French, T.E. Uehling and H.K. Wettstein eds *Midwest Studies in Philosophy, VII: Social and Political Philosophy*. Minneapolis: University of Minnesota Press.

1983. Public Goods Without the State. *Critical Review* 7: 505–23.

1992. Deliberative Democracy and Social Choice. *Political Studies* 40 (Special Issue): 54–67. Reprinted as Miller 1993.

1993. Deliberative Democracy and Social Choice in David Held ed. *Prospects for Democracy*. Cambridge: Polity Press: 74–92.

1995. *On Nationality*. Oxford: Clarendon Press.

1999. Social Justice and Environmental Goods in Andrew Dobson ed. *Fairness and Futurity: Essays on Environmental Sustainability and Social Justice*. Oxford: Oxford University Press.

2000. *Citizenship and National Identity*. Cambridge: Polity Press.

Miller, Gary and Schofield, Norman. 2003. Activists and Partisan Realignment in the US. *American Political Science Review* 97: 245–60.

Miller, William. 1995. *Arguing about Slavery*. New York: Knopf.

Mills, C. Wright. 1956. *The Power Elite*. Oxford: Oxford University Press.

Mirabeau. 1789. *Courrier de Provence* XXIV. August 5–7: 3.

Montaigne, Michel E. de. 1992. *Essays* (M.A. Screech trans.). Harmondsworth: Penguin.

Montesquieu, Charles. 1990 [1748]. The Spirit of the Laws in Melvin Richter ed. *Montesquieu: Selected Political Writings*. Indianapolis: Hacket.

Morris, Christopher W. 2000. The Very Idea of Popular Sovereignty: 'We the People' Reconsidered. *Social Philosophy and Policy* 17(1): 1–26.

Morriss, Peter. 1987/2002. *Power: A Philosophical Analysis*. Manchester: Manchester University Press.

Moynihan, Daniel Patrick. 1993. *Pandaemonium: Ethnicity in International Politics*. Oxford: Oxford University Press.

Mueller, Dennis C. 1989. *Public Choice II: A Revised Edition of Public Choice*. New York: Cambridge University Press.

Murphy, Liam. 1999. Institutions and the Demands of Justice. *Philosophy and Public Affairs* 27: 251–91.

2000. *Moral Demands in Non-Ideal Theory*. Oxford: Oxford University Press.

Murphy, Liam and Nagel, Thomas. 2002. *The Myth of Ownership: Taxes and Justice*. New York: Oxford University Press.

Myles, G.D. 1995. *Public Economics*. Cambridge: Cambridge University Press.

Naess, Arne with Christophersen, Jens A. and Kvalø, Kjell. 1956. *Democracy, Ideology and Objectivity: Studies in the Semantics and Cognitive Analysis of Ideological Controversy*. Oxford: Blackwell.

Nagel, E. and Newman, J.R. 1958. *Gödel's Proof*. New York: New York University Press.

Narveson, Jan F. 1976. A Puzzle about Economic Justice in Rawls' Theory. *Social Theory and Practice* 4: 1–27.

1978. Rawls on Equal Distribution of Wealth. *Philosophia* 7: 281–92.

Neill, J.R. 2000. The Benefit and Sacrifice Principles of Taxation: A Synthesis. *Social Choice and Welfare* 17: 117–24.

Nelson, William. 1980. *On Justifying Democracy*. London: Routledge and Kegan Paul.

New, B. 1999. Paternalism and Public Policy. *Economics and Philosophy* 15: 63–83.

Ng, Yew-Kwang. 1996. Happiness Surveys: Some Comparability Issues and an Exploratory Survey Based on Just Perceivable Increments. *Social Indicators Research* 38(1): 1–29.

2003. From Preference to Happiness: Towards a More Complete Welfare Economics. *Social Choice and Welfare* 20: 307–50.

North, Douglass. 1961. *The Economic Growth of the United States, 1790–1860*. Englewood Cliffs, NJ: Prentice-Hall.

North, Douglass and Weingast, Barry. 1989. Constitutions and Commitment: The Evolution of Institutions Governing Public Choice in Seventeenth Century England. *Journal of Economic History* 49: 803–32.

Nozick, Robert. 1974. *Anarchy, State and Utopia*. Oxford: Blackwell.

O'Donnell, Guillermo, Schmitter, Philippe C. and Whitehead, Laurence, eds. 1986. *Transitions from Authoritarian Rule*. Baltimore: John Hopkins University Press.

Okin, Susan Moller. 1989. *Justice, Gender and the Family*. New York: Basic Books.

1998. Feminism and Multiculturalism: Some Tensions. *Ethics*. 108: 322–48.

Okin, Susan Moller (with respondents). 1999. *Is Multiculturalism Bad for Women?* (Joshua Cohen, Matthew Howard and Martha C. Nussbaum eds.) Princeton, NJ: Princeton University Press.

Palley, C. 1966. *The Constitutional History of Southern Rhodesia*. Oxford: Oxford University Press.

Parfit, D. 1984. *Reasons and Persons*. Oxford: Oxford University Press.

Parkinson, John. 2001. Deliberative Democracy and Referendums in Keith Dowding, James Hughes and Helen Margetts *Challenges to Democracy: Ideas, Involvement and Institutions*. Houndmills: Palgrave: 131–52.

Pascal, Blaise. 1991. *Pensée* 520 (P. Seller ed.). Paris: Bordas.

Pateman, Carole. 1970. *Participation and Democratic Theory*. Cambridge: Cambridge University Press.

1988. *The Sexual Contract*. Oxford: Polity Press.

1989. *The Disorder of Women*. Oxford: Polity Press.

2003. Freedom and Democratization: Why Basic Income is to be Preferred to Basic Capital in Dowding *et al.* 2003: 130–48.

Peterson, M.D., ed. 1984. *Thomas Jefferson: Writings*. New York: Library of America.

Pettit, Philip. 1982. Habermas on Truth and Justice. *Marx and Marxisms*. (G.H.R. Parkinson ed.). Cambridge: Cambridge University Press.

1997. *Republicanism: A Theory of Freedom and Government*. Oxford: Oxford University Press.

2000. Democracy, Electoral and Contestatory. *Nomos* 42: 105–44.

2001. *A Theory of Freedom: From the Psychology to the Politics of Agency*. Cambridge: Polity.

2002a. Is Criminal Justice Politically Feasible? Buffalo Criminal Law Review 5(2): 427–50.

2002b. *Rules, Reasons, and Norms: Selected Essays*. Oxford: Oxford University Press.

2003. Deliberative Democracy, the Discursive Dilemma, and Republican Theory in Fishkin and Laslett 2003: 138–62.

Phillips, Anne. 1991. *Engendering Democracy*. Oxford: Polity Press.

1995. *The Politics of Presence: Democracy and Group Representation*. Oxford: Clarendon Press.

Plumb, John H. 1967. *The Growth of Political Stability in England: 1675–1725*. London: Macmillan.

Polsby, Nelson W. 1963/1980. *Community Power and Political Theory*. New Haven, CT: Yale University Press.

Putnam, Robert. 2000. *Bowling Alone*. New York: Simon and Schuster.

Rae, Douglas W. 1969. Decision-Rules and Individual Values in Constitutional Choice. *American Political Science Review* 63: 40–56.

1975. The Limits of Consensual Decision. *American Political Science Review* 69: 1270–94.

Rakove, Jack, ed. 1999. *James Madison: Writings*. New York: Library of America.

Rawls, John. 1971. *A Theory of Justice*. Cambridge, MA: Harvard University Press.

1978. The Basic Structure as Subject in Alvin Goldman and Jaegwon Kim *Values and Morals: Essays in Honor of William Frankena, Charles Stevenson and Richard B. Brandt*. Dordrecht: D. Reidel.

1993. *Political Liberalism*. New York: Columbia University Press.

1996. *Political Liberalism: With a New Introduction and 'Reply to Habermas'*. New York: Columbia University Press.

1997. The Idea of Public Reason Revisited. *University of Chicago Law Review* 94:765–807.

1999. *A Theory of Justice*. Cambridge, MA: Harvard University Press (revised edn).

Reeve, Andrew and Ware, Alan. 1992. *Electoral Systems: A Comparative and Theoretical Introduction*. London: Routledge.

Rhodes, R.A.W. 1997. *Understanding Governance: Policy Networks, Governance and Accountability*. Buckingham: Open University Press.

Richardson, L. and Le Grand, Julian. 2002. Outsider and Insider Expertise: the Response of Residents of Deprived Neighbourhoods to an Academic Definition of Social Exclusion. *Social Policy and Administration* 36(5): 496–515.

Riker, William H. 1982. *Liberalism Against Populism: A Confrontation Between the Theory of Democracy and the Theory of Social Choice*. San Francisco: W.H. Freeman and Co.

1986. *The Art of Political Manipulation*. New Haven: Yale University Press.

Riker, William and Ordeshook, P.C. 1968. A Theory of the Calculus of Voting. *American Political Science Review* 62: 25–43.

Rogowski, Ronald. 1974. *Rational Legitimacy*. Princeton, NJ: Princeton University Press.
1989. *Commerce and Coalitions*. Princeton, NJ: Princeton University Press.
Rohrschneider, Robert. 1988. Citizens' Attitudes toward Environmental Issues: Selfish or Selfless? *Comparative Political Studies* 21: 347–67.
Saari, Donald. 2001. *Decisions and Elections: Explaining the Unexpected.* Cambridge: Cambridge University Press.
Samuelson, Paul. 1954. The Pure Theory of Public Expenditure. *Review of Economics and Statistics* 36: 387–9.
Sartori, Giovanni. 1987. *The Theory of Democracy Revisited.* Chatham, NJ: Chatham House.
Sawer, Marian. 1990. *Sisters in Suits*. Sydney: Allen and Unwin.
Sawer, Marian and Simms, Marian. 1993. *A Woman's Place: Women and Politics in Australia*. Sydney: Allen and Unwin.
Scanlon, Thomas M. 1975. Preference and Urgency. *Journal of Philosophy* 72: 665–9.
1982. Contractualism and Utilitarianism in Amartya Sen and Bernard Williams eds *Utilitarianism and Beyond*. Cambridge: Cambridge University Press: 101–28.
1998. *What We Owe to Each Other*. Cambridge, MA: Harvard University Press.
2002. The Diversity of Objections to Inequality in Clayton and Williams 2002.
Schmidtz, David. 1991. *The Limits of Government: An Essay on the Public Goods Argument*. Boulder, CO: Westview Press.
Schmitter, Philippe. 1981. Interest Intermediation and Regime Governability in Suzanne Berger ed. *Organizing Interests in Western Europe*. Cambridge: Cambridge University Press: 285–327.
Schofield, Norman. 2001. Constitutions, Voting and Democracy. *Social Choice and Welfare* 18: 571–600.
2002a. Evolution of the Constitution. *British Journal of Political Science* 32: 1–23.
2002b. Quandaries of War and Union. *Politics and Society* 30: 5–49.
2003a. Power, Prosperity and Social Choice. *Social Choice and Welfare* 20: 85–118.
2003b. Valence Competition in the Spatial Stochastic Model. *Journal of Theoretical Politics* 15(4): 371–83.
2003c. Madison and the Founding of the Two Party System in the US in Kernell ed. *James Madison: The Theory and Practise of Republican Government*. Stanford: Stanford University Press: 302–27.
2003d. Constitutional Quandaries and Critical Elections. *Politics, Philosophy and Economics* 2: 5–36.
2004. Equilibrium in the Spatial 'Valence' Model of Politics. *Journal of Theoretical Politics* 16(4): forthcoming.
Schofield, Norman, Miller, Gary and Martin, Andrew. 2003. Critical Elections and Political Realignment in the US: 1860–2000. *Political Studies* 51: 217–40.
Schumpeter, Joseph A. 1950. *Capitalism, Socialism and Democracy*. New York: Harper and Row, (3rd edn).

Sellers, M.N.S. 1995. *American Republicanism: Roman Ideology in the United States Constitution*. New York: New York University Press.
Sen, Amartya. 1982. Rights and Agency. *Philosophy and Public Affairs* 11: 3–39.
1994. Well-being, Capability and Public Policy. *Giornale Degli Economisti e Annali de Economica* LIII (7–9): 333–47.
1995. *Inequality Re-examined*. Oxford: Clarendon Press.
Shachar, Ayelet. 2001. *Multicultural Jurisdictions: Cultural Differences and Women's Rights in a Liberal State*. Cambridge: Cambridge University Press.
Shapiro, Ian. 1999. *Democratic Justice*. New Haven, CT: Yale University Press.
Shapley, Lloyd S. and Shubik, Martin. 1969. A Method for Evaluating the Distribution of Power in a Committee System in R. Bell, D.V. Edwards and R.H. Wagner eds *Political Power: A Reader*. London: Collier-Macmillan: 209–13.
Shweder, Richard A. 2000. What about 'Female Genital Mutilation'? And Why Understanding Culture Matters in the First Place. *Daedalus* (Fall): 209–32.
Sidgwick, H. 1891. *The Elements of Politics*. London: Macmillan.
1901. *The Methods of Ethics*. London: Macmillan (6th edn).
Simon, Herbert A. 1991. Bounded Rationality and Organizational Learning. *Organizational Science* 2: 125–34.
Simon, Herbert A., Smithburg, Donald W. and Thompson, Victor A. 1950. *Public Administration*. New York: Knopf.
Skidelsky, Robert. 2000. *John Maynard Keynes: Fighting for Britain 1937–1946*. London: Macmillan.
Skinner, Quentin 1998. *Liberty Before Liberalism*. Cambridge: Cambridge University Press.
Skocpol, Theda and Fiorina, Morris eds. 1999. *Civic Engagement and American Democracy*. Washington, DC: Brookings Institution.
Smith, Adam. 1981 [1776]. *An Inquiry into the Nature and Causes of the Wealth of Nations*. Indianapolis: Liberty Fund.
Smith, M. 1994. *The Moral Problem*. Oxford: Blackwell.
Social Security Estimates. 2000. www.dwp.gov.uk/publications/dss/2000/spending /main (accessed 24 April 2003).
Stasavage, David. 2003. Credible Commitment in Early Modern Europe: North and Weingast Revisited. *Journal of Law, Economics and Organization* 18: 155–86.
Steenbergen, Marco R., Bächtiger, André, Spörndli, Markus, and Steiner, Jürg. 2002. Measuring Deliberation: a Discourse Quality Index. *Comparative European Politics* 1: 21–48.
Stigler, George J. 1970. Director's Law of Public Income Redistribution. *Journal of Law and Economics* 13: 1–10.
Stigler, George J., ed. 1988. *Chicago Studies in Political Economy*. Chicago: University of Chicago Press.
Stokes, Donald. 1963. Spatial Models of Party Competition. *American Political Science Review* 57: 368–77.
Sugden, R. 1992. How People Choose in Shaun Hargreaves Heap *et al. The Theory of Choice*. Oxford: Blackwell: 36–50.

1993. Justified to Whom? in Copp *et al.* 1993: 149–54.
Sunstein, Cass R. 1991. Preferences and Politics. *Philosophy and Public Affairs* 20: 3–34.
1993. *The Partial Constitution*. Cambridge, MA: Harvard University Press.
2001. *Designing Democracy: What Constitutions Do*. New York: Oxford University Press.
Sunstein, Cass R., ed. 1990. *Feminism and Political Theory*. Chicago: University of Chicago Press.
Tamir, Yael. 1993. *Liberal Nationalism*. Princeton, NJ: Princeton University Press.
Tangney, J. 1990. Assessing Individual Differences in Proneness to Shame and Guilt: Development of the Self-conscious Affect and Attribution Inventory. *Journal of Personality and Social Psychology* 59: 102–11.
Taylor, Michael. 1969. Proof of a Theorem on Majority Rule. *Behavioral Science* 14: 228–31.
Taylor, Peter. 1999. *Behind the Mask*. New York: TV Books.
Taylor, Serge. 1984. *Making Bureaucracies Think: The Environmental Impact Statement Strategy of Administrative Reform*. Stanford, CA: Stanford University Press.
Temkin, L. 2002. Equality, Priority and the Levelling Down Objection in Clayton and Williams 2002.
Thompson, William. 1825. *Appeal of One Half of the Human Race, Women, Against the Pretensions of the Other Half, Men, to Retain Them in Political and Thence in Civil and Domestic Slavery*. London: Longman.
Tocqueville, Alexis de. 1953. Fragments et Notes inédites sur la Révolution in *L'Ancien Régime et la Révolution*, vol. II:. Paris: Gallimard.
Tronto, Joan C. 1993. *Moral Boundaries: A Political Argument for an Ethic of Care*. London: Routledge.
Tucker, Robert and Hendrickson, David. 1990. *Empire of Liberty*. Oxford: Oxford University Press.
Tversky, Amos and Kahneman, Daniel. 1982. Judgment under Uncertainty: Heuristics and Biases in Daniel Kahneman, Paul Slovic and Amos Tversky eds *Judgement under Uncertainty: Heuristics and Biases*. Cambridge: Cambridge University Press.
Urken, Arnold. 1991. The Condorcet-Jefferson Connection and the Origins of Social Choice Theory. *Public Choice* 72: 213–36.
Van Parijs, Phillipe. 1995. *Real Freedom for All*. Oxford: Oxford University Press.
Van Parijs, Phillipe, ed. 1992. *Arguing for Basic Income*. London: Verso.
Verba, Sidney. 2000. Representative Democracy and Democratic Citizens: Philosophical and Empirical Understandings. *Tanner Lectures on Human Values* 21: 229–88.
Verba, Sidney, Nie, Norman H. and Kim, Jae-on. 1978. *Participation and Political Equality*. Cambridge: Cambridge University Press.
Viroli, M. 2002. *Republicanism*. New York: Hill and Wang.
Waldron, Jeremy. 1999a. *Law and Disagreement*. Oxford: Oxford University Press.
1999b. *The Dignity of Legislation*. Cambridge: Cambridge University Press.
Walzer, Michael. 1980. Pluralism: A Political Perspective in Stephen A. Thernstrom ed. *Harvard Encyclopedia of American Ethnic Groups*. Cambridge, MA: Harvard University Press: 781–7.

Weale, Albert. 1998. From Contracts to Pluralism? in Paul Kelly ed. *Impartiality, Neutrality and Justice: Re-reading Brian Barry's Justice as Impartiality*. Edinburgh: Edinburgh University Press: 9–34.

1999. *Democracy.* Houndmills: Macmillan.

Weber, Eugen. 1979. *Peasants into Frenchmen: The Modernization of Rural France, 1870–1914*. Stanford: Stanford University Press.

Whitehead, Laurence. 2002. *Democratization: Theory and Experience*. Oxford: Oxford University Press.

Wicksell, Knut. 1958. A New Principle of Just Taxation in R.A. Musgrave and A.T. Peacock eds *Classics in the Theory of Public Finance*. London: Macmillan.

Wikan, Unni. 2000. Citizenship on Trial: Nadia's Case. *Daedalus* (Fall): 55–76.

Williams, Andrew. 1998. Incentives, Inequality, and Publicity. *Philosophy and Public Affairs* 27: 225–47.

Williams, Bernard. 1981. Internal and External Reasons in Bernard Williams *Moral Luck*. Cambridge: Cambridge University Press.

Williams, Melissa. 1998. *Voice, Trust and Memory*. Princeton, NJ: Princeton University Press.

Wilson, W. 1987. *The Truly Disadvantaged: The Inner City, the Underclass and Public Policy*. Chicago: Chicago University Press.

Wolfinger, Raymond. 1971. Nondecisions and the Study of Local Politics. *American Political Science Review* 65: 1063–80.

Wollheim, Richard. 1962. A Paradox in the Theory of Democracy in Peter Laslett and W.G. Runciman eds., *Philosophy, Politics and Society*, 2nd series. Oxford: Blackwell.

Wollstonecraft, Mary. 1792. *A Vindication of the Rights of Woman* in Mary Wollstonecraft *Political Writings* (Janet Todd ed.). Toronto: University of Toronto Press. 1993.

1798. *Maria: or The Wrongs of Woman* (M. Ferguson ed.). New York: WW Norton. 1975.

Wood, G. 1987. Interest and Disinterestedness in the Making of the Constitution in R. Beeman, S. Botein and E. Carter II eds *Beyond Confederation: Origins of the Constitution and American National Identity*. Chapel Hill: North Carolina Press.

Zagarri, R. 1987. *The Politics of Size: Representation in the United States 1776–1850*. Ithaca NY: Cornell University Press.

Brian Barry's publications

BOOKS

1. *Political Argument* (London: Routledge and Kegan Paul, 1965); *Political Argument: A Reissue with a New Introduction* (Berkeley and Los Angeles: University of California Press, 1990; London: Harvester-Wheatsheaf, 1990).
2. *Sociologists, Economists and Democracy* (London: Collier-Macmillan, 1970). Reprinted (with a new introduction and updated bibliographical essay) by the University of Chicago Press, 1978; Spanish translation 1974.
3. *The Liberal Theory of Justice* (Oxford: Clarendon Press, 1973). Spanish translation 1993; Italian translation 1994.
4. *Theories of Justice*, vol. I of *A Treatise on Social Justice* (Berkeley and Los Angeles: University of California Press, 1989; London: Harvester-Wheatsheaf, 1989). Korean translation 1990; Spanish translation 1996.
5. *Democracy, Power and Justice: Essays in Political Theory* (Oxford: Clarendon Press, 1989).
6. *Democracy and Power: Essays in Political Theory* 1 (Oxford: Clarendon Press, 1991) (contains material from *Democracy, Power and Justice: Essays in Political Theory*).
7. *Liberty and Justice: Essays in Political Theory* 2 (Oxford: Clarendon Press, 1991) (Contains material from *Democracy, Power and Justice: Essays in Political Theory*).
8. *Justice as Impartiality*, vol. II of *A Treatise on Social Justice* (Oxford: Clarendon Press, 1995). Spanish translation 1997.
9. *Culture and Equality: An Egalitarian Critique of Multiculturalism* (Cambridge: Polity Press, 2001; Cambridge, MA: Harvard University Press, 2001).
10. *Why Social Justice Matters* (Cambridge: Polity Press, 2004).

BOOKS EDITED

1. *Power and Political Theory: Some European Perspectives* (London: Wiley, 1976).
2. *Obligations to Future Generations*, with Richard Sikora (Philadelphia: Temple University Press, Philosophical Monograph Series, 1978, reprinted Cambridge: White Horse Press, 1997).
3. *Rational Man and Irrational Society? An Introduction and Source Book*, with Russell Hardin (Beverly Hills, CA: Sage Publications, 1982).

4. *Free Movement: Ethical Issues in the Transnational Migration of People and of Money*, with Robert Goodin (London: Harvester-Wheatsheaf, and University Park: Pennsylvania State University Press, 1992).
5. *The British Study of Politics in the Twentieth Century*, with Jack Hayward and Archie Brown (Oxford: Clarendon Press for the British Academy, 1999).

ARTICLES

1. Justice and the Common Good (1961) *Analysis* 1 n.s. 82: 86–91.
2. Preferences and the Common Good (1962) *Ethics* 72: 141–42.
3. The Use and Abuse of 'The Public Interest', *NOMOS 5: The Public Interest*, (Carl J. Friedrich ed., New York: Atherton Press, 1962) 191–204.
4. The Public Interest (1964) *Proceedings of the Aristotelian Society*, supp. vol. 38: 1–18.
5. The Roots of Social Injustice (1966) *The Oxford Review* (Michaelmas) 33–46.
6. On Social Justice (1967) *The Oxford Review* (Trinity) 29–52.
7. Warrender and His Critics (1968) *Philosophy* 48(1):17–37.
8. Recent Developments in the Study of Political Choice (1970) *Advancement of Science*130: 394–99.
9. Liberalism and Want-Satisfaction (1973) *Political Theory* 1: 134–53.
10. John Rawls and the Priority of Liberty (1973) *Philosophy and Public Affairs* 2: 274–90.
11. Economic Approach to the Analysis of Power and Conflict (1974) *Government and Opposition* 9: 189–223.
12. Political Evaluation, with D.W. Rae, in *Handbook of Political Science* (Fred I. Greenstein and Nelson W. Polsby eds, Reading, MA: Addison-Wesley, 1975) vol. 1, 337–401.
13. On Analogy (1975) *Political Studies* 23: 208–24.
14. The Consociational Model and its Dangers (1975) *European Journal of Political Research* 3: 393–412. (Reprinted in *Democracy, Power and Justice: Essays in Political Theory* and *Democracy and Power: Essays in Political Theory* 1).
15. Power: An Economic Analysis in *Power and Political Theory: Some European Perspectives* 67–101. (Reprinted in *Democracy, Power and Justice: Essays in Political Theory* and *Democracy and Power: Essays in Political Theory* 1).
16. Justice Between Generations in *Law, Morality and Society: Essays in Honour of H.L.A. Hart* (P.M.S. Hacker and J. Raz eds, Oxford: Clarendon Press, 1977) 268–84. (Reprinted in *Democracy, Power and Justice: Essays in Political Theory* and *Liberty and Justice: Essays in Political Theory* 2).
17. Rawls on Average and Total Utility (1977) *Philosophical Studies* 31: 317–25.
18. Circumstances of Justice and Future Generations in *Obligations to Future Generations* 204–48.
19. Contribution to *Political Participation: A Discussion of Political Rationality*, initiated by Stanley Benn (Canberra: Australian National University Press, 1978) 37–48.
20. Is Democracy Special? in *Philosophy, Politics and Society* (Peter Laslett and James Fishkin eds, 5th series, Oxford: Basil Blackwell, 1979) 155–96. (Reprinted in *Rational Man and Irrational Society? An Introduction and Source*

Book; *Democracy, Power and Justice: Essays in Political Theory*; and *Democracy and Power: Essays in Political Theory* 1).

21. Justice as Reciprocity in *Justice* (E. Kamenka and A. Erh-Soon Tay eds, London: Edward Arnold, 1979) 50–78. (Reprinted in *Democracy, Power and Justice: Essays in Political Theory* and *Liberty and Justice: Essays in Political Theory* 2).
22. Don't Shoot the Trumpeter – He's Doing His Best! Reflections on a Problem of Fair Division (1979) *Theory and Decision* 11: 153–80.
23. Ethnicity and the State in *Politics and Language: Spanish and English in the United States* (D.J.R. Bruckner ed., University of Chicago: Center for Public Policy, 1980) 31–48.
24. Is It Better to Be Powerful or Lucky? (1980) *Political Studies* 28 Part I: 183–94; Part II: 338–52. (Reprinted in *Democracy, Power and Justice: Essays in Political Theory* and *Democracy and Power: Essays in Political Theory* 1).
25. The Strange Death of Political Philosophy (1980) *Government and Opposition* (Special Issue: A Generation of Political Thought) 15: 276–88. (Reprinted in *Democracy, Power and Justice: Essays in Political Theory* and *Democracy and Power: Essays in Political Theory* 1).
26. Is Social Justice a Myth? in *Justice, Social and Global: Papers Presented at the Stockholm International Symposium on Justice* (Lars. O. Ericsson, Harold Ofstad and Giuliano Pontara eds, Stockholm: Akademilitteratur, Filosofiska studier 3, 1980) 9–19.
27. Do Countries Have Moral Obligations? The Case of World Poverty in *The Tanner Lectures on Human Values* II (Sterling McMurrin ed., Salt Lake City: University of Utah Press, 1981) 2–44.
28. Do Neighbors Make Good Fences? Political Theory and the Territorial Imperative (1981) *Political Theory* 9: 293–301.
29. Social Science and Distributive Justice in *Value Judgement and Income Distribution* (Robert A. Solo and Charles W. Anderson eds, New York: Praeger Publishers, 1981) 107–37.
30. Humanity and Justice in Global Perspective in *NOMOS 24: Ethics, Economics, and the Law* (J. Roland Pennock ed., New York: New York University Press, 1982) 219–52. (Reprinted in *Democracy, Power and Justice: Essays in Political Theory* and *Liberty and Justice: Essays in Political Theory* 2).
31. Methodology Versus Ideology: The 'Economic' Approach Revisited in *Strategies of Political Inquiry* (Elinor Ostrom ed., Beverly Hills, CA: Sage Publications, 1982) 123–47.
32. Intergenerational Justice in Energy Policy in *Energy and the Future* (Douglas Maclean and Peter G. Brown eds, Totowa, New Jersey: Rowman and Littlefield, Maryland Studies in Public Policy, 1983) 15–30. (Reprinted in *Democracy, Power and Justice: Essays in Political Theory* and *Liberty and Justice: Essays in Political Theory* 2 as The Ethics of Resource Depletion.)
33. Self-Government Revisited in *The Nature of Political Theory* (David Miller and Larry Siedentop eds, Oxford: Clarendon Press, 1983) 121–54. (Reprinted in *Democracy, Power and Justice: Essays in Political Theory* and *Democracy and Power: Essays in Political Theory* 1).
34. Does Democracy Cause Inflation? in *The Politics of Inflation and Economic Stagnation* (L. Lindberg and C. Maier eds, Washington, DC: The

Brookings Institution, 1985) 280–317. (Reprinted in *Democracy, Power and Justice: Essays in Political Theory* and *Democracy and Power: Essays in Political Theory* 1).

35. Can States Be Moral? in *Ethics and International Relations* (Anthony Ellis ed., for the Centre for Philosophy and Public Affairs, University of St. Andrews, Scotland, Manchester University Press, 1986). Also appears as Justice and International Society in *International Ethics in the Nuclear Age* (Robert J. Myers ed., vol. 4 of the Ethics and Foreign Policy Series for the Carnegie Council on Ethics and International Affairs, Lanham, MD: University Press of America, 1987) 85–110. (Reprinted in *Democracy, Power and Justice: Essays in Political Theory* and *Liberty and Justice: Essays in Political Theory* 2).
36. Lady Chatterley's Lover and Doctor Fischer's Bomb Party: Liberalism, Pareto Optimality, and the Problem of Objectionable Preferences in *Foundations of Social Choice Theory* (Jon Elster and Aanund Hylland eds, Cambridge: Cambridge University Press, 1986) 11–43. (Reprinted with additional material in *Democracy, Power and Justice: Essays in Political Theory* and *Liberty and Justice: Essays in Political Theory* 2).
37. The Continuing Relevance of Socialism in *Thatcherism* (Robert Skidelsky ed., London: Chatto and Windus, 1988) 143–58. (Reprinted in *Democracy, Power and Justice: Essays in Political Theory* and *Liberty and Justice: Essays in Political Theory* 2).
38. Equal Opportunity and Moral Arbitrariness in *Equal Opportunity* (Norman E. Bowie ed., Boulder, CO and London: Westview Press, 1988) 23–44.
39. Utilitarianism and Preference Change (1989) *Utilitas* 1: 278–82.
40. The Welfare State versus the Relief of Poverty (1990) *Ethics* 100: 503–29; and in *Needs and Welfare* (Robert Goodin and Alan Ware eds, London: Sage, 1990) 73–103.
41. How Not to Defend Liberal Institutions (1990) *British Journal of Political Science* 20: 1–14; and in *Liberalism and the Good* (R. Bruce Douglass, Gerald M. Mara and Henry S. Richardson eds, New York: Routledge, 1990) 44–58. (Reprinted in *Liberty and Justice: Essays in Political Theory* 2).
42. Chance, Choice, and Justice in *Liberty and Justice: Essays in Political Theory* 2, 142–58.
43. The Quest for Consistency: A Skeptical View in *Free Movement: Ethical Issues in the Transnational Migration of People and of Money* 279–87.
44. Equality Yes, Basic Income, No in *Arguing for Basic Income* (Philippe Van Parijs ed., London: Verso, 1992) 128–141.
45. Justice, Freedom, and Basic Income in *The Ethical Foundations of the Market Economy* (Horst Siebert ed., Tübingen: J.C.B. Mohr [Paul Siebeck], 1994) 61–89.
46. In Defence of Political Liberalism (1994) *Ratio Juris* 7: 325–30.
47. Spherical Justice and Global Injustice in *Pluralism, Justice, and Equality* (David Miller and Michael Walzer eds, Oxford: Clarendon Press, 1995) 67–80.
48. Is Social Justice a Mirage? (1995) *Greek Economic Review* 17: 137–44; also as Ist soziale Gerechtigkeit eine Illusion? (1995) *Prokla* 99: 235–43.
49. Does Society Exist? The Case for Socialism in *Socialism and the Common Good* (Preston King ed., London: Frank Cass, 1996) 115–43.

50. Political Theory, Old and New in *A New Handbook of Political Science* (Robert E. Goodin and Hans-Dieter Klingemann eds, Oxford: Oxford University Press, 1996) 531–48.
51. A Commitment to Impartiality (1996) *Political Studies* 44: 382–42. (Reply to critiques of *Justice as Impartiality*, vol. II of *A Treatise on Social Justice*.)
52. Contractual Justice: A Modest Defence (1996) *Utilitas* 8: 357–80. (Reply to critiques of *Justice as Impartiality*, vol. II of *A Treatise on Social Justice*.)
53. The Politics of Free Will (1997) *Tijdschrift voor Filosofie* 59: 615–30.
54. The Attractions of Basic Income in *Equality* (Jane Franklin ed., London: Institute for Public Policy Research, 1997).
55. International Society from a Cosmopolitan Perspective in *International Society: Diverse Ethical Perspectives* (David Mapel and Terry Nardin eds, Princeton, NJ: Princeton University Press, 1998) 144–63.
56. Is More International Trade Better than Less? in *The Legal and Moral Aspects of International Trade* (Geraint Parry, Asif Qureshi and Hillel Steiner eds) vol. III of *Freedom and Trade* (Geraint Parry and Hillel Steiner eds, London and New York: Routledge, 1998) 12–25.
57. Drepotatea [Justice], with Matt Matravers in *Filosofia Morala Britanica* (Alan Montefiore and Valentin Muresan eds, Bucharest: Editura Alternative, 1998).
58. Something in the Disputation not Unpleasant in *Impartiality, Neutrality and Justice: Re-reading Brian Barry's Justice as Impartiality* (Paul Kelly ed., Edinburgh: Edinburgh University Press, 1998) 186–257. (Reply to critiques of *Justice as Impartiality*, vol. II of *A Treatise on Social Justice*.)
59. The Limits of Cultural Politics (1998) *Review of International Studies* 24: 307–19.
60. Statism and Nationalism: A Cosmopolitan Critique in *NOMOS 41: Global Justice* (Ian Shapiro and Lea Brilmayer eds, New York: New York University Press, 1999) 12–26.
61. Sustainability and Social Justice in *Fairness and Futurity: Essays on Environmental Sustainability and Social Justice* (Andrew Dobson ed., Oxford University Press, 1999) 93–117.
62. The Study of Politics as a Vocation in *The British Study of Politics in the Twentieth Century* (Oxford: Clarendon Press for the British Academy, 1999) 425–67.
63. Is There a Right to Development? The John Austin Lecture in *International Justice* (Tony Coates ed., Aldershot: Ashgate, 2000) 9–22.
64. UBI and the Work Ethic in *What's Wrong with a Free Lunch?* with Philippe Van Parijs (Joshua Cohen and Joel Rogers eds, Boston: Beacon Press, 2001) 60–69.
65. Social Exclusion, Social Isolation and the Distribution of Income in *Understanding Social Exclusion* (John Hills, Julian Le Grand and David Piachaud eds, Oxford: Oxford University Press, 2002) 13–29.
66. Second Thoughts – and Some First Thoughts Revived in *Multiculturalism Reconsidered: Culture and Equality and its Critics* (Paul Kelly ed., Cambridge: Polity, 2002) 204–38. (Reply to critiques of *Culture and Equality: An Egalitarian Critique of Multiculturalism*.)
67. Capitalists Rule OK? Some Puzzles about Power (2002) *Politics, Philosophy and Economics* 1: 155–84.

68. Capitalists Rule. OK? A Commentary on Keith Dowding (2003) *Politics, Philosophy and Economics* 2: 323–341. (Reply to a critique of Capitalists Rule OK? Some Puzzles about Power.)
69. What Did We Learn? contribution to proceedings of a conference on cultural differences and the welfare state (Philippe Van Parijs ed., forthcoming).
70. A Hundred Years of Studying Politics: What Have We Got to Show for It? in British Academy Centenary Lecture Series (John Morrill ed., forthcoming).
71. Rationality and Want-Satisfaction in *Justice, Political Liberalism and Utilitarianism: Themes from Harsanyi* (Maurice Salles and John A. Weymark eds, Cambridge: Cambridge University Press, forthcoming).

REVIEW ARTICLES

1. Reflections on Conflict: A Review of Richard Rose, *Governing Without Consensus* (1972) *Sociology* 6: 443–49.
2. Review Article: *Exit, Voice and Loyalty* (Albert Hirschman) (1974) *British Journal of Political Science* 4: 79–107. (Reprinted in *Democracy, Power and Justice: Essays in Political Theory* and *Democracy and Power: Essays in Political Theory* 1).
3. Review Article: *Political Accommodation and Consociational Democracy* (Arend Lijphart) (1975) *British Journal of Political Science* 5: 477–505. German translation in Konkordanzdemokratie (Martin Geiling ed., Cologne: Böhlau). (Reprinted in *Democracy, Power and Justice: Essays in Political Theory* and *Democracy and Power: Essays in Political Theory* 1).
4. Review Article: *Anarchy, State, and Utopia* (Robert Nozick) (1975) *Political Theory* 3: 331–36.
5. Review Article: *Crisis, Choice, and Change* (Gabriel Almond), Part I: Plus ça change?; Part II: Games Theorists Play (1977) *British Journal of Political Science* 7: 99–113 and 217–53.
6. Review Article: Robert Paul Wolff, *Understanding Rawls* (1978) *Canadian Journal of Philosophy* 8: 753–83.
7. And Who Is My Neighbor? A Review of Charles Fried, *Right and Wrong* (1979) *Yale Law Journal* 88: 629–58. (Reprinted in *Democracy, Power and Justice: Essays in Political Theory* and *Liberty and Justice: Essays in Political Theory* 2).
8. Superfox. A Review of Jon Elster, *Logic and Society* and *Ulysses and the Sirens* (1980) *Political Studies* 28: 136–43.
9. Review Article: James Buchanan, *The Limits of Liberty and Freedom in Constitutional Contract* (1980) *Theory and Decision* 12: 95–106.
10. Review Article: Mancur Olson Jr., *The Rise and Decline of Nations* (1983) *International Studies Quarterly* 27: 17–27.
11. Tragic Choices. A Review of Guido Calabresi and Philip Bobbitt, *Tragic Choices* (1984) *Ethics* 84: 303–18. (Reprinted in *Democracy, Power and Justice: Essays in Political Theory* and *Liberty and Justice: Essays in Political Theory* 2).
12. Intimations of Justice. A Review of Michael Walzer, *Spheres of Justice* (1984) *Columbia Law Review* 84: 806–15.
13. The Uses of 'Power'. A Review of Peter Morriss, *Power: A Philosophical Analysis* (1988) *Government and Opposition* 23: 340–53. (Reprinted in *Democracy,*

Power and Justice: Essays in Political Theory and *Democracy and Power: Essays in Political Theory* 1).

14. The Light that Failed? A Review of Alasdair MacIntyre, *Whose Justice? Which Rationality?* (1989) *Ethics* 100: 160–68. (Reprinted in *Liberty and Justice: Essays in Political Theory* 2).
15. Social Criticism and Political Philosophy. A Review of Michael Walzer, *Interpretation and Social Criticism* and *The Company of Critics* (1990) *Philosophy & Public Affairs* 19: 360–73. (Reprinted in *Liberty and Justice: Essays in Political Theory* 2).
16. John Rawls and the Search for Stability. A Review of John Rawls, *Political Liberalism* (1995) *Ethics* 105: 874–915.
17. Real Freedom and Basic Income. A Review of Philippe Van Parijs, *Real Freedom for All* (1996) *Journal of Political Philosophy* 4: 242–76; reprinted in *Real Libertarianism Assessed: Political Theory after Van Parijs* (Andrew Reeve and Andrew Williams eds, New York: Palgrave, 2003) 53–79.
18. Nationalism versus Liberalism? A Contribution to a Symposium on David Miller, *On Nationality* (1996) *Nations and Nationalism* 2: 430–35.
19. The Muddles of Multiculturalism. A Review of Bhikhu Parekh ed., *The Future of Multicultural Britain* (2001) *New Left Review* (2nd series) (March/April) 8: 49–71.

BOOK REVIEWS

1. G. Catlin, *Science and Method of Politics*; H. Lasswell, *The Future of Political Science*; D. Pickles, *Introduction to Politics*; G. Catlin, *Political and Sociological Theory and Its Applications* (1966) *Political Studies* 14: 399–402.
2. K.C. Brown ed., *Hobbes Studies* (1967) *Political Studies* 15: 83–86.
3. Gidon Gottlieb, *The Logic of Choice* (1968) *Mind* 77 n.s. 308: 613–14.
4. Michael Young ed., *Forecasting and the Social Sciences* (1969) *Universities Quarterly* 23: 235–37.
5. J.R. Lucas, *The Principles of Politics* in (1969) *Philosophical Review* 78: 105–7
6. Hugh Stretton, *The Political Sciences* (1970) *Public Law* (Spring) 101–2.
7. A.H. Halsey and M.A. Trow, *The British Academics* (1971) *Universities Quarterly* 25: 240–44.
8. Joseph Frankel, *National Interest* (1971) *Sociology* 5: 269–70.
9. Stephen Withy ed., *A Degree and What Else* (1972) *Universities Quarterly* 26: 517–20.
10. Prasanta Pattanaik, *Voting and Collective Choice* (1972) *Political Studies* 20: 257–58.
11. George Lichtheim, *Imperialism* (1972) *Sociological Review* 20: 126–28.
12. Abram de Swaan, *Coalition Theories and Cabinet Formations* (1974) *Quality and Quantity* 8: 381–94.
13. Bernard Gert ed., *Man and Citizen* by Thomas Hobbes (1974) *American Political Science Review* 68: 759–60.
14. Robert A. Dahl and Edward R. Tufte, *Size and Democracy* (1974) *Government and Opposition* 9: 492–503.

15. The Obscurities of Power. A Review of Steven Lukes, *Power: A Radical View* (1975) *Government and Opposition* 10: 250–54. (Reprinted in *Democracy, Power and Justice: Essays in Political Theory* and *Liberty and Justice: Essays in Political Theory* 2).
16. James Cornford ed., *The Failure of the State* (1976) *Government and Opposition* 11: 117–20.
17. Richard Flathman, *The Practice of Rights* (1977) *International Studies in Philosophy* 9: 191–93.
18. C.B. Macpherson, *The Life and Times of Liberal Democracy* (1979) *The Journal of Modern History* 51: 331–33.
19. Norman Daniels ed., *Reading Rawls* (1976) *Canadian Journal of Political Science* 9: 720–21.
20. Harvey C. Mansfield, *The Spirit of Liberalism* (1979) *American Political Science Review* 73: 859–60.
21. David Lewis Schaefer, *Justice or Tyranny?: A Critique of John Rawls's Theory of Justice* (1980) *Social Science Quarterly* 60: 716–17.
22. Leon Shaskolsky Sheleff, *The Bystander: Behavior, Law, Ethics* (1980) *Ethics* 90: 457–62.
23. J.R. Lucas, *On Justice* (1980) *Political Studies* 28: 651.
24. Alkis Kontos ed., *Powers, Possessions and Freedom: Essays in Honour of C.B. Macpherson* (1981) *Canadian Journal of Political Science* 14: 174.
25. Bonnie Steinbock ed., *Killing and Letting Die*; John Harris, *Violence and Responsibility* (1982) *Ethics* 92: 555–58
26. Michael Walzer, *Radical Principles: Reflections of an Unreconstructed Democrat* (1982) *Ethics* 92: 369–73.
27. Tony Benn, *Arguments for Democracy*; Ian Bradley, *Breaking the Mould*; Anthony Crosland, *The Future of Socialism*; David Lipsey and Dick Leonard eds, *The Socialist Agenda*; David Owen, *Face the Future*; Shirley Williams, *Politics is for People* (1982) *Political Quarterly* 53: 351–57.
28. The Private Morality of Public Servants. A Review of *Public Duties: The Moral Obligations of Government Officials* (1982) *The Hastings Center Report* 12: 38–40.
29. Daniel Callahan and H. Tristam Engelhardt, Jr. eds, *The Roots of Ethics: Science, Religion, and Values*; Arthur L. Caplan and Daniel Callahan eds, *Ethics in Hard Times* (1983) *Ethics* 94: 138–40.
30. Michael J. Sandel, *Liberalism and the Limits of Justice* (1984) *Ethics* 94: 523–25.
31. J.H. Wellbank, Dennis Snook and David T. Mason, *John Rawls and his Critics: An Annotated Bibliography* (1984) *Ethics* 84: 351–53.
32. Neil MacCormick, *Legal Right and Social Democracy: Essays in Legal and Political Philosophy* (1984) *Ethics* 94: 525–27.
33. Edward N. Luttwak, *Strategy: The Logic of War and Peace*; Ian Clark, *Waging War: A Philosophical Introduction* (1988) *Government and Opposition* 23: 496–500.
34. Dennis F. Thompson, *Political Ethics and Public Office* (1988) *Journal of Public Policy* 8: 108–9.
35. John R. Freeman, *Democracy and Markets: The Politics of Mixed Economies* (1991) *Ethics* 102: 176–77.

36. Russell Hardin, *One for All: The Logic of Group Conflict* (1995) *American Political Science Review* 89: 1008–9.
37. Will Kymlicka, *Multicultural Citizenship* (1996) *Ethics* 107: 153–55.
38. James Griffin, *Value Judgement: Improving Our Ethical Beliefs* (1997) *Utilitas* 9: 361–63.
39. Ian Shapiro and Russell Hardin eds, *NOMOS: 38, Political Order* (1998) *American Political Science Review* 92: 211.

NOTES AND SHORT COMMENTS

1. Conflict of Interest and Coalition Formation (1971) *British Journal of Political Science* 1: 255–56.
2. Comments on 'The Pork Barrel and Majority Rule' (1972) *Journal of Politics* 33: 530.
3. Wollheim's Paradox: Comment (1973) *Political Theory* 1: 317–22.
4. In Defense of a Review (1977) *Political Theory* 5: 113–16.
5. Comment on Elster (1985) *Ethics* 96: 156–58.
6. Modern Knowledge and Modern Politics (1989) *Government and Opposition* 24: 387–90.
7. A Reader's Guide in *Free Movement: Ethical Issues in the Transnational Migration of People and of Money* 3–5.

ENTRIES IN ENCYCLOPEDIAS

1. 'Nationalism' and 'Rationality' in David Miller ed., *The Blackwell Encyclopedia of Political Thought* (Oxford: Basil Blackwell, 1987).
2. 'Equality' and 'Political Systems, Evaluation of' in Lawrence C. Becker and Charlotte B. Becker eds, *Encyclopedia of Ethics* (New York: Garland Publishing, Inc., 1992).
3. 'Justice' and 'International Justice' (with M. Matravers) in E. Craig ed., *Encyclopaedia of Philosophy* (London: Routledge, 1998).

OTHER PUBLICATIONS

1. Contributions to *Times Literary Supplement, London Review of Books, Guardian, The New Republic, Times Higher Education Supplement, Financial Times.*
2. *Does Society Exist? The Case for Socialism* (Fabian Society Tract 536, November 1989).
3. An Interview with Professor Brian Barry (1999) *Cogito* 13: 77–85.
4. Liberal Egalitarianism, Impartiality, and Multiculturalism: An Interview with Brian Barry (2002) *Imprints* 6: 100–7.

Index